Abnormal Psychology across the Ages

Recent Titles in
Abnormal Psychology

Mental Disorders of the New Millennium, Volumes 1–3
Thomas G. Plante, Editor

Bleeding to Ease the Pain: Cutting, Self-Injury, and the Adolescent
Lori G. Plante

Understanding and Treating Depression: Ways to Find Hope and Help
Rudy Nydegger

The Praeger International Collection on Addictions, Volumes 1–4
Angela Browne-Miller, Editor

Sexual Abuse in the Catholic Church: A Decade of Crisis, 2002–2012
Thomas G. Plante and Kathleen L. McChesney, Editors

ABNORMAL PSYCHOLOGY ACROSS THE AGES

Volume 1
History and Conceptualizations

Thomas G. Plante, Editor

Praeger Perspectives

Abnormal Psychology

Thomas G. Plante, Series Editor

 PRAEGER

AN IMPRINT OF ABC-CLIO, LLC
Santa Barbara, California • Denver, Colorado • Oxford, England

Library of Congress Cataloging-in-Publication Data

Abnormal psychology across the ages / Thomas G. Plante, editor.
    volumes cm. — (Abnormal psychology)
    Includes bibliographical references and index.
    ISBN 978-0-313-39836-0 (hardback : acid-free paper) — ISBN 978-0-313-39837-7 (Ebook)
    1. Mental illness—History.   2. Psychiatry—History.   3. Psychology, Pathological.
I. Plante, Thomas G.
    RC438.A238   2013
    616.89—dc23   2013001196

ISBN: 978-0-313-39836-0
EISBN: 978-0-313-39837-7

17 16 15 14 13   1 2 3 4 5

This book is also available on the World Wide Web as an eBook.
Visit www.abc-clio.com for details.

Praeger
An Imprint of ABC-CLIO, LLC

ABC-CLIO, LLC
130 Cremona Drive, P.O. Box 1911
Santa Barbara, California 93116-1911

This book is printed on acid-free paper ∞
Manufactured in the United States of America

*For all those who have suffered with mental illness and for all those
who have used their personal and professional gifts to ease their distress.*

Contents

Preface

What is normal? What is abnormal? What is acceptable human behavior, and what is not? How do we understand why people do what they do, and what can we do to help those who behave in ways that are unhealthy, disturbing, and dangerous to themselves or to others? To attempt to answer these important questions, which often have had very different answers during various times in history, this book, *Abnormal Psychology across the Ages*, in three volumes, examines the past, present, and predicted future of our understanding and diverse perspectives regarding psychopathology and abnormal behavior, broadly defined. Leading experts from across multiple perspectives come together in this book to offer their views on abnormal psychology across the ages.

The first volume focuses on the history of abnormal behavior throughout time. This volume follows our understanding of abnormal behavior from ancient times through the Renaissance and Enlightenment eras, and through the 20th century. Additionally, this volume highlights different organizing principles and themes that have informed our views of psychopathology, such as biological, psychological, social, and cultural perspectives. The second volume provides a contemporary understanding of abnormal psychology in the present that reviews what we know about psychopathology from different diagnostic categories, such as eating disorders, mood disorders, cognitive disorders, and addictive disorders, to name just a few. The third volume examines current and future trends in abnormal psychology, such as the role of pharmaceuticals, legal issues, and global concerns.

In all, the reader is presented with thoughtful reflections and state-of-the art understandings of abnormal psychology across the ages from leading experts.

This book is a companion to various books on this topic published by Praeger/Greenwood/ABC-CLIO, most notably *Mental Disorders of the New Millennium (Vols. I, II, and III)*, published in 2006.

Acknowledgments

Many people other than the author or editor assist in the completion of a book project. Some contribute in a direct way while others help in a more supportive manner. I would like to acknowledge the assistance of the people who worked to make the idea of this book a reality.

First and foremost, I would like to thank the contributors to this volume. They include some of the leading scholars in the field, who have worked like an all-star team to provide the reader with state-of-the-art reflection and scholarship. Second, it is important to recognize the wonderful people at ABC-CLIO who published this book. Most especially, many thanks go to my editor Debbie Carvalko for her many efforts not only with this book project but with many other book projects that I have published with her assistance during the past decade. Finally, I would like to thank my wife Lori and son Zach, who are daily reminders that life is good and sacred and that I am blessed beyond words to have them both in my life.

Chapter 1

Influences of the Greeks and Romans

Janet R. Matthews and Lee H. Matthews

Interest in abnormal behavior, or psychopathology, appears to have existed from the time of early written records. Our understanding of both the causes and treatment of behavior that differs from the typical has not been a steady movement of learning but rather has had periods of intense interest and writings followed by periods when prior knowledge seems to have been lost. The following chapter presents some of the highlights of this process from the perspective of the early Greek and Roman cultures. Brief information about some of the early people, myths, etiology, and treatments related to abnormal behavior is presented to illustrate the breadth of information they provided as a foundation that influenced thoughts about psychopathology for many centuries.

THE GREEKS

Personalities

For many scholars, the most influential Greek physician was Hippocrates of Cos (460–377 B.C.). Because he believed that the brain was the central control of human activity, he felt that disrupted behavior was the result of brain pathology. Scientists of this era believed that the four basic elements of the world were earth, air, fire, and water. These elements had the attributes of heat, cold, moistness, and dryness. A combination of these attributes led to the development of bodily fluids known as *humors*. These bodily fluids were influenced by many factors, including the weather and the foods one has eaten. According to Hippocrates, abnormal behavior was the result of an imbalance of the humors. The four basic humors in this system were black bile (cold + dry), yellow bile (hot + dry), phlegm (cold + moist), and blood (hot + moist). For example, a person who had an excessive amount of yellow bile would be expected to exhibit symptoms of mania. Such a person would engage in a range of excessive and frenzied activities. However, a person who had an excessive amount of black bile in contrast to the other humors would be expected to exhibit symptoms of melancholia, or extreme sadness.[1] Hippocrates also believed that such environmental factors as air and water quality, altitude, and time of the year contributed to the development of these imbalances. He noted that abnormal behavior sometimes seems to impact more than one member of a family and thus suggested that heredity also plays a role in the development of psychopathology. Finally, Hippocrates hypothesized the presence of a life force that was psychological in nature. Although this force typically operated through the senses and motor system in a traditional biological fashion, when sleeping it could produce dreams that were important to understanding the person's problems. In order to have an adequate understanding of a person's psychopathology, Hippocrates noted the necessity of close behavioral observation of the patient.

Based on this theory and his detailed patient observations, Hippocrates developed one of the earliest systems for classifying mental illness: mania, melancholia, and phrenitis (brain fever). This theory provided an early foundation for viewing abnormal behavior (mental illness) as an illness. This *mental illness* was comparable to the physical illnesses and therefore should be treated in a similar manner. This approach was different from the more general belief of viewing people who exhibited abnormal behavior as moral degenerates. His biopsychosocial theory has some basic similarities to current thoughts. This theory of abnormal behavior was in marked contrast to that of many of his colleagues, who believed that such behavior was the result of the work of gods and demons.

Hippocrates made treatment recommendations based on his theory of mental illness. He suggested that learning about the person's dreams would help the physician have a better understanding of the individual's personality. He also believed that the person's environment was potentially relevant to the treatment process. In many cases he recommended that patients be treated away from the influence of their families. Depending upon the specific form of abnormal behavior being treated, he recommended having a regular schedule and calm life situation, vigorous exercise, abstinence from all forms of excessive behavior, and a mild diet (often vegetarian). In the case of *hysteria*, a disease limited to women and attributed to a strong desire to have a child, he recommended marriage as the best treatment. On the other hand, he also believed in *medicinal days*. These were the days when it was safe for the physician to administer medications. Medical historians have suggested that this concept may have been the result of his careful observation of patients and noting that behavior changes from day to day.

When the Macedonian king Alexander III (356–323 B.C.), known popularly as Alexander the Great, founded the city of Alexandria in 332 B.C., Hippocrates' theories were transported to Egypt. Alexandria became a center of Greek culture where medical practices developed to a high level. Many of the temples dedicated to the god Saturn became similar to sanatoria, thus acknowledging the importance of the environment to the healing process. Mental patients in these sanatoria were given many activities that would be considered part of 21st-century activity therapy. They included dancing, gymnastics, walks in the garden, concerts, and rowing on the Nile. Although they did use such treatments as bleeding and restraints, they also provided massage, hydrotherapy, and dieting. Alexander the Great also lends his name to a disorder that would be described in the 19th century—*alexanderism*. Alexanderism is a form of psychopathology in which the individual has uncontrollable desires to destroy or exterminate entire societies or cultures.

Among the early Greeks, philosophers also wrote about abnormal behavior. For example, Plato (429–347 B.C.) seemed to have had a strong interest in mentally ill people who had committed criminal acts. He suggested that such individuals should be made to pay for any damages they had caused but that no other punishment should be given. He believed that these people should be treated in hospitals within their own community. His ideas about treatment centered on a form of conversation analogous to modern psychotherapy, although he also recommended the use of both incantations and drugs.[2] As Freud and others would suggest much later, Plato stressed the importance of dream interpretation. He noted that dreams were the result of frustrated desires and thus an important part of understanding the person. Unlike Hippocrates, who felt the center of human behavior was the brain, Plato said the spirit or soul was the core. Plato suggested that problems originating in the soul led to physical illness, and in his system abnormal behavior was one form of physical illness. Abnormal behavior was caused by problems in the part of the soul that controls reason. This part of the soul, for Plato, was located in the person's head. When describing the causes of abnormal behavior, Plato felt that some forms of abnormal behavior were naturally caused while others were the result of action by the gods. In some of his writings, therefore, Plato suggested that there were two different types of mental illness. One type was inspired by the gods. This mental illness gave the person the ability to see into the future. Since prophetic ability was viewed positively, this type of mental illness should not be altered. The other type of mental illness was caused by physical disease and therefore needed to be treated.[3] Thus, he held to both traditional ideas about madness and a more biological approach. Another topic about which Plato disagreed with Hippocrates was the role of the gods in mental illness. Hippocrates took the position that no illnesses were caused by the gods; however, Plato supported the ancient belief of *holy disease*. Plato wrote that a form of insanity was due to the divine breath of the gods. This breath was actually a gift to the person who might experience such characteristics as holy delirium and clairvoyance.

Plato's student, Aristotle (384–322 B.C.), also wrote about mental illness but seemed to agree with some of Hippocrates' ideas about causation. He wrote especially careful descriptions of affective states and the relationship between epilepsy and mental illness. Like his mentor Plato, Aristotle also wrote about the role of the soul in the development of abnormal behavior. Since difficulty with reason was a major component of abnormal behavior, it is not surprising that Aristotle suggested the importance of logic and reason in conversations with these individuals. In modern psychotherapy these factors are core to the cognitive therapies. Another of Aristotle's concepts, *catharsis*, is an important part of psychodynamic therapies. He was not, however, referring to a part of psychotherapy but rather the reaction of the audience during the performance of one of the Greek tragedies. Aristotle suggested that emotional cleansing occurred as a result of the person experiencing feelings of strong terror and pity, which were elicited by the actors in the play. As tutor to Alexander the Great, Aristotle also conveyed Hippocrates' ideas to his student, who would later carry them to Egypt, as noted previously. Another of Aristotle's concepts, earlier also emphasized by Socrates, was *physiognomy*. According to this concept, there is a correlation between a person's personality and his or her outward appearance. Twentieth-century personality theorists, like William Sheldon, would use this concept as the foundation for their work. Aristotle was especially interested in people's facial features and how they related to the personality. In a book attributed to Aristotle, the concept of physiognomy was carried even further by suggesting that people have the temperament of the animals they resemble. He even suggested that this principle could be applied more broadly to an entire race of people since there are broad commonalities in facial features that are found within such groups.

Myths

The role of myths and the numerous gods they described was an important part of Greek life. Many of these myths described both the behavior and treatments that in modern times are included in the diagnostic classification systems of abnormal behavior. In Greek mythology there was even a goddess of madness, Lyssa. According to mythology, if you offended Lyssa, she would possess you and cause you to lose your mind. These myths also provide further insight about how such behavior was viewed within the Greek culture. For example, the *maenads* were a group of women in myth who had superhuman strength. They did not follow the social customs of their times but rather roamed the countryside hunting wild animals. Their rites led to frenzies, which became identified in the culture as a form of madness.

Medea was a sorceress in Greek mythology. In one of the stories about Medea, she falls in love with a man named Jason. Jason is, however, engaged to be married. Her jealousy leads her to kill his fiancée. Because of the conflict she feels about having committed this murder, she later kills her own children. This myth forms the basis of the *Medea complex*, a term first used in the 1940s to describe mothers who have feelings that they want to kill their children. This death wish is often associated with a desire to seek revenge against the children's father.[4]

Narcissus was described in Greek mythology as the beautiful son of a river god and a nymph. According to myth, he never experienced love until the first time he saw his own reflection in a pool of water. What happens next varies, depending on which version of the myth you read. One version of the myth says that he thought this reflection was a nymph and he dove into the water to reach her. The result was that he drowned. In a different version of the myth about Narcissus, however, he spent the remainder of his life pining for the love he could not reach. This myth forms the basis of the narcissistic personality disorder found in modern classification systems. The person who is given this diagnosis today is considered to have an exaggerated sense of his or her self-worth and importance.

The story of Oedipus in Greek mythology not only describes abnormal behavior but has had a major impact on psychological theory over time. According to this myth, an oracle predicted that the king of Thebes, Laius, would be killed by his son. When his wife Jocasta gave birth to a boy, Laius had the child taken to the mountains to be left to die. The shepherd who was given this task gave the child to the childless king of Corinth, Polybus. This child was named Oedipus. When Oedipus became an adolescent, an oracle told him that his destiny was to kill his father and marry his mother. Oedipus was horrified by this prediction. In order to avoid this outcome, he decided to leave home. As he traveled toward Thebes, he met Laius on the road, had an argument with him, and killed him. He then married Jocasta. When he realized that the oracle's prediction had actually come true, he blinded himself and Jocasta committed suicide. This myth forms part of the basis for Freud's theory of infantile sexuality.[5] Sexual attraction between parent and child was also the theme of the myth about Phaedra, who fell in love with her stepson. The term *Phaedra complex* was later used to refer to a mother's sexual attraction to her son.[6]

Treatment

Historically, there has been a strong tradition of using herbal medication. Many of these remedies can be traced to the early Greeks and Romans. Colonial Americans used many home remedies based on herbs. In recent years people in the United States have begun to show an interest in herbal medicine. Prior to that time, herbal medicine was popular in many Eastern countries and in central Europe. The early Greeks made use of many natural products in the treatment of abnormal behavior. Consideration of a few of these items illustrates the range of plants and herbs that were used in ancient times. The peony is a plant that has been used in several different ways as a treatment for mental disorders. It was recommended that if you wore the root of a peony around your neck, you would prevent the onset of epilepsy. You could also take it in powder form by mouth as a cure for various forms of abnormal behavior. An infusion of peppermint leaves was considered a stimulant and thus could be used to treat depression. Practitioners who subscribed to the evil spirit theory of causation of abnormal behavior might use the wild herb, St. John's wort, as a treatment because it was believed that evil spirits did not like this herb. Vervain was another plant often used in the treatment of mental disorders. Hippocrates often used it with his patients. In the 21st century, with the popularity of tales of vampires, werewolves, and witchcraft, other uses of this plant may be more familiar to the reader. Black hellebore, also known as the Christmas rose, was used to treat severe mental illness in ancient Greece and continued to be popular well into the 19th century. The best black hellebore was considered to come from Anticyra, a peninsula on the Gulf of Corinth. People who were seen as seriously mentally ill were told to "sail to Anticyra." This was a gentle way of telling the person or family that the individual was really mentally ill and needed to have hellebore. The use of hellebore was also popularized in Greek mythology when the character Melampus was granted part of the kingdom of Argos because he used hellebore to treat an epidemic of mental illness there. The women of this kingdom had a group delusion that they were all cows and roamed the countryside accordingly.

GREEKS TO ROME

Personalities

Greek and Roman cultures have a degree of overlap. As the cultural center of the times moved from Greece to Rome, a number of prominent Greeks moved as well. Some of them brought the Greek ideas about abnormal behavior with them. Aretaeus of Cappadocia was a Greek physician born in the first century A.D. He studied in Alexandria prior to moving to Rome to practice medicine.

Aretaeus was among the first to note the importance of the person's premorbid personality. He devoted time to investigating and describing the personality of mental patients prior to the onset of their overt symptoms. Aretaeus also expanded on the classification system developed by Hippocrates. His system had seven categories of mental disorder: epilepsy (both ordinary and the hysterical variety, which was found only in women), melancholia, mania, phrenitis, drug delirium (a temporary disorder), senile dementia, and secondary dementia. He believed that melancholia was the basis of all psychotic disorders.

Another first-century Greek physician with an interest in mental illness was Dioscorides Pedanius. He served as a physician to the Roman emperor Nero. He brought the herbal tradition to Rome. His writings covered over 600 different plants and have been preserved in an illustrated manuscript that is now in the Bibliotheque in Paris. Nero had multiple emotional problems, which are described later in this chapter. One of the remedies Dioscorides prescribed for Nero was mandragora, or mandrake. This plant has been used in many cultures, including China, Palestine, Spain, and Italy, for the treatment of symptoms of mental illness. Although he gave it to Nero for insomnia, Hippocrates also found it useful for the treatment of depression. According to modern analysis of this plant, it actually has depressant, hallucinogenic, and hypnotic properties, usually producing both delirium and hallucinations. Later cultures would describe mandrake as having magical properties which not only cured various forms of mental illness but also served as an aid to fertility and an aphrodisiac. These latter uses were based on the specific shape of the plant.

Galenus Claudius (A.D. 129–199), better known as Galen, was also a Greek physician who trained in Alexandria and later moved to Rome. He integrated the concepts of Hippocrates, Plato, and Aristotle with his own ideas to form a holistic system of medicine. Rather than just talk about a single soul, Galen wrote that humans have two distinct subsouls. The brain was the site of the rational soul, but not the subsouls. The female subsoul was located in the liver while the male subsoul was located in the heart. Galen did such an impressive job of synthesizing and organizing the medical knowledge of his time that his works became the medical standard for about 1,500 years. His theories were based, to a great degree, on his dissection of animals. Human autopsies were not yet permitted, so he had to work with lower animals and then apply these findings to humans. He agreed with Hippocrates' theory about the importance of the humors but developed a somewhat different classification system for them. His eight-part system included anoia (reasoning problems), moria (retardation), phrenitis, melancholia, mania, lethargus, hysteria (found in both males & females), and epilepsy. Because he saw these problems as the same as physical disorders, his treatments were those used at the time for physical disorders—bleeding, drugs and herbs, and diet.

Alexander of Tralles (A.D. 525–605) was another of the well-known physicians who trained in Alexandria but later practiced in Rome. Some authors have described him as second only to Hippocrates among Greek physicians.[7] His writings were translated into numerous languages, including Latin, Greek, and Hebrew. Like Hippocrates, he strongly favored humane forms of treatment for his patients. Among his common treatments were baths, special diets, drinking wine, and taking sedatives. He also prescribed amulets to be worn by his patients. These amulets were custom-designed for the patient and frequently included religious sentiments. He discussed the importance of developing individualized treatments for unique patient problems. For example, one of his deluded patients believed that she had swallowed a snake. Not surprisingly, she became quite distressed by this belief. Alexander, in a fashion somewhat similar to the move of a modern magician, produced a snake for her to see. She thus believed he had removed that snake from her and was cured. He developed a classification system similar to that of Hippocrates but seemed to have a particular interest in melancholia. Alexander's classification system included six types of this disorder. When he became elderly and found the practice of medicine too tiring, he wrote about medicine, his major work titled *Twelve Books on Medicine*.

ROMANS

Personalities

Although most people think of Cicero (Marcus Tullius Cicero, 106 B.C.–43 B.C.) as an orator and philosopher, he also wrote about medicine. He was not a physician but expressed strong feelings about the incorrect nature of parts of Hippocrates' humoric theory. Specifically, he objected to the idea that an excess of black bile was the cause of melancholia. Cicero wrote that melancholia was due to psychological factors such as fear or anger. He also wrote that strong emotions can lead to physical symptoms. He did support Hippocrates' theory, however, that such disorders should be treated by skilled healers rather than one's depending on the gods to heal people.

Publius Ovidius Naso (43 B.C.–A.D. 17), better known as Ovid, was an early Roman poet who wrote about ways to deal with problems of sexuality. Although he was born into a rich family and educated as an attorney prior to dedicating himself to writing poetry, Ovid seems to have been an early specialist in an area of psychopathology that was often hidden until modern times. Because his lifestyle was found offensive by Roman authorities of his time, he was exiled. His writings after that period indicate that he found isolation to be a problem for people who have some form of psychopathology. Perhaps because of his own rather harsh treatment by the culture of the times, he also noted that harsh forms of treatment do not help those with mental problems.

Aulus Cornelius Celsus (25 B.C.–A.D. 50) wrote on a range of medical topics including mental illness. He was a nobleman but not a physician because that profession was considered below his social status. He is credited with being the first person to use the term *insanity* in relation to abnormal behavior. Today that term is used in legal rather than medical settings. He said that the presence of a mental disorder influences the entire personality. His classification system was similar to the one developed by Hippocrates. He was one of the early writers who also emphasized the importance of the doctor-patient relationship, or what in modern times is called the establishment of *rapport*. His treatment suggestions were quite broad. They included the common medical procedure of bleeding, various potions such as emetics and herbal treatments, as well as activities ranging from sports to listening to music or travel. He also suggested the use of *gestation*, or a process of gentle rocking, of the mental patient in a suspended bed. One of his more unique concepts was the idea that epilepsy was cured differentially in males and females. He noted that epilepsy in boys may be cured by their first coitus while for girls the cure may be the onset of menstruation.

Scribonius Largus (A.D. 14–54) was an early Roman physician who had an interest in the use of a range of medications for the treatment of abnormal behavior. He was the first of the Roman physicians to describe the use of the sting of the torpedo or electric fish to treat the pain of intractable headaches. This treatment can be viewed as a somewhat crude precursor of ECT (electroconvulsive therapy), which remains a treatment in the 21st century. Although most industrialized countries now use electronic equipment for this procedure, some African tribes in the 21st century continue to use the Nile electric catfish (malopterurus electricus) as a form of shock treatment, which their ancestors learned from early Greek and Roman healers. He also described the use of an opium extraction, as well as the drinking of one's own blood, for the treatment of various problems. He wrote one of the early books on the use of various drugs, *Compositiones Medicamentorum*. He took some of his ideas about the treatment of psychopathology to Britain when he visited there in A.D. 43.

Gaius Plinius Secundus, also known as Pliny the Elder (A.D. 23–79) appeared to have more interest in the treatment of abnormal behavior than in the development of a classification system. As a naturalist, he emphasized the use of natural products as remedies. For example, he suggested that calf's dung which had been boiled in wine was a remedy for melancholia. He said a safe remedy for epilepsy was the hollyhock (althea officinalis), a small plant found most often near the sea. In more modern times, British healers suggested harvesting the leaves in the summer to treat lung and kidney problems and harvesting the root in the late autumn to treat digestive problems. He realized that even natural products, when used excessively, could have a negative effect. One example of this problem was the use of henbane. Henbane, an annual plant, may be the oldest anesthetic known to humanity. It was used as a pain-killer. When it was used to deal with earaches, people of the time often poured its juice into their ears. According to Pliny this application of henbane could cause mental disorders, including hallucinations. Its hallucinogenic properties would be used in the Middle Ages as part of the practice of witchcraft. Another useful product was the juice of the poppy. Pliny noted that it was helpful for inducing sleep but was easily abused. The Greeks first used the modern term *opium* for this product. For depression, a problem found throughout the ages, Pliny recommended the use of the herb *borage*, also known as starflower, to elevate a person's mood. Although this annual herb originated in Syria, it is found commonly throughout the Mediterranean area. Today, homeopathic practitioners still use borage as a mood elevator, most often for the treatment of PMS in women. Like Scribonius Largus, Pliny described the use of electric eels in the treatment of severe headaches.

Nero Claudius Caesar (A.D. 37–68), a Roman emperor, lived during the time that Pliny was writing about the treatment of abnormal behavior. Perhaps if he had received treatment from Pliny, his life might not have ended the way it did. Nero's behavior has been described as depressed at some times and manic at others, or what 21st-century mental health professionals would call bipolar disorder. He was also reported to have suffered from epilepsy. Historians have noted that both his father and mother came from families that were considered to have exhibited mental illness. From the time of Nero's birth, he seems to have been viewed in a negative way. Historians say he was born feet first, and this was considered a bad omen at the time. When he was only two years old, his father died and he was adopted by Emperor Claudius. As an adult, he was described as having difficulty controlling his anger. This behavior may well have been a symptom of his mania. During these periods he murdered his first two wives, the second of whom some sources say he kicked to death while she was pregnant. He also ordered the execution of his mother. Nero is said to have set the city of Rome on fire and then recited poetry about the burning of the city of Troy while he watched Rome burn. He committed suicide on the anniversary of the death of his first wife, Claudia Octavia, who was also his stepsister, during a period when he was in hiding and learned that factions within the country were rising against him. Descriptions of his behavior illustrate the fact that although there were some who wrote about psychopathology at that time, leaders of the country were not willing to seek such treatment.

The modern definition of sociopathy can be traced to the life experiences of Lucius Aelius Aurelius Commodus, better known as Emperor Marcus Antonius

(A.D. 161–192). Historians have described his behavior as both extravagant and cruel. Among his characteristic behaviors were his sexual demands of his 300 concubines and young boys, offering human sacrifices to the gods, fighting with wild animals in the arena, and torturing men by making multiple cuts on them with surgical implements. He exhibited no shame or regret for his behavior but rather ordered that his most infamous actions should be included in public records.

Myths

The belief that the moon has a major impact on human behavior dates from ancient times. Although the role of the moon is part of many cultures, the modern term *lunacy* comes from the Latin word *luna*, which means moon. Pliny noted that the moon could cause both nightmares and complete insanity. Many Roman physicians believed that the moon caused epilepsy. The influence of the moon on mental state persisted through many subsequent cultures.[8] Even in the 21st century, it is not uncommon to hear someone note, during times of upheaval, that there "must be a full moon." Modern science, however, does not support the idea that the presence of a full moon correlates with increased psychopathology.[9]

Another important part of Roman folk lore was the role of spirits of the woods, known as *fauni*. Many people of this era believed that mental illness was caused by the fauni. Pliny the Elder, the naturalist previously described, referred to several forms of mental illness as "mockeries of the fauni."

Treatment

Somatic and psychic illnesses were initially seen as part of the same whole, therefore were treated using the same substances as well. Psychic and somatic symptoms were considered as separate phenomena only in later times, before finally being progressively considered once more as different manifestations affecting the *same body* in the course of the *same disease*.

Instead of looking just at natural sources for remedies from pain, illness, and death, the ancients looked to magic and the supernatural for cures. In fact, the word *remedy* comes from the Latin *mederi* and is related to the Latin origin of the word *medicine*. Thus, the original goal of medicine, regardless of the source of the cure (environmental, herbal, magic or supernatural), was to provide relief from suffering.[10]

One example of the interaction between herbal and supernatural treatment is mistletoe. The word *mistletoe* is related to the Latin name of the god of medicine, Asclepius. The Greeks thought of mistletoe as a life-giving plant, a symbol of sexuality. For the Romans, it was tied to Saturn, an agricultural god, and used as part of fertility rites. Harvesting mistletoe, especially that growing on oak trees, was seen as symbolically castrating the tree because the juice from mistletoe berries, seen as the *oak sperm*, was considered to be charged with therapeutic powers. Due in part to mistletoe's role in fertility rites, the Greeks used it for menstrual complaints. Both the Greeks and Romans also used it to treat epilepsy and other neurological disorders and for external tumors and cancers. Mistletoe is just one among many different herbs and trees used in ancient medical practice; the bark of willow trees surrounding the temple of Athena contained salicylate, an antipyretic and anti-inflammatory drug still widely prescribed.[11]

In many ways, Roman medicine can be viewed as illustrating the overall view of humanity of the culture at the time. There was a focus on pleasure and comfort, especially for the leaders of the society. Thus, treatment of abnormal behavior was often designed to make the patient comfortable. Physicians made extensive use of such physical treatments as massage and warm baths. One principle that was quite popular at the time was *the use of contraries*, which refers to the importance of opposites. Thus, a physician might recommend sitting in a warm tub while drinking a chilled wine. Another unusual treatment from this era was first described for Rome's empress Faustina Augusta (A.D. 124–175). She developed such strong sexual desires for one of the gladiators that she became seriously ill from her desires. When she confessed her problem to her emperor husband, he had the gladiator killed. He then had his wife's body anointed with the warm blood of the gladiator, which cured her passion. This case led to the use of the warm blood of killed gladiators to treat certain forms of mental illness.

Although modern society has specific laws that relate to the mentally ill, the Roman culture seems to have been somewhat more organized in codifying this material. The main body of Roman law, *Corpus Juris Civilis*, was developed during the reign of Justinian (A.D. 483–565). This document recognized the importance of *soundness of mind*, rather than the health of the body, when making a will. This legal code not only defined the criminal responsibility of the mentally ill but also addressed their ability to testify in court, to make such legal documents as wills, their ability to marry and divorce, and to sell their possessions. This system even covered the influence of drunkenness and strong emotions on criminal behavior.

CONCLUSIONS

This chapter has provided an overview of the way abnormal behavior was explained and treated by the early Greek and Roman civilizations. There are many other people who could have been cited. We have attempted to discuss a representative sample with the hope that interested readers will continue to explore this topic in both other secondary sources and primary sources. The work of these early cultures forms the foundation for viewing psychopathology as an *illness*. Despite the counterargument that psychopathology is really a cultural phenomenon,[12] the overriding position today seems to have moved only slightly to a biopsychosocial position rather than a purely biological one.

Although the views of modern professionals are probably not as diverse as those of ancient times, the field continues to be divided in terms of both causality and treatment. Demon possession is no longer viewed as a cause of psychopathology by mental health professionals. On the other hand, the role of nature in contrast to nurture, relative to many forms of psychopathology, remains a point of debate. Whereas early cultures had myths depicting various forms of abnormal behavior, modern society has films.[13] The lay public continues to have sufficient fascination with the behavior of those who differ from themselves that these films are often large-budget items, winning major awards.

The early Greeks and Romans used a wide variety of natural products in their treatment of abnormal behavior. Today in the United States, we see such terms as homeopathy or naturopathy as alternatives to traditional medical interventions for a range of problems including psychopathology. Although these approaches have been used in this country since the early 19th century,[14] there seems to be a rising interest in them in the 21st century. Today some states even license professionals in the specialty "homeopathic physician" (e.g., Arizona, Connecticut, and Nevada), but these individuals are typically graduates of either traditional or osteopathic medical schools. The natural products recommended by these practitioners are regulated by the federal government in the same manner as over-the-counter drugs.

REFERENCES

1. Arikha, N. (2007). *Passions and tempers: A history of the humors.* New York: Ecco/ HarperCollins.
2. Milns, R. D. (1986). Squibb academic lecture: Attitudes towards mental illness in antiquity. *Australian and New Zealand Journal of Psychiatry, 20,* 454–462.
3. Ackerknecht, E. H. (1959). *A short history of psychiatry.* New York: Hafner.
4. Stern, E. S. (1948). The Medea complex: Mother's homicidal wishes to her child. *Journal of Mental Sciences, 94,* 321.
5. Freud, S. (1954). *The origins of psychoanalysis: Letters to Wilhelm Fliess, drafts and notes: 1887–1902.* M. Bonaparte, A. Freud, & E. Kriss (Eds.). New York: Basic Books.
6. Graves, R. (1993). *The Greek myths: Combined edition.* New York: Penguin.

7. Howells, J. G., & Osborn, M. L. (1984). *A reference companion to the history of abnormal psychology: A-L*. Westport, CT: Greenwood Press.
8. Oliven, J. F. (1943). Moonlight and nervous disorders: A historical study. *American Journal of Psychiatry, 99*, 579–584.
9. Wilkinson, G., Piccinelli, M., Roberts, S., & Fry, J. (1997). Lunar cycle and consultation for anxiety and depression in general practice. *International Journal of Social Psychiatry, 43*(1), 29–34.
10. Hoffman, D. (2003). *Medical herbalism: The science and practice of herbal medicine*. Rochester, VT: Healing Arts Press.
11. Evans, J. (2005). Mistletoe: Good for more than free kisses. *Herbal Gram, 68*, 50–59.
12. Szasz, T. S. (1960). The myth of mental illness. *American Psychologist, 15*, 113–118.
13. Wedding, D., Boyd, M. A., & Niemiec, R. M. (2010). *Movies and mental illness: Using films to understand psychopathology* (3rd ed.). Cambridge, MA: Hogrefe & Huber.
14. Ballard, R. (2000). Homeopathy: An overview. *Australian Family Physician, 29*, 1145–1148.

Chapter 2

Perceptions, Thoughts, and Attitudes in the Middle Ages

Eva D. Papiasvili and Linda A. Mayers

From the fall of the Western Roman Empire in 476 CE to Columbus's discovery of the New World in 1492, massive geo-political reconfigurations coincided with profound transformations in a wide range of human activities, norms, and abnormalities. This millennium embraces the Early Middle Ages (476 CE–11th century CE), High Middle Ages (12th century–1347 CE), and Late Middle Ages (1347 CE–1492 CE).

A once dominant view saw the Middle Ages as a detour between the Classical period and its Renaissance. Twentieth-century historians, however, came to characterize the years of the Middle Ages as leaving legacies in their own right, including the inception of the parliamentary system, the nation state, trial by jury, and the legal definition of mental incapacity; the birth of banking, the university, and experimental science; achievements in philosophy, architecture and the fine arts; and the invention of eye glasses, the clock, and the printing press.

The creative output of the period is all the more remarkable for having transpired amid multiple epic traumas. Pestilence, famine, and plague matched territorial reconfiguration and war throughout the Middle Ages, marking the people who lived and thrived through them for their adaptability and uncommon resilience.

The Middle Ages were born out of the trauma of cultures clashing over the ruins of Rome. When the Greco-Roman ideals of rationality and self-reliance were no longer viable, they were replaced by the adaptation model of early Christian theology. This new model emphasized faith over reason, and reliance on supernatural forces to transcend everyday threats to physical survival.

Rooted in Neo-Platonic subjectivism, early Christian theology paired with a post-traumatically fragile connection with physical reality to effect thinking rich in symbols, metaphors, imagery, and mysticism, and perceptual phenomena such as visions and hallucinations. With the High Middle Ages came Neo-Aristotelian Christian theology and the renewed legitimacy of reason, part of a multifaceted recovery halted only by the Black Plague. The posttraumatic, regressive adaptation which followed characterized the Late Middle Ages and was manifest in behaviors such as group rituals, self-flagellation, pogroms, and cults.

In the Middle East, where the Eastern Roman Empire survived as Byzantium until 1453, mental conditions were identified and treated as illnesses, as they were in parts of North Africa and non-Christian Spain. Early Christian Europe, in contrast, conceptualized "madness" in theological terms, as a mixture of the divine, diabolical, magical, and transcendental. In the High and Late Middle Ages, new developments in philosophy and law, together with new empirical findings and the rediscovery of ancient knowledge, contributed to more diverse practices in every field, including mental health assessment and treatments.

This chapter will begin with the consideration of norms and abnormalities with regard to the Middle Ages. It will proceed with a historical-cultural review focusing on the two major traumas of the Middle Ages, the aftermath of the Fall of Rome and the Black Plague. In examining their respective posttraumatic adaptations, special emphasis will be placed on attitudes, perceptions, lifestyles, behaviors, and thought. The chapter will conclude by contrasting Christian Europe's approaches to mental conditions with those of the Middle East and the non-Christian Mediterranean.

NORMS AND ABNORMALITIES

"Contemporary research now supports the idea that the social environment has important consequences for mental health. Within a social context therefore, behaviors that are considered abnormal are those that deviate significantly from those standards of behavior generally regarded as normal by the majority of people in a society"[1] (p. 2).

Where behaviors of any era belong to the norm, and where they cross the abnormality border, can be assessed according to several criteria: historical/cultural, objective/universal/legal, subjective, and statistical. The Historical-Cultural view holds that certain lifestyles, behaviors, attitudes, perceptions, and thoughts might be deemed pathological in one historical-cultural context and not in another. The Objective/Universal/Legal view holds that there are certain states of extreme withdrawal, states of disorientation, incoherent thoughts, and unconventional, disorganized behaviors, which will be universally considered the product of mental affliction, regardless of the attributed etiology. In the Middle Ages, this view was articulated in early medical models of mental disorder deriving from the Four Humor classification and the legal definition of insanity originating in Thomas Aquinas's *Canon Law*. Aquinas's High Middle Ages text postulated the "Sick of Mind" category, identifying degrees of insanity rather than varieties in kind. The objective was the evaluation of an individual's legal competence to participate in valid contracts. The Subjective Report concerns the individual's experience. The first Subjective Report written in English was the Late Middle Ages autobiographical account of Margery Kempe. The Statistical Assessment (prevalence, incidence) addresses the frequency with which a given condition occurs in a general population. In the absence of statistics, inferences may be drawn from available sources, such as chronicles, public records, and literature.

HISTORICAL-CULTURAL CONTEXT: EVOLUTION OF ATTITUDES, BEHAVIORS, THOUGHTS, AND PERCEPTIONS

Initial Traumas and Posttraumatic Adaptations

Rome was sacked by "Barbarians" in 410, 453, and 476 CE. While the resulting physical devastation was great, the psychological effect was greater still. As the institutions and the identity of the Western Empire crumbled, the Greco-Roman ideal of the independent, rational, self-reliant man was decapitated. Amidst death, destruction, and chaos, terrorized survivors fled the city en masse: at the end of the fifth century, Rome retained only 30,000 inhabitants, one tenth of the imperial city's population at its height. Attempting to grasp the incomprehensible, Christian Neo-Platonists of the Academy invoked faith as reason's guiding light in the pursuit of truth. In 410 CE, this new adaptation model was articulated by Augustine in *The City of God*. Augustine drew on his own transformative experience, his consuming lust having become love for God, his soul's catastrophe becoming salvation, all through his conversion to the Christian faith[2] (p. 27). Augustine formulated the Early Medieval Christian conceptualization of man as God's beloved instrument, a helpless child-creature occupying a pre-ordained position in the divinely designed order, wholly dependent on supernatural forces, rewarded for his suffering by the eternal salvation of his soul. Compared to this transcendental super-reality, the traumas and miseries of physical reality were temporary and insignificant. Based on Augustine and later Boethius's (480–525 CE) philosophical synthesis, stressing the mystical and subjective elements of Plato's philosophy, Early Christian theology offered the comfort of continuity with the Classical world within the context of monotheism, transcendence, and community. It wrote a meaningful narrative around society's trauma, defining the mentality of Christian Europe until the 13th century.[3]

Early posttraumatic attempts at adaptation touched and linked every constituent of the clash of cultures and every emerging segment of Early Medieval Society. As with ideologies, old identities had to be transformed and new identities forged. Disorientation, withdrawal, and depression were countered by attempts at mobilization and integration, as were disassociation, vigilance, paranoia, and aggressive enactment against others and self.

The posttraumatic adaptation process of Rome's senatorial aristocracy was tracked by Sidonius Apollinaris (unknown–489 CE), Senator-turned-bishop: from disorientation, literary escapism and disillusionment with Rome to widespread clericalization and, finally, identification with the adopted "Barbarian" culture (p. 4).[4] Even while monks around the Mediterranean suffered widespread depression and holy anorexia[5] and prepared for the end of the world, another Roman aristocrat, St. Benedict (480–547 CE), established the first Western monastic order rigorously organized around daily work, prayer, and study. A third Roman noble, Pope Gregory the Great (540–604 CE), effected an "integration of Lombard and Anglo-Saxon invaders into the Christian world by a deliberate missionary program"[4] (p. 41).

Just as some Romans came to identify with the culture of their conquerors, the Barbarians strove to become those whom they had decapitated, keeping totems of Rome everywhere. The heads of emperors adorned the Roman currency they circulated. They used Roman titles and wrote Roman inscriptions on their state buildings. Between the 5th and 9th centuries, they teamed with the Roman clergy to establish stratified feudal monarchies with written legal codes, integrating Latin law, ecclesiastic law, and tribal customs.[6] The Ascendency celebrated its new identity in 800 CE, when the Pope crowned the Frankish Charlemagne Roman Emperor. The new emperor treated his own "Barbarians," the Saxons, with violence comparable to Caesar's. The ensuing "Carolingian Renaissance" rivaled antiquity in intellectual achievement, only to collapse shortly after Charlemagne's death.

Having become Roman, the Franks now suffered their own Fall of Rome,[7] and years of chaos ensued.[4] Reports of barbaric behavior, of young men engaging in raids, rape, and slaughter, and terrorizing neighborhoods[8] coincided with early records of lycanthropy.[9] Communities apparently lived in terror of werewolf attacks, just as Romans once lived in terror of Barbarian raids. The werewolf was a projection or a direct manifestation of the Devil.[9] Local violence and the lycanthropic response may be illustrative of posttraumatic regression, with loss of identity spawning a vigilant paranoid adaptation in insulated manorial communities. Echoing the fifth-century Mediterranean monks, some communities were reported to fear the imminent end of the world.[4]

In this mad world hid an unlikely voice of reason. By assuming the role of Fool, men of keen insight and caustic wit enjoyed a special "freedom of speech" in the courts of Medieval princes.[10] Under the cover of asses' ears and mismatched colors, the Greco-Roman institution of independent thought survived.

Some Holy and Normative Lifestyles
Peculiar to the Middle Ages

Once the mystical and the transcendental were elevated to the status of "super-reality," what distinguished between "holiness" and aberration was the ideological content of the behavior. Content-fitting theological aspirations were pronounced "holy," therefore indisputable by reason.

Typically for the Middle Ages, several social groups engaging in the study, defense, and service of God, renouncing some or most of their physical and social needs, were deemed to be close to God. Hermits, monks, clerics, anchorites, and some knights all held recognized holiness in varying degrees, and it was generally among them that specific perceptual, attitudinal, or behavioral phenomena termed "holy" occurred. Some monks and clerics, most knights, and all anchorites began rigorous schooling at the age of eight, boarding away from their families.[11] Consequently, some measure of emotional and physical deprivation may have started early in life.

Some hermits reportedly castrated themselves to prevent temptation. Some monks perpetually fasted, experiencing "holy anorexia." Although organized monastic orders did not institutionalize extreme deprivation measures, their spiritual training and religious involvement included various restrictions of social and sexual behaviors. Apart from speaking with animals, St. Francis, founder of the Franciscan monastic order, reported scores of visions and painful physical sensations, including stigmata (bleeding from "Christ's wounds"). Monks regularly engaged in self-flagellation to expiate their desires of the flesh.[2]

The lifestyle of Anchorite women included seclusion in the proximity of a church or a cathedral, serious study, and prayer. As a viable alternative to marriage, it provided some with a unique opportunity for self-realization. One of the most famous anchorites of the twelfth century was Hildegard von Bingen,[11] who went on to become an abbess, writer, and illustrator, as well as a composer of liturgical music and poetry. She traveled through Europe on "preaching tours" and corresponded with monarchs and popes. Hildegard's description and illustrations of her visions in *Scivias*[11] show them to be symbolic expressions of emotional conflicts, highly condensed "picture-insights" into the essence of events inside and around her. From childhood on, she was consistently able to differentiate them from the real physical world around her.

A Knight's code of honor included a religious aspect, a martial aspect, and, from the High Middle Ages on, an aspect of chivalry as well. The early prototype of St. George slaying the Dragon is a symbolic expression of a knight fighting the evil forces. In the High Middle Ages, knights evolved into a complex cultural group. Twelfth-century Romances portrayed knights as Men in Robes, decorated with emblems of arithmetic, geometry, astronomy, and music.[12] Of particular psychological interest is chivalry, whose provision for platonic courtly love served as a potent motivation for a knight's heroic military service. A knight's worshipping the "pure lady" and devaluing the "whore" (all other women) was a cultural norm, while his aggression on a Holy Crusade was sanctioned and blessed by church authorities.[13]

Some Specific Patterns of Perceptions and Thought in the Early and High Middle Ages

Regarding perception, the posttraumatic fluidity of the boundary between the real and the transcendental was evidenced by abundant reports of visions and hallucinations. These fall on a continuum of distinction from physical reality. However, the divisions between them were often blurred, as people tended to call "visions" all they heard and saw that was not perceived by others. Many personalities besides Hildegard and St. Francis reported visions and/or hallucinations, including Abelard, Joan of Arc, and St. Augustine. Visions were often described as two-dimensional translucent images, like stained glass windows in Gothic cathedrals.[11] Visions of saints and scenes of piety, subjectively beneficent, were believed to be divinely inspired. Visions of menacing characters, subjectively disturbing, were believed to be devil-inspired, and therefore pathological.[8,14]

Written and spoken speech was rich with metaphors, allegories, and condensed symbolism[11]–abstract principles and generalizations were illustrated allegorically, metaphorically, and symbolically. The dominant pattern was of symbolic relational associations rather than causal logical abstract connections. For some, amidst traumatic chaos, suggestibility and superficial associations of co-occurrences substituted for causality and bred popular superstitions, which guided the regressive magical thinking.[9] For others, heavily symbolized associative-relational thought, even under stress, lacked neither depth nor complexity, nor organization and structure. A fifth-century example of in-depth analysis of internal psychological processes is Augustine's *Confessions*, which describe "the poignant inner experience of the soul catastrophe in a catastrophic world"[2] (p. 27). Dante's *Divine Comedy* offers a 14th-century example, describing as it does a soul-healing journey through a hierarchical, internal world. The Inferno translates as the seat of the Id's Sexual and Aggressive drives, while Purgatory serves as the seat of the Ego's insight and working through of one's problems, and Paradise forms the Superego's moral and ideal superstructure. The *Divine Comedy* thus parallels Freudian psychoanalysis of the 20th century.[15]

Hildegard's twelfth-century *Scivia* comprises volumes on philosophy, music and poetry, society, economics, and the natural sciences, including the biology of sexual organs. Even when she wrote on economics and the natural sciences, allegories, metaphors, and condensed relational symbols were invoked to convey information.[11]

Thinking was heavily influenced by primary process (characterized by condensation and displacement, as in dreams and poetry). Thought was predominantly relational, everything being defined by its relation to something else, as nothing exists alone.[3,11] An example of this is Augustine's "first relational definition" of time which foreshadowed the Big Bang Theory. It posited that God created the world *with* time, *not in* time, as time and matter could not exist separately. Neo-Aristotelian thought broke this pattern, whether in the 13th-century deductive reasoning of Aquinas and Abelard, or in Grosseteste's and Bacon's 11th- and 12th-century inductive, empirical reports on optics.[4,11]

The High Middle Ages, a stage for cultural recovery, the birth of cities, the Magna Carta, universities, commerce, and Gothic cathedrals, re-engaged the problem of Faith and Reason. Aquinas' Neo-Aristotelian thesis defended the legitimacy of reason by arguing that both Reason and Faith present different ways to discovering the truth. Aquinas's revolutionary thesis became central to scholastic philosophy, reflecting the need for a conceptual framework for diversification in all fields, including approaches to mental conditions.

Later Trauma and Posttraumatic Developments

The Black Plague of 1347–1348, following the Famine of 1315, killed one-third of the population of Europe and the Mediterranean.[12,16] Death and decay were everyday occurrences. As once with the approaching armies of Barbarians, so now with the advent of the Black Death, terror was general. Citizens fled town amidst a sense of impending doom, disorientation, helplessness, and disillusionment. The multigenerational, traumatic psychological effects were immense.[16] Specific to this period were repentance, self-flagellation, penitential exercises, and the "macabre culture." This complex phenomenon involved Dances of Death, a "devil-may-care" attitude of excess, and the fascination with magic, rumored to spread in the form of witchcraft and satanic cults. Ultimately the macabre culture provoked a backlash of religious excitement and ensuing pogroms against "The Others," who became the targets of projected guilt.[9,16]

The art of this time reflected its mood: torture, death, and decay were all portrayed naturalistically, particularly in Bosch's "Temptations of Saint Anthony," depicting the Witches' Sabbath, Brueghel's "Last Judgment" and "Apocalypse", and the Block books "La Danse Macabre" and "Ars Moriendi" by Antonio Verard.[17]

Among examples of regressive group behavior surrounding famine and plague were epidemics of wild dancing, jumping, and drinking, which spread all over Europe as "St. Vitus' Dance." First noted in Italy in the tenth century as "Tarantism," it began spreading during the Plague and continued after the Plague subsided.[9,16] Tarantism was triggered by the real or imagined bite of a spider, which was to be cured by music. Reports of major outbreaks of the St. Vitus' dance in Aachen, Germany, in 1374 describe men, women, and children breaking into dance, for no discernable reason, and continuing until they collapsed. Musicians often accompanied dancers to ward off the mania, but often this backfired because the music encouraged more people to join in.[9]

From the 11th century on, the mysticism of the Cult of the Free Spirit appeared, a strand of mysticism separate from that which was sanctioned by the Church. Although both "sprang from a craving for immediate communion with God; both stressed the value of ecstatic experiences; and both took their conceptual apparatus from Neo-Platonist philosophy"[18] (p. 51), there were crucial differences. While the Church recognized the experience of the mystical union with God as a momentary illumination, the adept of the Free Spirit felt himself to be utterly transformed, identical with and surpassing God. After such a transformative experience, the adepts of the Free Spirit adopted an amoral stance, claiming that "practicing free love re-created the state of innocence enjoyed by Adam and Eve in earthly paradise"[18] (p. 65).

Sin-expiating, self-flagellation processions flared up in the wake of the Black Death, famine, and typhus in the High and Late Middle Ages. Flagellants attributed sin to themselves. Those perpetuating pogroms, on the other hand, attributed sin to another group of people. Flagellants usually formed a public procession, inflicting wounds on themselves until blood squirted from their bodies, expiating sins that caused deadly epidemics.[9] The predominance of magical thinking under conditions of extreme trauma is illustrated in accounts of Pope Clement VI's attempt to stop French Farmers' Pogroms of Jews during famine and plague. No logical arguments got through. Only when the Pope threatened the farmers with God's wrath did the killing cease.[9] The attribution of evil by one group to another or to an individual who became the target of a crowd's aggression continued during the Later Middle Ages in various forms.

Creative adaptations of a different kind to the horrors of plague and famine were depicted in literature, for example, Chaucer's *Canterbury Tales* and Boccaccio's *Decameron*, describing groups of survivors comforting each other with humorous, lascivious stories. This was an era of pilgrimages, lay piety, and growing interest in the Cult of Virgin Mary and her mother St. Anne, the saviors of Plague survivors.[16]

While some historians see the post-Plague depression extending into all spheres of human functioning,[16] others[4,12] argue that, economically, post-Plague Europe may have yielded improved conditions for the survivors. With fewer people to share available resources, wages grew, land was cheaper, and while some cultural centers were afflicted, new ones rose to replace them. New universities were founded in Prague in 1348, Warsaw in 1358, and Heidelberg in 1360. Viewed synthetically, both trends—the normative, posttraumatic depression of older cultural centers (France) and the posttraumatic mobilization of ascendant ones (Germany, Bohemia, Poland, Flanders, England, and the Low Countries)—co-existed. The Late Middle Ages are known for such monumental advances as the inventions of the astronomical clock and the printing press and new precision and dynamism in paintings, ushering in the Renaissance.[17] The access to information, art, and culture was promoted in the Late Middle Ages by written and printed vernacular languages. While in the High Middle Ages, new texts were written primarily in Latin and French, the Late Middle Ages saw the dominance of English, Italian, Flemish, Catalonian, and Czech. The development of vernacular production was promoted by religious reformers, knights, merchants, bankers, and poets alike. In the Late Middle Ages, Europe became a complex civilization of new diversities, reflecting resilience in the face of unfathomable traumas.[4]

MENTAL ILLNESS AND TREATMENT IN THE MIDDLE AGES

The Middle East and the Non-Christian Mediterranean

In the Middle East, where classical knowledge survived, abnormalities in perception, thought, mood, and behavior were identified and treated as illnesses in psychiatric hospitals as early as 707 CE. Patients were treated with hydrotherapy, music, and activities that could be viewed as forerunners of projective doll play, therapeutic puppetry, and psychodrama. Middle Eastern scholars and physicians combined the Greco-Roman tradition with Muslim religious influences and their own empirical findings. Some of the most important personalities and their contributions are listed below.

Expanding on Hippocrates' (460–370 BC) Four Humor Theory and Galen's (129–200 CE) extension, which identified the brain as the seat of mental functioning and illness, Al Balkhi (787–886 CE) classified fears, sadness, and obsession; Al Tabari (839–923 CE) identified the need for counseling; Rhazes (865–925 CE), the head of the "psychiatric unit" at the general hospital in Baghdad, advocated the importance of hope in addressing psychological, moral, and spiritual problems. His *Liber Continens* included the successful employment of "shock psychotherapy." His shocking of an unsuspecting, long-term paralyzed patient by attacking him in a steam room with a knife, screaming "run or be killed!" demonstrated an awareness of psychogenic factors in hysterical paralysis (p. 52).[2] Avicenna (980–1037 CE) combined physiological and psychological approaches, addressing insomnia, hallucinations, vertigo, mania, and melancholia in his *Canon of Medicine*. He "exerted deep and lasting influence on all the great scholastic thinkers of the Middle Ages (p. 53)."[2] Avicenna's *Canon of Medicine* proved to be a daring attempt to synthesize the Greek and Arabic healing arts and served as the standard for European medicine for five centuries to come. His belief in the influence of the mind over the body was apparent in his version of the free-associative method. Averroes (1126–1198 CE) identified Parkinson's disease. A personal physician to the Caliphs and a critic of charlatanry and superstition, he authored the important concept of "double truth"—what is true in theology may be false in philosophy, and vice versa, which opened the scientific inquiry at a time of religious fervor.[2] Unhamad (870–925 CE) identified nine classes of psychopathology with treatment recommendations: Febrile Delirium; Dementia; Obsessive Compulsive Syndrome; Involutional Psychotic Reaction; Paranoid and Melancholic Disorders; Paranoid Mania; Antisocial Personality; and Depressive-Loss Reaction. Humoral pathology and interaction with other somatic symptoms, as well as the importance of interpersonal relations and self-concept, were seen as etiologically prominent. Dietary and other treatments varied according to how acute or chronic the symptomatology was. If inflammation was present, treatment included a mild form of bloodletting and a milk diet. In most other cases, a high caloric diet was recommended with occupational therapy, games, and hydrotherapy. Patients were never permitted to sit in the dark. Patients with agitation or aggressive behavior were restrained to prevent injury to themselves and others. Attempts were made to help patients to develop attitudes and behaviors to reengage with the world after a loss.[2]

Psychiatric Hospitals

The first psychiatric hospitals were founded in Baghdad and Fes in the early eighth century, in Cairo in 800, and in Damascus and Aleppo in 1270. Patients were benevolently treated with hydrotherapy, music, and activities. Restraint was used only sporadically to prevent injury to self and others. In the thirteenth century, Rabbi Benjamin of Toledo wrote: ". . . demented people who have become insane in the towns through the great heat of the summer . . . are provided with the food from the house of the Caliph. Every month the officers of the Caliph inquire and investigate whether they have regained their reason, in which case they are discharged"[19] (p. 88).

One of the best-known institutions in the Arab world was the Mansuri Hospital of Cairo, whose designated sections for various diseases included a wing for the treatment of mental disorders with the practice of "bibliotherapy." In a collegial atmosphere, male and female patients were encouraged to select books on a wide range of subjects from the hospital library, attend lectures and seminars, and communicate their feelings and suffering in "therapy" groups (p. 57).[2] By the 12th century the Arabs introduced the puppet shows to entertain the sick. In the 13th century, a Jewish physician of Arab origin, Al-Mawsili, wrote about a highly developed form of shadow play under the title *Phantoms of the Imagination and the Knowledge of Shadow Play*, which anticipated projective doll play, psychodrama, and puppetry. Other developments included modern methods for research, diagnosis, and psychotherapy.[2]

Overall, the Greco-Roman traditions of empirical inquiry, including research, diagnosis, and treatments, remarkably unobstructed by ideologies, with an admixture of non-conflicting cultural values of the region, continued until the sacking of Baghdad in 1258 and the end of Byzantium in 1453.[2]

LATIN WEST—CHRISTIAN EUROPE

Theological Approach

Medieval attitudes and perceptions of mental illness as possession stem from the Bible: According to St. Mark, Jesus cured a madman by casting out the devils within him into a herd of swine. The swine stampeded and fell to their deaths, thus destroying the evil spirit.[14]

In Early Medieval Europe, the conception of "madness" was largely under the jurisdiction of theologians as a mixture of the divine, diabolical, magical, and transcendental. For a society that perceived all events as a cosmic struggle between good and evil (schism), madness was evidence of a battle lost. If madness was possession and a moral malady, then the remedies were spiritual. An example from Early Medieval England was Prince Guthlac.[8] After nine years of rape and slaughter, at twenty-four, Guthlac experienced an existential crisis. Subsequently, he entered a monastery and began rigorous spiritual training. He did not fit in, so he left to live alone (with servants) on a nearby island. There he was assailed by hallucinations and visions of screaming demons. Reportedly, Guthlac overcame all of his infernal opponents through the power of self-flagellation and prayer and became known for his ability to cure insanity through exorcism and prayer.

Within Medieval Christianity's concept of divine harmony, the purpose of treatment was to repair the "illness" of schism and to re-institute the previous order. Because Christian theology saw mental illness as a moral issue, a test of faith or punishment for sins, it endorsed various therapies such as fasting, music, and prayer for those estranged from God and various forms of exorcism, including self-flagellation, torture, and occasional death by fire for those possessed by the devil. The "possessed" were termed witches. The first recorded witch's trial in Toulouse in 1275 was not yet part of a systematized effort.[20] In the Early and High Middle Ages, the inconsistencies in the application of theological concepts left a window open for creative strivings in the face of chaos, culminating in the High Middle Ages Renaissance. It took two hundred more years of traumas of plague, famine, and wars for a vigilant systemic counterattack to mobilize effectively.

Towards the end of the Late Middle Ages, the theological trend became systematized in the *Hammer of Witches, Malleus Maleficiarum*, by the two monks Henry Kramer and James Sprenger, endorsed by Pope Innocent and Emperor Maxmilian. This approach was seconded by *Letters of Approbation* in 1487, written by the Faculty of Theology of the University of Cologne. Both documents accused countless people of witchcraft, among them many on the spectrum of mental afflictions, who stood out with their observable behavioral abnormalities. The chief Texts of Anti-Satanism in Europe, defining "The Devil" and "The Witch," described how Lucifer could induce Evil Love in both sexes, bewitch them to procure abortion, induce disease in any organ, deprive individuals of reason, and make them impotent. According to Kramer and Sprenger, the witches were primarily women because "all witchcraft derived from carnal lust, insatiable in women"[1] (p. 11). The *Hammer of Witches*, together with the *Letters of Approbation*, provided an early taxonomy of perceived deviant behavior and proposed guidelines for prosecution and "treatment." It was designed to reassert control over the maddening chaos and the staggering loss of population in the aftermath of the 100 Year War, famine, and plague. It set up the Witch Trial System of the Inquisition for centuries to come.

Medical Approach

From the 11th century, Latin translations of Islamic medical texts began to appear in Europe and were incorporated into the teaching of medicine at the universities of Naples and Montpellier, spreading into all European medical schools. By the beginning of the high Middle Ages, *Canon of Medicine*, by Avicenna, extending Galen's tradition, became the medieval physicians' curriculum. Towards the fall of Byzantium in 1453, there was an influx of Greek scholars and manuscripts into the West, which established two traditions: the Conservative Arabian and the Greek Liberal, offering a direct comparison between the original Greek texts and Arabic translations and commentaries.

In England, by the 13th century classical notions of humoral imbalance had become the standard explanation of psychiatric conditions in medical treatises and encyclopedias, thanks to the brothers Anglicus and others who summarized ancient learning on the subject. Bartholemew Anglicus (1203–1272) distinguished mental retardation from mental illness and described depression and treated it with music therapy, dietary, herbal, and surgical regimes of classical medicine.[19,21] The regulation of diet was mostly effected through the use of spices in cooking. Pepper, cumin, cinnamon, cloves, etc., were perceived as the essential regulators of the different humors. For the peasant class there were poultices made by healers from local herbs. Surgical techniques were limited to bleeding. In practice, the most widely used method to contain disorganized, aggressive, disruptive behaviors was confinement in chains.[20]

Synthetic Approaches

Arnaldus de Villanova (1235–1313) combined Galenic principles with beliefs in the devil and astrology. Specifically, he recommended trepanning as a treatment to let both demons and excess humors escape. His poem *Flos Medicinae* became a mainstay of applied psychotherapy through the Renaissance.[21]

Trepanning or trepanation related to an old idea, that mental illness was caused by foreign bodies lodged in the head. Starting in the Late Middle Ages, a series of paintings by Peter Breughel the Elder, Hieronymus Bosch, and others portrayed the removal of stones from the head and other parts of the body, addressed themselves to the conflicts of the culture, and incorporated religious, intellectual and social trends. Depicting the interrelationship between mental illness and sin, madness, and sexuality, the paintings illustrated the salient issue of the religious and secular Middle Ages—the loss of control and sinfulness related to the kind of passions which make people "lose their minds." The stones operation was a means of controlling madness and its correlative sexual passions.[22]

Legal Definition and Evaluation of Insanity

Thomas Aquinas (1224–1274) provided the first legal definition of mental incompetence, designating the "Sick of Mind" category in his *Canon Law*. Aquinas's *Canon Law* differentiated between the "insane from infancy without periods of lucidity" and those "with periods of lucidity," those who "were at one time sane but have suffered loss of reason," and the "mentally deficient [who] can take thought for their salvation"[2] (p. 72).

In High and Late Medieval England, the application of the legal definition of mental illness rested on somatic understanding. During the reign of Henry III

(1216–1272), the crown assumed the right to the guardianship of "congenital idiots." A government-appointed commissioner investigated the matter in front of twelve local jurors, selected for their knowledge of the subject. A verdict was suggested, the commissioner proceeded to interview the subject, and a ruling was reported to Chancery, where guardianship provisions were determined.[14] The implementation of such procedures is illustrated by the case of Emma de Beeston. An inquest in 1382 determined that she had not been an idiot from birth but had been insane for only four years. Consequently, the king ordered her person, lands, and goods to be entrusted to her kinsman during her infirmity. Emma, supported by the mayor and several other townsmen, challenged the decision. She charged that the inquisition had been suborned by her kinsman and unnamed accomplices, who hoped to benefit from her idiocy. Emma petitioned for her guardianship to be granted to burgesses unconnected with either party. In 1383 a second inquest was held in Lincoln to determine her state of mind. The abbreviated record stated that Emma was asked where she was born, and she answered that she did not know. Being asked in what town she was, Emma said that she was at Ely. Being asked what day that Friday was, she said that she did not know. Being asked how many days there were in the week, she said seven but could not name them. Being asked how many husbands she had had in her time, she said three, giving the name of one only and not knowing the names of the others. Being asked whether she had ever had issue by them, she said that she had had a husband with a son but did not know his name. After such commonsense questions, the justices found her not to be of sound mind, having no sufficient intelligence to manage herself or her property. The questions considered her experience and circumstances. Assessment of her general awareness was related to memory, life skills, and general knowledge. In the end, Emma herself was placed in the guardianship of her kinsman, but her property was managed by four burgesses on her behalf.[23] The same pragmatism and empiricism inform the vast majority of cases from 1349, for which records survive. Many returned a verdict of congenital idiocy, while some cases found post-natal insanity and detailed the circumstances, for example, being struck on the head by a lance during jousting, after fever,[19,21,23] etc. Even in cases with no known cause, there were no appeals to supernatural influences.[14,23]

Subjective Report

The first subjective account of mental disorder in the English language is the autobiography of Margery Kempe from the 1430s. At the time she wrote her autobiography, she was in her 60s[24] (pp. 39–44). The daughter of the mayor of a town, she married well, but after her first confinement she suffered what would contemporarily be called postpartum psychosis. After giving birth to 14 children, she tried to sever marital relations with her husband and was subject to sexual fantasies and temptations. She suffered bouts of incessant weeping and later in life reported constant visions and conversations with God the Father and various female saints. She restlessly traveled to authorities and shrines throughout England and Europe to justify her experiences. Margery described herself as "like a mad woman," "a drunk woman," "without reason." She recognized her illness as insanity, but this recognition was useless to her. Her life became a constant struggle with the devil to realize her spiritual essence. What for most were symptoms of disease were for Margery a cosmic drama. And through that drama, Margery attained the peace that she longed for. By the time she wrote her autobiography, she "realized her essence," living a pious life, surrounded by her family and friends. By investing her illness with meaning, she gained control over it. In some cases metaphysical representations of mental illness were more effective. The perception of mental illness as containing a metaphysical meaning took into account the person and the mind.[14]

Treatment Institutions

During the Early and High Middle Ages, the mentally ill were cared for by their communities and families. As we saw in the case of Prince Guthlac, already at that time monasteries functioned officially or unofficially as asylums and spiritual "training" centers for mentally afflicted, who may have "checked themselves in" voluntarily. In some countries of Eastern Europe, where Orthodox Christianity became a state religion, as in Russia, the monasteries' role was legitimized as early as the 10th century by Prince Vladimir's statute. It was now "mandatory for the church to provide shelters for widows, orphans, and the mentally ill"[26] (p. 34).

In the Late Middle Ages, the more formal segregation between the mentally afflicted and physically ill was under way. The London hospital of St. Mary of Bethlehem, founded in 1247, later known as "Bedlam," sheltered (and exhibited) exclusively mentally ill individuals from 1402.[26] By then, the Flemish village of Gheel, which housed the shrine of St. Dymphna, had gained a reputation as a healing center for the mentally disturbed. Asylums were also founded at an early date under religious auspices in 15th-century Spain. In 1410 CE, the first mental asylum opened in Valencia, Spain, when Friar Jofre witnessed a mob abusing several insane people. Local tradesmen financed the construction and functioning of their city's asylum. Similar situations arose in Zaragoza, Seville, Valladolid, Toledo, and Barcelona.[14,24,25,26]

To summarize, Middle Ages Christian Europe's approach to mental abnormalities has shown great variability. While originally firmly in the grip of Early

Christian ideology, with monks and monasteries taking on the role of mental health arbiters, gradually the empirically driven medical models and pragmatically driven legal models emerged more and were applied with varying success and varying degrees of humanity. The 21st-century observer must exercise caution in ascribing an unquestioningly positive value to the "progressive" medical model and a negative value to the "regressive" theologically derived approaches, for in some instances engagement with a theological "cosmic struggle" between good and evil actually proved curative while medical assessment and treatment did not. We could conjecture that especially with the legacy of intergenerational traumas, the access to the irrational, magical, and transcendental proved to be a needed resource in adapting and healing.

CONCLUSION

An era of massive generational traumas and posttraumatic developments, the Middle Ages ended with a "diversity of the hundred centers of political and cultural aspirations competing for success"[4] (p. 329). The fracturing and fragmentation of the large empires, causing the devastating trauma at the earliest point of the Middle Ages, became a resource of creative resilience and recovery amidst the pandemic trauma of the Late Middle Ages, as competing perceptions, opinions, attitudes, and remedies became accessible to more people. This diversity posed the opportunity for various avenues of adaptation, which ushered in the Renaissance and the Ages of Discovery, Humanism, and Reason. In the area of approaches to mental conditions, this diversity guarded against an exclusive application of any one empirical/scientific or philosophical system over another without regard for the suitability to an individual. In general, those with mental abnormalities constitute a minority in any society, and they are therefore, by definition, at risk. Throughout history, when diversity was suppressed, abuses followed.[26]

REFERENCES

1. Cockerham, W. C. (2010). *Sociology of mental disorder*, 8/E. Upper Saddle River, NJ: Pearson, Prentice Hall.
2. Graham, T. F. (1967). *Medieval minds: Mental health in the Middle Ages*. London: George Allen & Unwin LTD.
3. Russell, B. (1972). *History of western philosophy*. New York, NY: Simon & Schuster.
4. Holmes, G. (1988). *The Oxford history of medieval Europe*. New York, NY: Oxford University Press.
5. Bruno, W. (1993). Holy and profane mental anorexia. *Rivista Psicoanal*, 39, 81–99.

6. Drew, K. F. (1991). *The laws of the Salian Franks (Pactus legis Salicae).* Philadelphia: University of Pennsylvania Press.
7. Pirenne, H. (1980). *Medieval cities: Their origin and the revival of trade in Europe.* Princeton, NJ: Princeton University Press. (Reprinted from 1925 and 1952 editions)
8. Colgrave, B. (Ed.) (1956). *Felix's life of Guthlac.* Cambridge, UK: Cambridge University Press.
9. Ginsburg, C. (2003). *Nocni Pribeh.* Prague: Argo. (Translated from the Italian Original *Storia Nocturna,* 1995 by J. Hajny)
10. Swain, B. (1934). Fools and folly during the Middle Ages and the Renaissance. *Psychoanalytic Review, 21,* 119–120.
11. Cahill, T. (2006). *The mysteries of the Middle Ages.* New York, NY: Random House.
12. Keen, M. (1984). *Chivalry.* New Haven, CT: Yale University Press.
13. Blanchard, W. H. (1956). Medieval morality and juvenile delinquency. *American Imago, 13,* 383–398.
14. Roffe, D., & Roffe, C. (1995). Madness and care in the community: A medieval perspective. *British Medical Journal, 311,* 1708–12.
15. Chessick, R. D. (2001). Dante's *Divine Comedy* revisited: What can modern psychoanalysis learn from a medieval "psychoanalysis"? *Journal of American Academy of Psychoanalysis, 29,* 281–304.
16. Langer, W. L. (1958). The next assignment: Epidemics and underlying psychological states at the time of the Black Death 1348–1349. *American Imago, 15,* 235–266.
17. Myers, B., & Copplestone, T. (Eds.) (1990). *The history of art.* New York, NY: Dorset.
18. Cohn, N. (1961). The Cult of the Free Spirit: A Medieval Heresy Reconstructed. *Psychoanalytic Review, 48A,* 51–68.
19. Adler, M. N. (1907). *Itinerary of Rabbi Benjamin of Tuleda* (Translator Henry Frowde). London: Oxford University Press.
20. Kroll, J. (1973). A reappraisal of psychiatry in the Middle Ages, *Archives of General Psychiatry, 29,* 276–283.
21. Neubegauer, R. (1979). Medieval and early modern theories of mental illness. *Archives of General Psychiatry, 36,* 477–483.
22. Hartman, J. J., White, S. H., Ravin, J. G., & Hodge, G. P. (1976). The stones of madness. *American Imago, 33,* 266–295.
23. CIM (1957). *Calendar of inquisitions miscellaneous preserved in the public record office, iv, 1377–1388; 1348–1350.* Public Record Office (London).
24. Porter, R. (1988, April). Margery Kempe and the meaning of madness. *History Today, 38,* 39–44.
25. Bloch, S., & Reddaway, P. (1977). *Russia's political hospitals.* London: Victor Gollanzc, Ltd.
26. Millon, T. (2004). *Masters of the mind: Exploring the story of mental illness from ancient times to the new millennium.* Hoboken, NJ: John Wiley and Sons.

Chapter 3

Abnormal Psychology in the Renaissance

Diane E. Dreher

The Renaissance was a time of dramatic change and rising individualism, leading men and women to examine their lives with greater introspection, a passionate interest in their own consciousness, and a new awareness of abnormal states of mind. This dynamic era inspired countless journals and spiritual autobiographies as well as John Donne's *Devotions*, Robert Burton's *Anatomy of Melancholy*, and Shakespeare's greatest tragedies. Renaissance healers and medical practitioners attributed mental illnesses to divine retribution, demonic possession, witchcraft, astrological influences, excessive passions, and imbalanced humors. They treated mental disorders with a combination of magic, medicine, science, and religion and saw balance—in humors, passions, diet, and activities—as the key to health.

Balance was essential to the Renaissance, a time when people saw life as a complex set of correspondences in which each person was a microcosm, a small reflection of the larger world around them. Human consciousness was comprised of 1) the vegetal soul, the ability to take in nourishment, grow, and reproduce, shared with plants; 2) the sensible soul, the senses, movement, and passions, shared with animals; and 3) the rational soul, the powers of reason, understanding, and will, shared with angels. The four elements of air, fire, water, and earth in the physical world were paralleled on the personal level by the four humors: blood, choler, phlegm, and melancholy. Blood was hot and moist, choler hot and dry, phlegm cold and moist, and melancholy cold and dry. There were four personality types, determined by one's dominant humor: "*sanguine*"— lively, energetic, good-natured, and amiable; "*choleric*"—hot-tempered, impulsive, with great strength and courage; *"phlegmatic"*—lethargic, sluggish, inactive; or *"melancholy"*—sober, serious, intellectual, sad, and often wryly witty.[1,2,3] In Renaissance art, philosophy, and literature, the plan of all creation was portrayed as a "Great Chain of Being," in which human life was a precarious balancing act. People were positioned midway on the chain between angels and animals, the powerful polarities of reason and passion, and predisposed to inherent tension and inner conflict between these two polarities of our nature.

MENTAL DISORDERS IN THE RENAISSANCE

The Renaissance has been called "the most psychically disturbed era in European history."[4] Rapid changes in science, religion, culture, politics, and the arts produced widespread anxiety and a vast panorama of mental disorders, some bizarre and extreme, while others are still familiar to us today.

The term "lunacy," a term for insanity dating back in England to the 13th century, was originally associated with the influence of the moon. From the 15th century onward, "lunatic" and *non compos mentis* were legal terms for the mentally ill, who could experience lucid intervals or even a complete recovery. These cases contrasted with the mentally retarded, who were known as "natural fools" or "idiots." By an act of Parliament in 1540, lunatics and fools were made wards of the court, and their properties and personal care overseen by the state. Early papers from the English Court of Wards and Liveries recorded Renaissance cases of lunacy caused by physical illness, a blow to the head, sudden emotional shock, extreme and prolonged grief, the stress of economic ruin, and excessive drinking.[5,6]

Renaissance descriptions of lunatics emphasized their wild, animalistic qualities. Imbalanced and deprived of reason, the quality distinguishing us from beasts on the Great Chain of Being, the mentally ill often ran around disheveled and nearly naked, like Tom O'Bedlam in *King Lear*. English astrological physician Richard Napier described how one of his patients, Elizabeth Knot, tore her dress and ran around naked on the cold, wet ground.[7] Lunatics were known to stick weeds in their hair, run wildly about, or lie motionless and passive for hours at a time. They refused to eat or gobbled down garbage and often attempted suicide. Beset by jerks, gyrations, and convulsions, they babbled, shrieked, ran or wandered aimlessly, fell into fits of weird laughter, and howled at the moon.[7,8]

Richard Napier diagnosed his mentally ill patients with three levels of insanity: "madness," "distraction," or "lightheadedness." Mad patients were wild and violent, distracted patients babbled and raved incoherently and could also be violent, while light-headed patients were nonviolent, engaging in nonsensical babbling.[7] Renaissance sources described a panorama of mental illnesses.

In cases of *mania* (which Napier called madness), people behaved like wild animals, unable to control their passions.[5,9] They were frightening and dangerous, lashing out with phenomenal physical strength and prone to fits of rage, raving, and violent acts.[7] A 1663 treatise by English physician Robert Bayfield described cases of *lycanthropy* or "wolf-madness" in which people ran around the fields at night, barking and howling like dogs.[5]

One form of madness, known as *melancholy*, became especially prevalent during this period. According to Robert Burton, melancholy was "a kind of dotage without a fever, having for his ordinary companions fear and sadness, without any apparent occasion."[2] In this condition, known today as Major Depressive Disorder, symptoms included sadness, exhaustion, heaviness of mind, anxiety, delusions, the inability to experience pleasure, withdrawal from social activities, fearfulness, and thoughts of suicide.[2,10] Richard Napier diagnosed some of his patients as melancholy and others as "mopish," suffering from a chronic and less acute form of melancholy involving idleness, gloom, and excessive solitude, which we might diagnose today as Dysthymic Disorder.[7,10]

In what was known as *religious melancholy*, the afflicted were plagued by religious doubts, fears, guilt, visions of their sins, the fires of hell, and the belief that they were incorrigibly damned. One form of religious melancholy was *scruples*, a condition described by English Bishop Jeremy Taylor in which sufferers were riddled with anxiety, focusing obsessively on the details of their daily lives, afraid to eat for fear of gluttony, afraid to sleep for fear of the sin of sloth, or afraid of offending God through some mistaken action, no matter how small.[5] Today we might see this behavior as a form of phobia or Obsessive-Compulsive Disorder.[10]

Specifically female mental disorders included the "green sickness," a species of melancholy affecting young women, with episodes of sorrow, headaches, difficulty breathing, indigestion, faintness, pallor, absence of menses, anxiety, and abdominal pain for which, Burton says, the best cure was marriage. Many women supposedly suffered from "suffocation of the mother," a form of melancholy blamed on a wandering uterus that migrated upward toward the heart and lungs, causing anxiety, choking, convulsions, difficulty breathing, and in some cases a fainting fit, in which the victim fell down unconscious, appearing dead to the world for up to three days.[2,3,7,11]

Renaissance physicians recognized what we now know as *Dementia*, the cognitive deficits and loss of memory that can afflict the aged.[10] English physician William Salmon described one such case in *The Practice of Curing Diseases* (1694), in which Sir John Roberts, a man he had known for years, became "decayed in his intellectuals," laughing and crying for no apparent reason. Unable to remember what his doctor had just said to him, he asked the same question, then forgot and asked again five or six times in a row.[5]

Because the Renaissance was still a patriarchal, authoritarian society, people who refused to blindly submit to authority were frequently regarded as mentally ill, including wives who refused to obey their husbands and children who rebelled against their parents. Napier records the case of Ellen Hixon, a young woman brought to him as a mental patient simply because she refused to obey her parents.[7]

RENAISSANCE EXPLANATIONS FOR MENTAL DISORDERS

A variety of causes were proposed for mental illnesses: the influence of the moon, the stars, the weather, earwigs in the head, and an imbalanced life involving excessive or insufficient drink, diet, sleep, exercise, passions, and humors, along with witchcraft and the devil himself. Excess in any form was considered unhealthy. Timothy Bright saw an overly rich diet as a major cause of melancholy, advising people to avoid cabbage, beets, dates, olives, chestnuts, acorns, pancakes, rye bread, beans, pork, beef, mutton, goat, boar, venison, mutton, water fowl, quail, eels, porpoises, milk, cheese, eggs, red wine, and dried and salted meats.[12] Excessive passions could cause a dramatic case of "melancholy adjust." According to Bright, melancholy adjust burned the humors with excessive heat, which would bring about symptoms associated today with a Major Depressive or Manic Episode:[10] "the greatest tempest of perturbations and most of all destroys the brain with all his faculties, and dispositions of action, and makes both it, and the heart more uncomfortable: and if it rise of the natural melancholy, beyond all likelihood of truth, frame monstrous terrors of fear and heaviness without cause. If it rise of choler, then rage plays her part, and fury joined with madness, puts all out of frame. If blood minister matter to this fire, every serious thing for a time, is turned into a jest and tragedies into comedies, and lamentation into jigs and dances: thus the passion whereof the humor ministers occasion, by this unkindly heat advances itself into greater extremities."[12]

As in the Middle Ages, mental illness was often associated with demonic possession. Religion, popular culture, and medical practice attributed many cases of melancholy, madness, and anxiety, as well as sadism and sexual addictions to witchcraft and the devil's powers. Martin Luther associated madness with the wages of sin and the work of the devil, describing hardened sinners as mentally deranged, raging, possessed, and lunatic.[13] People often attributed their unconscious urges to the devil's work and referred to supernatural causes to explain mysterious illnesses and accidents. Belief in witchcraft was widespread throughout the Renaissance. More than 500 of Richard Napier's patients believed that they or their family members were bewitched. Many of his bewitched patients exhibited symptoms of schizophrenia and other psychotic disorders. Hearing bizarre voices, they believed themselves possessed by devils, were tempted to extreme acts, and often screamed out in terror.[7,10]

Suicide was considered a civil and religious crime in Tudor England, believed to be the devil's work because it involved the loss of one's immortal soul. Religious leaders taught that melancholy made people vulnerable to the devil's temptations, as dramatically portrayed in Marlowe's *Doctor Faustus*. Chief among these temptations was "the sin of despair," leading to suicide.[14] Yet with the increased focus on melancholy and the influence of new scientific attitudes during the late 16th and 17th centuries, suicide came to be seen more as a symptom of mental illness.[7]

New scientific attitudes and direct observation gradually led to less magical thinking and more objective conclusions about mental illness. German physician Johann Weyer maintained, in *De Praestigiis Daemonum* (1563), that many old women persecuted as witches were actually suffering from melancholy delusions.[15,16] In 1584, Reginald Scot, an English justice of the peace, noted that people accused of witchcraft, as well as the accusers, were often mentally ill, recording his views in his book, *The Discoverie of Witchcraft*.[5] Concerned that science was not giving the devil his due, in 1597 James I, then king of Scotland, wrote *Daemonologie*, condemning Weyer and Scot, while warning of the devil's powers.[17] When he became king of England in 1603, he ordered Scot's book burned. His Witchcraft Act of 1604 condemned witches to death, leading, for a time, to increased witch hunts and persecutions.[3,5,14] In this heightened atmosphere, Shakespeare wrote *Macbeth* in 1606. However, science ultimately prevailed. The last witch was hanged in England in 1684, and in 1691 English minister Timothy Rogers warned people not to confuse the disease of melancholy with the work of the devil, advocating kindness and compassion for people with this disorder.[5]

Physician Richard Napier kept detailed records of his patients' symptoms and causes of their mental disorders, many of which are still relevant today. Although more than 264 of his patients believed they were bewitched, 99 suffered from financial distress, experiencing severe anxiety over losses and debts. Grief at the loss of a loved one was a common cause of mental illness. One patient, Agnes Stiff, suffered from extreme melancholy months after her mother's death, unable to work, and given to fits of weeping and aimless wandering. Nearly one-third of Napier's patients suffered from illness or insanity after the death of a spouse. Relationship problems were another common cause of mental illness. Nearly 40 percent of his patients complained of mental disturbances caused by courtship and married life. Forty-one patients attributed their insanity to the fact that their families would not let them marry the person they loved, and 135 complained about marital problems, including alcoholic spouses and spousal abuse.[7]

RENAISSANCE TREATMENTS FOR MENTAL DISORDERS

Treatment for mental illness depended upon the diagnosis and cultural contexts. In the early Renaissance, religious rituals and aggressive treatments were used to expel evil spirits or excessive humors. Catholic priests performed exorcisms, and Puritan ministers employed ritual, prayer, and fasting, while astrologers and folk healers used charms and talismans. Richard Napier purged and exorcised patients and also gave them sigils, metal disks inscribed with astrological signs, to wear on ribbons around their necks.[7,13,18,19] Medical treatments were often extreme, painful, and brutal. Patients were whipped, chained, given a diet of bread and water, and left in darkness and solitary confinement, like Malvolio in Shakespeare's *Twelfth Night*. The mentally ill were subjected to a debilitating course of emetics, laxatives, and bleeding to purge the offending humors.[20,21] Yet the German doctor Paracelsus rejected the humors theory. Believing that health and sickness were part of our spiritual journey, he used prayer, herbs, minerals, opium grains, and spiritual alchemy to treat his patients. Diagnosis and treatment of mental illness often differed with social class. In Germany upper-class patients were treated medically to expel the excess of melancholy humors while lower-class patients with the same disorder would be exorcised as sinful or demonically possessed.[19,22]

In addition to prayer, exorcism, and astrological cures, common medical treatments included removing the cause of the disturbance, as well as beginning a regimen of diet, healthy activities, and herbal remedies to restore the patient to a state of balance. Since body and mind were intrinsically related in Renaissance beliefs, physical remedies were commonly used to treat mental illness. Special diets were prescribed to balance the humors. A person suffering from a hot and dry disease was to avoid spicy foods and eat lettuce and other cold and moist foods. Activities, too, were prescribed to promote balance. Sleep was believed to warm the body while activity cooled and dried it.[3] Healers used kitchen remedies, rubbing the patients' heads with vinegar and potions of herbs and ground ivy leaves. They gave patients oxtail soup for breakfast and cooled their humors with drinks of lettuce water or lemonade.[8,13] Timothy Bright recommended a diet of broth; tender young meat, preferably fowl; bread made from oats and wheat; carrots, parsnips, and lettuce; cherries, figs, grapes, apricots, and either orange or lemon juice; and eggs, oysters, sole, haddock, and trout. Some healers shaved their patients' heads and applied split chickens, capons, or other animal parts to reduce fever.[12,13]

The traditional purge, advocated by Bright, involved emptying the excessive humors by applying a "clister" or laxative, then bleeding the patient and often making the poor soul vomit as well.[12] The clinical records of Daniel

Oxenbridge, an early-seventeenth-century English physician, provide an insight into the medical treatment suffered by one patient:

> Mrs. Miller, aged 24, a cloth-worker's wife, was mad for two years, though she took many remedies. I was called in 1628, in the spring. After a common clister, I bled her plentifully in the cephalic vein, on both arms, at the saphena in both feet, at both the salvatellas, in the forehead, under the tongue, and by leaches to the hemorrhoid vein. I made her drink much cider made fresh in the house, with apples and water. I tempered the atribilarious humors, with syrup of borage, buglos, endive, ... apples ... and ... after the general evacuations, once in three of four days, I either bled her or vomited her strongly, or purged her ... she would vomit 12 times, and purge two of three times downward. ... After she was generally thus evacuated, I shaved off all the hair of her head, and used a stillicidium daily to her head of warm water, wherein the herbs rosemary, sage, lavender, betony were boiled, and ... cloths wet in the same about her head, and anointed her head with mandrake oil. At bed-time she bathed her feet in warm water to dispose her to sleep; other opiates she used inwardly, as laudanum, paracelsi sometimes or lettuce boiled and sweetened with sugar or an emulsion of barley, with ... lettuce seed or white poppy seed, ... Oil of violets, of nympheae, roses, and to her head shaved, I applied the warm lungs of lambs, sheep, young whelps, pigeons alive.[5]

Like Oxenbridge, Richard Napier also prescribed laudanum, an opium tincture developed by Paracelsus, to calm the raging madness of some patients and help others sleep.[7]

Other treatments for mental disorders were also recorded, some unusual and extreme. Drowning or dunking was advocated by Dutch physician Franciscus Mercurius Van Helmont in 1694.[5] In 17th-century England, Oxford physician Thomas Willis treated a young woman for madness by throwing her naked into a river for a quarter of an hour, then had her taken out, whereupon she experienced profound sweats, fell asleep, and then recovered her wits.[20] Willis also practiced trephination or trepanning, making a hole in the patient's skull to release the foul vapors and excessive humors.[23] In 1667, the French Doctor Denis performed a transfusion on a 34-year-old man suffering melancholy after an unhappy love affair, first bleeding the patient of ten ounces of blood, then replacing some of it with cow's blood. Remarkably, the patient recovered from the operation as well as the melancholy.[15] Among less vehement herbal cures, English doctors treated victims of melancholy with St. John's Wort.[23] Robert Hooke, M.D., Fellow of the Royal Society, even proposed using marijuana to relieve symptoms.[5]

England's first mental institution, the priory of St. Mary of Bethlehem in London, founded in 1247, had been used to house and treat lunatics since 1377.

In 1547 it became a public insane asylum, managed by a court of governors and by Bridewell, a house of correction. In the asylum, known as "Bedlam," patients were whipped, chained, bled, and subjected to a meager diet, a bed of straw, and exhibited like circus animals for curious visitors, who regarded Bedlam as one of the "must-see" sights of London. By the end of the 17th century, as many as 96,000 a year visited the asylum.[7,8,20]

Yet some raised their voices against inhumane treatment of the mentally ill. As early as 1538, Juan Luis Vives wrote that mental patients were first and foremost human beings, to be treated with compassion and kindness. He believed that our primary motivation was to love and be loved, recognizing that when this desire is thwarted, it produces anger, shame, and a mixture of mental illnesses.[15] While acknowledging that the treatment should correspond to the condition, he encouraged healers to create an atmosphere of tranquility to quiet patients' minds and settle their spirits. In 1542, Andrew Boorde wrote that the mentally ill were to be comforted, withdrawn from noise and bothersome thoughts, and cheered with pleasant music before sterner measures were tried.[21] In 1586 Timothy Bright also advocated a clean, pleasant atmosphere, with clean clothes, pleasant surroundings, and the solace of a garden.[12]

Gradually, people recognized that the mentally ill needed greater compassion. In the 17th century, the Quakers, inspired by their founder, George Fox, cared for the mentally ill with kindness.[7,24] English medical writer Thomas Tryon criticized the use of blood-letting and sedatives, as well as the exposure of Bedlam inmates to public viewings. In *A Treatise of Dreams & Visions* (1689), he wrote that observation had disproved and invalidated medical treatments based on the humors theory. Madness, he argued, came from extreme passions which unsettled the balance of the soul and could best be treated by a simple, balanced diet, peaceful atmosphere, and caring friends, who could listen with compassion.[5] In 1691 English minister Timothy Rogers wrote that the mentally ill needed the kindness, gentleness, and companionship of a friend who would listen to their feelings, no matter how extreme, with acceptance and empathy. Above all, he felt, the compassionate friend must convey hope, telling the patient of others who have suffered and recovered, as he himself had recovered from a prolonged bout of melancholy.[5]

MELANCHOLY: DEPRESSIVE DISORDER IN THE RENAISSANCE

Melancholy was the most popular and prevalent mental disorder of the Renaissance. From the 1580s onward, references to this disorder abounded in English medical, legal, and literary texts, including Bright's *Treatise of Melancholy* (1586); Shakespeare's *Hamlet* (1602); John Donne's treatise on suicide,

Biathanatos (1644); and Burton's *Anatomy of Melancholy* (1621), which became a best-seller, with eight editions in the 17th century. In this cultural context, educated men and women who found themselves sad, anxious, or troubled, often concluded that they had come down with the melancholy and sought out treatment.[7]

As mentioned earlier, symptoms of melancholy included overwhelming anxiety, fearfulness, sadness, and gloom, restlessness, dissatisfaction, emotional instability, suspicion, weeping, complaining, ill-tempered and aggressive behavior, withdrawal from social life, disturbed sexual relations, torpor, the inability to feel pleasure, lethargy, oppression with a sense of guilt and unworthiness, inability to sleep, delusions, hallucinations, profound weariness with life, and suicidal tendencies.[2,3,12,14] These symptoms anticipate Sigmund Freud's description of melancholia three centuries later: "The distinguishing mental features of melancholia are a profoundly painful dejection, cessation of interest in the outside world, loss of the capacity to love, inhibition of all activity, and a lowering of the self-regarding feelings to a degree that finds utterance in self-reproaches and self-revilings, and culminates in a delusional expectation of punishment."[25,26]

Reflecting a profound inner imbalance, the melancholic's emotional state was extreme, out of all proportion to any external conditions. As Timothy Bright explained: "We do see by experience certain persons which enjoy all the comforts of this life whatsoever wealth can procure, and whatsoever friendship offers of kindness, and whatsoever security may assure them: yet to be overwhelmed with heaviness, and dismayed with such fear, as they can neither receive consolation nor hope of assurance, notwithstanding there be neither matter of fear, or discontentment, nor yet cause of danger, but contrarily of great comfort. This passion being not moved by any adversity present or imminent, is attributed to melancholy the grossest part of all the blood, either while it is yet contained in the veins: or abounds in the spleen, (ordained to purge the blood of that dross and settling of the humors) surcharged therewith for want of free vent, by reason of obstruction."[12]

As today Depressive Episodes are often recognized to be preceded by anxiety,[10] so in the Renaissance melancholy persons were seen as driven by an underlying fear. According to Bright, "fear is the very ground and root of that sorrow, which melancholy men are thrown into. For a continuance of fear, which is of danger to come, so overlays the heart that it makes it as now present, which is only in expectation, and although the danger feared be absent, yet the assuredness thereof in the opinion of a melancholy brain is always present, which engenders a sorrow always accompanying their fears."[12] With their cognition disordered by "melancholy fumes," patients often misperceived reality, suffering from delusions, believing themselves kings or emperors, or, in the case of religious melancholy, tormented by ghosts and visions of devils and hellfire. Although today the term *melancholy* is synonymous with sadness or depression, the Renaissance disorder also included symptoms of what we would now call Schizophrenia, as well as Anxiety and Obsessive-Compulsive Disorders.[10] Six of Napier's patients were tormented by devils' voices that told them to kill their relatives, and one patient, Alice Davy, diagnosed with "extreme melancholy," was phobic about dirt, obsessively washing her clothes, and afraid to touch anything or go out to church for fear of the dust soiling her clothes.[7]

Causes and Types of Melancholy

Burton's *Anatomy*, at over 1,200 pages, provides the most compendious Renaissance description of melancholy, its causes, types, and treatment. According to Burton, melancholy could have natural or supernatural, internal or external causes. Supernatural causes involved God (causing a dark night of the soul in a call to conversion), the devil, or the devil's agents, namely magicians and witches, luring a sinner to damnation. Natural causes involved the stars (astrological influences); and congenitally, our temperament and heredity (for Burton observed that melancholy is "an hereditary disease"), as we derive our temperament in large part from our parents;[2] as well as old age, which makes people's humors cold and dry, predisposing them to melancholy. Outward causes included imbalanced relationships, adverse experiences with parents, nurses, and schoolmasters (for Burton recognized the powerful influence early childhood experience has on our emotional development); as well as imbalanced external conditions such as accidents, misfortune, loss, poverty, and death of friends. Inward causes involved physical diseases and imbalanced humors. Burton described three categories of melancholy:

1. *head melancholy*—brought about inwardly by excessive passions and imbalanced humors, an adjust humor, disease, or excessive or deficient sexual activity; and outwardly by a heat stroke, a blow on the head, hot wines, excessive spices, lack of sleep, idleness, loneliness, and excessive study or work.
2. *hypochondriacal or windy melancholy*—involving imbalance in the digestive system, affecting the spleen, belly, stomach, and bowels.
3. *whole body melancholy*—brought about by an imbalanced diet, distempered liver, or excessive worry.[2]

Yet even as he drew these distinctions, Burton recognized the interrelation of the body and mind—"For as the body works upon the mind by his bad humors, troubling the spirits, sending gross fumes into the brain, and so *per consequens* disturbing the soul, and all the faculties of it, . . . with fear, sorrow, etc., which are ordinary symptoms of this disease: so, on the other side, the mind most effectually works upon the body, producing by his passions and per-turbations miraculous alterations, as melancholy, despair, cruel diseases, and sometimes death itself."[2]

A major cause of melancholy was "perturbations of the mind" or excessive passions: intense grief, anger, jealousy, sexual desire or love melancholy (to which Burton devotes 300 pages), or religious melancholy. Melancholy was also caused by imbalanced activity and external conditions, such as idleness, excessive work, and insufficient fresh air and exercise. As an Oxford scholar, Burton was well aware of the hazards of a sedentary life, describing "the scholar's melancholy," in which the brain grew dry from overexertion, while the body languished from lack of exercise, proper circulation, and severe indiges-tion. Excess study, he said, "dries the brain and extinguisheth natural heat; for whilst the spirits are intent to meditation above in the head, the stomach and liver are left destitute, and thence come black blood and crudities by defect of concoction, and for want of exercise the superfluous vapors cannot exhale. . . . hard students are commonly troubled with gout, catarrhs, rheums, . . . bad eyes, stone, and colic, crudities, oppilations, vertigo, winds, consumptions, and all such diseases as come by overmuch sitting."[2] Renaissance physician Richard Napier treated 27 men and women who claimed they were mentally ill from excessive study, while research today has shown how excessive sitting and lack of exercise can adversely impact our physical and emotional health.[7,27]

Burton and his contemporaries believed melancholy was caused by an imbalanced or excessive diet. Thus scholars and physicians gave extensive—often contradictory—dietary advice. According to Burton, beef, "a strong and hearty meat" should be avoided as it could "breed gross melancholy blood." He also counseled people to avoid venison, pork, and goats; all shellfish and hard and slimy fish; milk, butter, and most cheeses; cucumber, melons, cabbage, onions, garlic, root vegetables such as turnips, carrots, and radishes; peas and beans; and raw fruits such as pears, apples, plums, cherries, and strawberries, as well as nuts. He also advised people to avoid spices such as salt, pepper, ginger, cinnamon, cloves, and mace, as well as sugar, oil, vinegar, and mustard. Food, he believed, should not be fried or broiled and should be eaten in moderation, and beer, cider, and all dark wines should be avoided since they were conducive to melancholy.[2] Denied most meats, vegetables, fruits, and spices, what remained, for his health-conscious Renaissance readers, was a decidedly bland diet.

Treatment of Melancholy

Unlike many of his countrymen, Burton advocated moderate means to treat melancholy patients, beginning with modifications in diet and living conditions to restore them to balance, resorting to more aggressive purging and bleeding only when needed. He offered a lengthy discussion of foods believed to balance the humors and cure the melancholy, including "such meats . . . which are moist, easy of digestion, and not apt to engender wind, not fried nor roasted," and predominantly fowl, such as hen, capon, and quail. He praised the restorative powers of broths, "especially of a cock boiled"—a 17th-century reference to chicken soup. Eggs, mild fish such as trout or perch, pure wheat bread, raisins, apples, oranges, parsnips, and potatoes were recommended by Burton while Bright also allowed oysters and a wider variety of fruits, including cherries, figs, grapes, and apricots as well as orange and lemon juice.[2,12]

Both Bright and Burton recommended fresh air, clean clothes, and a clean, light, pleasant atmosphere to restore a person's health, doing everything possible to reassure the patient and dispel any feelings of dejection—the antithesis of the sordid conditions of Bedlam.[2,12,14] They recommended prayer, as well as reading in Scripture and moral philosophy, and moderate exercise of body and mind to divert patients and raise their mood. Burton lists all manner of diversions: engaging in sports, hunting, fishing, going to plays, taking journeys with friends, going out socially, listening to music, or playing with dogs and cats. Especially effective, Burton believed, was to walk with friends "amongst orchards, gardens, bowers, mounts, and arbours . . . between wood and water, in a fair meadow, by a river-side," taking in the beauty and healing influence of nature.[2] Burton also advocated pleasant experiences and pleasant company, believing in the healing power of positive emotions, and felt that friendship was a powerful cure, that "the best way to ease is to impart our misery to some friend."[2]

If, after attempts to restore a patient's balance with diet and living conditions, the unfortunate person was still suffering from melancholy, then physic or medicinal means should be tried, beginning with moderate herbal remedies, which Burton called "alternative medicines," to balance the system. For he believed that "Many an old wife or country woman doth often more good with a few known and common garden herbs than our bombast physicians with all their prodigious, sumptuous, far-fetched, rare, conjectural medicines."[2] Herbal remedies included teas, infusions, ointments, and sachets made of borage, melissa, marigold, dandelion, roses, violets, rosemary, and chamomile. Ointments of fragrant herbs were to be rubbed on the skin after bathing the patient in warm water with rose petals and violets; little bags of herbs were applied to the head, heart, and stomach, and water lilies, lettuce, violets, and chamomile were to be applied to cool the head. Precious stones such as garnets, coral, emeralds, and sapphires were thought to dispel melancholy as well. Burton also recommended a newly-discovered caffeinated beverage said to increase energy and raise the spirits: "The Turks have a drink called coffa . . . so named of a berry as black as soot, and as bitter . . . which they sip still of, and sup as warm as they can suffer: they spend much time in those coffa-houses, which are somewhat like our alehouses or taverns, and there they sit chatting and drinking to drive away the time, and to be merry together, because they find by experience that kind of drink, so used, helpeth digestion and procureth alacrity."[2]

If herbal remedies were insufficient, then Burton felt, the next level of treatment should be tried, with purgatives "upward and downward," for which he offers herbal recipes; then bleeding or phlebotomy of the arm, head, or knee, using leeches to draw out the blood. He also mentions the use of trepanning— "Tis not amiss to bore the skull with an instrument to let out the fuliginous vapours"[2]—and sedatives made of laudanum to help with difficulty sleeping.

Hamlet and Melancholy

Although many Renaissance theories about the *causes* of melancholy and other mental illness were erroneous, their observations about symptoms were often quite accurate. Shakespeare's dramatization of melancholy in *Hamlet* is one notable example. Early in the play we learn that Hamlet, naturally of a healthy sanguine temperament, is suffering from melancholy, imbalanced by deep grief at the death of his father.[1,26] As he says to his friends, "I have of late—but wherefore I know not—lost all my mirth, forgone all custom of exercise; and indeed it goes so heavily with my disposition that this goodly frame, the earth, seems to me a sterile promontory" (II.2. 287–290).[28] The sadness, gloom, dissatisfaction, anhedonia, lethargy, withdrawal from exercise and social life, and profound weariness with life are apparent. His first soliloquy reveals more symptoms: thoughts of suicide and weariness and disgust with life, all associated with a Major Depressive Episode:[10]

O that this too too solid flesh would melt,
Thaw, and resolve itself into a dew.
Or that the Everlasting had not fixed
His canon 'gainst self-slaughter! O God, O God,
How weary, stale, flat, and unprofitable
Seem to me all the uses of this world!
Fie on't, ah fie, fie! 'Tis an unweeded garden
That grows to seed; things rank and gross in nature
Possess it merely. (I.2. 129–137)[28]

The soliloquy ends with a profound sense of foreboding—"It is not, nor it cannot, come to good"—and a deep sense of isolation. According to Shakespeare scholar Paul Jorgensen, Hamlet represses his anger and sense of betrayal at his father's death, mother's remarriage, and his bitter suspicions about his uncle:[26] "But break, my heart, for I must hold my tongue" (I.2.158–159).[28]

Hamlet's gradual recovery begins when his close friend Horatio comes from college at Wittenberg to console him. Horatio provides Hamlet with that powerful remedy for melancholy—a trusted friend in whom he can confide his grief, to whom he can unburden his conflicted soul. As Renaissance healers recognized, the emotional support of a caring friend was profoundly therapeutic,[2,5,12] and as Jorgensen has noted, Horatio was "also an extraordinarily good listener."[26] Throughout the play, Horatio is there to listen, to witness, and to support his friend, offering him steadiness and support in his journey through the darkness of melancholy to the light of deeper understanding.

Contrast Horatio's healing presence for Hamlet with the lack of support experienced by another young person suffering from the melancholy of deep grief. Ophelia, too, has lost a father. After Hamlet's violent rejection of her in Act III, he kills her father, Polonius, who is hiding beneath a curtain in the Queen's chamber. Emotionally devastated, Ophelia is bereaved, betrayed by love, and abandoned. Alone in her grief—for even her brother is out of the country—she collapses into madness. Singing songs of lost love and dirges for dead fathers, she drowns, clutching wildflowers that Shakespeare's contemporaries would have recognized as emblems of regret and phallic symbols, revealing her repressed sexuality, pain, and confusion.[29]

Hamlet's healing process continues, without the brutal Renaissance medical regimen—there are no purges or bleedings in *Hamlet*. Leading to his gradual recovery are support from Horatio and the cathartic episode with his mother when he finally expresses his repressed anger and outrage at her hasty marriage and his father's murder. Shakespeare's contemporaries believed that unexpressed rage (or choler) could cause melancholy.[26] Burton notes that unless expressed, "Anger, a perturbation, . . . carries the spirits outwards, preparing the body to melancholy, and madness itself."[2] Thus in *Macbeth*, Malcolm tells the bereaved Macduff not to let his anger fester inside but to express it: "Give sorrow words. The grief that does not speak/ Whispers the o'erfraught heart and bids it break" (IV.3.210–211).[28] Finally, in the last act of the play, with his inner balance restored by catharsis, time, and supportive friendship, Hamlet sees his life with new patience and perspective, telling Horatio: "There's a special providence in the fall of a sparrow. If it be now, 'tis not to come. If it be not to come, it will be now. If it be not now, yet it will come. The readiness is all" (V.2. 157–160).[28]

RENAISSANCE PERSPECTIVES ON MENTAL ILLNESS AND CURRENT PARALLELS

As we have seen in this chapter, the Renaissance offered a range of approaches to the cause and treatment of mental illness, from superstition and folklore to medical purges to expel offending humors, to prayer and spiritual practice, observations inspired by the new science, and therapeutic healings based on compassionate personal support. Some approaches are absurd, abhorrent, outdated and extreme, but others are still relevant today, including the holistic view of mental health. As Renaissance scholar Lily Bess Campbell has noted, "No modern psychologist has more strenuously insisted upon the fundamental relationship between body and mind or body and soul than did these writers of the 16th and 17th centuries in England."[1]

Centuries before research on love and attachment, in 1538 Juan Luis Vives wrote that our primary motivation was to love and be loved, and that frustrated love can cause all manner of mental illness.[15] In 1621, Burton attributed many cases of melancholy to lack of love and affection in childhood, criticizing the "offences, indiscretion, and intemperance" of parents who either neglect their children or "are too stern, always threatening, chiding, brawling, whipping, or striking; by means of which their poor children are so disheartened and cowed, that they never after have any courage, a merry hour in their lives, or take pleasure in anything. There is a great moderation to be had in such things, as matters of so great moment to the making or marring of a child."[2]

During the 17th century the perception of mental disorders gradually moved from humors theory, folklore, and superstition to more scientific approaches involving case studies and observations, inspired by Sir Francis Bacon, who advocated direct observation and detailed study of individual cases[5] (p. 78). In *The New Organon* (1620), Bacon proposed the investigation of the history, symptoms, and treatment of diseases, and the study of the emotions, sleep, dreams, the intellectual faculties, and memory—all now studied in contemporary psychology.[30]

Although one would hardly expect bleeding, purges, and trepanning from contemporary therapists, many Renaissance treatments for mental disorders are recognized today. Among them are:

- *The use of exercise to relieve depression*, advocated by Bright and Burton and validated by current research.[27] Closely related is the debilitating effect of what Burton called "overmuch sitting" on mental and physical health.[2] A contemporary parallel to the "scholar's melancholy" may well result from the sedentary solitary lifestyle of information workers, who spend hours sitting at the computer, sitting in their cars, or in front of television screens.
- *The effect of pets on mental health*, recognized by Burton and validated by current research.[2,31]
- *The therapeutic benefit of music*, noted by Burton and also recognized today.[2,32]
- *The therapeutic influence of nature*. Burton recommended that melancholy patients spend time walking in gardens and meadows, and research has demonstrated the healing effects of nature.[2,33]

- ♦ *The effect of caffeine on mood and mental acuity.* Burton listed coffee as a possible treatment for melancholy. Studies have shown that caffeine improves psychomotor performance, energy, and the sense of well-being, and in 2011 a longitudinal study revealed a possible protective effect of coffee consumption on the risk of depression.[2,34]
- ♦ *The importance of positive emotions.* Burton, citing Vives, said that "Mirth . . . 'purgeth the blood, confirms health, causeth a fresh, pleasing, and fine colour,' prorogues life, whets the wit, makes the body young, lively, and fit for any manner of employment. The merrier the heart, the longer the life.'"[2] Many of these insights have been validated by research in positive psychology.[35]

Above all, our Renaissance counterparts recognized the healing effect of what is now called the "therapeutic relationship," the presence of a caring friend who will listen, offering moral support, and what Carl Rogers called "unconditional positive regard."[36] In 1621, when many unfortunate mentally ill persons were relegated to solitary confinement, Burton recognized that "the best way to ease is to impart our misery to some friend, not to smother it up in our own breast . . . for grief concealed strangles the soul; but whenas we shall but import it to some discreet, trusty, loving friend, it is instantly removed."[2] In 1691, centuries before Carl Rogers, Timothy Rogers advocated kindness and compassion, saying, "You must be so kind to your Friends under this Disease, as to believe what they say. Or however, that their apprehensions are such as they tell you they are," advocating kindness, acceptance, and compassionate listening.[5] In the Renaissance, Rogers recognized that a soul in distress needs emotional acceptance, respect, and understanding, the qualities of an affective therapist today, for an atmosphere of trust can bring the light of hope to people working through the darkness of a mental disorder, helping them gain greater understanding, health, and personal balance.

REFERENCES

1. Campbell, L. B. (1966). *Shakespeare's tragic heroes: Slaves of passion.* New York, NY: Barnes & Noble. Quote on p. 79.
2. Burton, R. (1977). *The anatomy of melancholy.* H. Jackson (Ed.). New York, NY: Vintage Books. Originally published 1621. Quotes (in order by book) are from Bk. 1, pp. 169–170, 211, 250, 302, 217–223, 269, 333; and Bk. 2, pp. 22–23, 74, 107, 213, 246–247, 242, 119, 107.
3. Babb, L. (1951). *The Elizabethan malady: A study of melancholia in English literature from 1580 to 1642.* East Lansing, MI: Michigan State College Press.
4. White, L. (1974). Death and the devil. In R. S. Kinsman (Ed.). *The darker vision of the Renaissance.* Berkeley, CA: University of California Press. Quote on pp. 25–26.

5. Hunter, R., & Macalpine, I. (Eds.) (1963). *Three hundred years of psychiatry 1535–1860*. New York, NY: Oxford University Press. Quotes from pp. 258, 122–23, 249.

6. Neugebauer, R. (1979). Medieval and early modern theories of mental illness. *Archives of General Psychiatry, 36*, 477–483.

7. MacDonald, M. (1981). *Mystical Bedlam: Madness, anxiety, and healing in seventeenth-century England*. New York, NY: Cambridge University Press.

8. Porter, R. (2004). Madmen: A social history of madhouses, mad-doctors, & lunatics. Stroud, Gloucestershire, UK: Tempus Publishing Limited.

9. Feder, L. (1980). Madness in literature. Princeton, NJ: Princeton University Press.

10. American Psychiatric Association. (2000). *Diagnostic and statistical manual of mental disorders* (4th ed., text rev.). Washington, DC: Author.

11. Peterson, K. L. (2010). *Popular medicine, hysterical disease, and social controversy in Shakespeare's England*. Burlington, VT: Ashgate Publishing Company.

12. Bright, T. (1995). *A treatise of melancholy*. New York: Classics of Psychiatry & Behavioral Science Library. Facsimile edition of original London: John Windet, 1586. Quotes from pp. 107–108, 87–88, 129. Spelling modernized.

13. Midelfort, H. C. E. (1984). Sin, melancholy, obsession: Insanity and culture in 16th century Germany. In S. L. Kaplan (Ed.). *Understanding popular culture: Europe from the Middle Ages to the nineteenth century* (pp. 113–145). New York, NY: Mouton Publishers.

14. Evans, B., & Mohr, G. J. (1972). *The psychiatry of Robert Burton*. New York, NY: Octagon Books.

15. Zilboorg, G., with Henry, G. W. (1941). *A history of medical psychology*. New York, NY: W. W. Norton.

16. Weyer, J. (1991). *Witches, devils, and doctors in the Renaissance. De praestigiis daemonum*. G. Mora (Ed.). Binghamton, NY: Medieval & Renaissance Texts & Studies. Originally published in Latin 1563.

17. Harrison, G. B. (Ed.). (1966). *King James the First: Daemonologie*. New York, NY: Barnes & Noble. Originally published 1597.

18. MacDonald, M. (1981). Insanity and the realities of history in early modern England. *Psychological Medicine, 11*, 11–25.

19. Fabrega, H. (1991). The culture and history of psychiatric stigma in early modern and modern western societies: A review of recent literature. *Comprehensive Psychiatry, 32*, 97–119.

20. Silvette, H. (1938). Madness in seventeenth-century England. *Bulletin of the Institute of the History of Medicine, 6*, 22–33.

21. Kinsman, R. S. (Ed.). (1974). *The darker vision of the Renaissance*. Berkeley, CA: University of California Press.

22. Jacobi, J. (Ed.) (1979). *Paracelsus: Selected writings*. Princeton, NJ: Princeton University Press.

23. Gross, C. G. (1999). A hole in the head. *The Neuroscientist, 5*, 263–269.

24. MacDonald, M. (1982). Religion, social change, and psychological healing in England, 1600–1800. In W. J. Sheils (Ed.). *The church and healing* (pp. 101–125). Oxford, UK: Basil Blackwell.

25. Freud, S. (1957). *The standard edition of the complete psychological works of Sigmund Freud*. James Strachey (Ed. & Trans.). London: Hogarth Press, XIV, p. 244.

26. Jorgensen, P. A. (1964). Hamlet's therapy. *Huntington Library Quarterly, 27,* 239–258. Quote on p. 245.

27. Daley, A. (2008). Exercise and depression: A review of reviews. *Journal of Clinical Psychology in Medical Settings, 15,* 140–147. DOI.10.107/s10880-008-9105-z

28. Greenblatt, S. (Gen. Ed.) (1997). *The Norton Shakespeare*. New York: Norton. Quotes from the plays are noted by Act, scene, and line in the text.

29. Dreher, D. E. (1986). *Domination and defiance: Fathers and daughters in Shakespeare*. Lexington, KY: University of Kentucky Press.

30. Bacon, F. (1960). *The new organon and related writings*. F. H. Anderson (Ed.). New York, NY: Bobbs-Merrill. Originally published 1620.

31. Friedmann, E., Thomas., S. A., & Son, H. (2011). Pets, depression, and long-term survival in community living patients following myocardial infarction. *Anthrozoos, 24,* 273–285.

32. Mohammadi, A. Z., Shahabi, T., & Panah, F. M. (2011). An evaluation of the effect of group music therapy on stress, anxiety, and depression levels in nursing home residents. *Canadian Journal of Music Therapy, 17,* 55–68.

33. Kaplan, R., & Kaplan, S. (1989). *The experience of nature*. New York, NY: Cambridge University Press.

34. Lucas, M., Mirzaei, F., Pan, A., Okereke, O. I., Willett, W. C., O'Reilly, E. J., & Ascherio, A. (2011). Coffee, caffeine, and risk of depression among women. *Archives of Internal Medicine, 171,* 1571–1578.

35. Fredrickson, B. L. (2002). Positive emotions. In C. R. Snyder & S. J. Lopez (Eds.), *Handbook of positive psychology* (pp. 120–134). New York, NY: Oxford University Press.

36. Rogers, C. R. (1989). *The Carl Rogers reader*. H. Kirschenbaum and V. L. Henderson (Eds.). Boston, MA: Houghton Mifflin, 135–138. First published in Kutash, I., and Wolf, A. (Eds.). (1986). *Psychotherapist's Casebook*. Jossey-Bass, 197–208.

Chapter 4

From Colonial Constructs of Abnormality to Emerging Indigenous Perspectives

Mark S. Carlson

Europeans involved in the early colonization of Asia and Africa typically viewed the indigenous people they governed as psychologically inferior. Consistent with this view, medical writers of the late 1800s and early 1900s crafted accounts of primitive cultures populated by childlike, irresponsible natives. Only a few anthropologists and physicians were inclined or even able to think outside this dominant understanding of indigenous peoples and their folk psychologies. For most, practical colonial concerns of governance were of primary concern. The priority of European governors was maintaining order, thus ensuring stability and their authority. As such, one of the most disruptive elements in any colony was indigenous individuals who acted out violently, for whatever reason.

The governors of Asian and African colonies were quick to provide medical authorities there with the legal power to hospitalize individuals against their will. An early model for this was the Indian Lunatic Asylums Act of 1858.[1] With this act, the English gave authorities in India the power to hospitalize or imprison for ten days any individual who was found wandering at large, believed to be dangerous, or not under proper care or control, among other criteria.

What constituted dangerous behavior or improper control was, of course, highly subjective and easily influenced by political as well as community needs. Dozens of insane asylums were built across Asia and Africa from the 1850s through the 1920s, when they became more commonly known as mental hospitals. Often a colonial psychiatrist's primary knowledge of a culture's people would be based on the patients he treated in the asylum. It was in this context that a literature regarding abnormal psychology in colonial Asia and Africa began to emerge.

This chapter traces the broad development of theories of mental health disorders in non-Western cultures from the late 19th century to the present. It begins with an exploration of early diagnostic schemes and what came to be called *ethnopsychiatry* and then traces the progression of new research paradigms that followed. The history of this evolution of ideas of necessity becomes something of a history of our evolving attitudes towards other cultures as well.

KRAEPELIN AND COMPARATIVE PSYCHIATRY

Emil Kraepelin is appropriately lauded for his groundbreaking work in developing a comprehensive system for classifying the mental illnesses commonly recognized at the close of the 19th-century. Having established his elaborate diagnostic scheme, Kraepelin was naturally interested in whether his nosology was universally applicable to other cultures. Hoping to gain perspective on that question, Kraepelin traveled to Java in 1903 to observe mental health disorders there.

To the reader of 19th-century travelogues, the Dutch East Indies seemed to have more than their share of exotic disorders, among them the phenomenon known as running amok. Running amok, derived from a Malay word *mengamok*, meaning a furious and desperate charge, had been described as early as 1770.[2] Explorer James Cook noted that some Malay men would suddenly act out violently, often indiscriminately killing people in their vicinity. And in 1895 a health officer in the region noted the curious condition of *koro*, in which a man feared his penis was shrinking and literally disappearing into his body. An epidemic of "genital shrinking" would be reported in China only a few years later, fascinating European medical observers.[3]

These were just a few of the disorders Kraepelin hoped to learn about. Centering his investigations at the regional asylum, Kraepelin interviewed a hundred indigenous patients as well as a hundred European ones.[4] From these interviews, Kraepelin concluded that psychiatric disorders in all regions have an essential biological underpinning but that variation between regions was likely due to their differing levels of intellectual development and cultural complexity. Kraepelin adhered to an evolutionary theory popular at the time that suggested the maturational stages a European experienced in developing from childhood to adulthood was paralleled by the stages that various societies experienced in progressing from a primitive to advanced status. This perspective is characterized by the phrase *ontogeny recapitulates phylogeny*. So-called Western society, not surprisingly, was considered by Europeans to represent the most advanced manifestation of culture.

Kraepelin and other scientific thinkers typically characterized indigenous cultures as childlike, superstitious, and generally less intellectually developed. This carried over into their characterization of mental illness and the abnormal. For example, Kraepelin believed that the apparent lower incidence of delusional thinking and auditory hallucinations in Java could be attributed to a general lower level of cognitive development and an internal life dominated by sensory rather than linguistic consciousness.[5] Influenced by what he had observed, Kraepelin proposed a new discipline, which he named *vergleichende psychiatrie* or comparative psychiatry. Yet Kraepelin's ability to properly interpret the information he garnered from his interviews, given issues of translation and lack of relationship with the patients he interviewed, remains an open question.[6] Kraepelin's belief in the intellectual inferiority of "primitive" peoples, and its presumed impact on the manifestation of mental illness, continued to have an impact long after his death in 1926.

COLONIAL VERSUS INDIGENOUS PERSPECTIVES IN SOUTHEAST ASIA

Early in the 20th century, ethnopsychiatry was proposed as a sub-discipline of both psychiatry and anthropology. Its goals were very similar to those of Kraepelin's comparative psychiatry, though its name has come to be specifically associated with the practice of colonial psychiatrists. Both psychiatrists and anthropologists began taking note of unusual patterns of behavior in "native" peoples, now characterizing them with the new psychiatric terminology of syndromes and disorders.

Petrus Travaglino, a Dutch psychiatrist, took over the large mental hospital in Java in 1915.[7] According to medical historian Hans Pols, Travaglino agreed with Kraepelin that a simplistic inner life accounted for the difference in manifestation of psychoses among the Javanese. He found that psychotic breaks with acute emotional and sometimes aggressive outbursts were much more common in Java than in Europe. Travaglino felt these psychotic episodes were not due to an underlying schizophrenic process but rather to an emotional trauma such as humiliation or severe embarrassment. Travaglino concluded without empirical support that the individual identities of the Javanese were underdeveloped and thus less able to sustain the injury of social disapproval. Nor were Travaglino's conclusions unique.

Beginning in the 1920s, indigenous people educated in Europe led a critique of this colonial narrative. These indigenous critics argued that practitioners ought to speak the local language and be familiar with local cultural practices. Furthermore, practitioners ought to be careful about generalizing from psychiatric patients to the general population and from one ethnicity to

all the others in the region. Muhammad Hatta, a prominent voice in this response, was also actively engaged in the movement for political independence.
These two enterprises would often be linked in the critics of colonial psychiatry. The tension between European viewpoints and indigenous counterpoints
would be echoed throughout any part of the world where colonial powers
held sway.

COLONIAL PSYCHIATRY IN AFRICA

A look at the state of colonial psychiatry in North and Sub-Saharan Africa
reveals numerous parallels to that found in Southeast Asia. Writing in 1896,
the director of a French insane asylum blatantly declared that the "issue of race
dominates all psychopathology for the Algerian native," convinced that his
Arab patients displayed intellectual inferiority, childish affect and barbarous
behavior.[8]

Decades later, J. C. Carothers, a colonial physician in Kenya, was making
only slightly more evolved arguments. In 1953 Carothers wrote *The African
Mind in Health and Disease* for the World Health Organization.[9] In a chapter devoted to mental disorders, Carothers discussed a condition he called
frenzied anxiety in which an individual displayed agitation, loud behavior,
incoherent speech, and even violence in reaction to a stressful event, "perhaps
real only to an African," he added with apparent condescension. After acting
out, the individual would deny any memory of his behavior. But this dissociative aspect was not to be considered hysterical in nature, the physician
cautioned.

Carothers argued that Africans lacked the complex mental organization necessary for an internal mental conflict, a traditional hallmark of true
hysteria. Rather, this behavior occurred when there was a conflict between
the African and his immediate social circle and was processed through antisocial aggression. Carothers went so far as to suggest Africans lacked a working conscience, moral principles residing instead in their traditional healers.
As such, he felt confident asserting that the rate of insanity among Africans
living in tribal settings was remarkably low and only increased when Africans
lived amidst Europeans. Even with all of his extreme assertions, Carothers
seems unable to entirely avoid evidence of African cultures' more collectivistic nature. But the physician attributes this valuing of community to a
pathological lack of individualistic personality development and not to relative differences in mores. Carothers never considered the possibility that the
experience of oppressive colonial practices could be in any way pathogenic.

In the meantime, indigenous people in Africa continued to be psychiat-
rically hospitalized for reasons some recognized as grossly inappropriate.

H. L. Gordon pointedly declared in 1936: "No person in Kenya is quite as disordered as Kenya's Lunacy act," which was based on the 19th-century Indian statute.[10] In his review of hospital records, Gordon found admission rationales ranging from "he has behaved rationally but should be detained because he has cut his ear with a knife" to "throws his limbs about in an aimless way" or "behaves well but has no relations so should be detained in his own interests."

CALL FOR A CULTURALLY SENSITIVE GLOBAL PSYCHIATRY

When the Indonesian medical students raised their concerns about methodological and logical flaws in the colonial psychiatric paradigm, they were an articulate but decidedly non-dominant voice. This was true within the Western professional community as well. There were, however, glimmers of a less Euro-centric approach in scattered writings in the field.

In 1934, for example, John M. Cooper proposed a new discipline he hoped would replace what he saw as the methodologically flawed ethnopsychiatry.[11] Summarizing the existing research on five divergent ethnic groups from around the world, including the Eskimos of Alaska and the Malays of Southeast Asia, Cooper tentatively summarized what he had surmised:

1. There is no apparent correlation between incidence of mental illness and racial heredity, natural environment, and "level" of culture;
2. Mental illness has fundamentally the same patterns and likely the same etiology in both preliterate and so-called civilized cultures;
3. A role for either racial heredity or natural environment in the types or patterns of mental illness is unlikely;
4. Specific cultural patterns within an ethnic group are the most likely influence on patterns of mental illness; and finally,
5. The existing literature is extremely inadequate.

Cooper ended his article with a call for more systematic research focusing on statistically accurate incidence rates, descriptive rather than theoretical summaries of mental illnesses, and greater reliance on individual case studies. Similar critiques of so-called racial psychology were also occurring in the 1930s.

Cooper's sensible conclusions would do little to keep psychological anthropologists and colonial psychiatrists from drawing far less culturally sensitive conclusions. The new field Cooper imagined wouldn't manifest for several decades. It was overshadowed by what many would argue was a misapplication of a newly dominant psychoanalytic paradigm to culturally specific studies of abnormal psychology.

PSYCHOANALYTIC THEORIES
OF "PRIMITIVE" PATHOLOGY

A new interdisciplinary field was coming into being, heavily influenced by psychoanalytic theory, which came to be called Culture and Personality or, alternatively, psychological anthropology.[12] In 1932, Geza Roheim wrote the seminal article in the new discipline titled "The psychoanalysis of primitive culture types." Roheim specifically advised anthropologists to begin focusing on dreams, sexuality, child-rearing, joking behavior, and detailed life histories, among other data domains, in order to better understand unconscious process and psychopathology in other cultures.

Ruth Benedict followed in 1934 with her *Patterns of Culture*. In it she argued that while similar individual temperaments existed in all cultures, specific cultures only let some of those personality types flourish. Benedict argued that deviance in any culture would remain small, due to her belief that the vast majority of any group would generally take whatever shape that culture most valued.

For many of these writers, individual weakness was often understood in early childhood or constitutional terms, predicting a failure to conform. National character was attributed to child-rearing patterns. Patterns of behavior that might be seen as pathological in Western culture, such as dissociation, could be seen as both normative but also indicative of a less developed, childlike culture.

Indigenous philosophers and psychologists alike began to question how universally applicable psychodynamic concepts were to their culture. In 1929 the Indian psychoanalyst Girindrasekhar Bose, for example, questioned the prominence of castration anxiety in the Indian cultural context.[13] Even though Bose maintained a consistently psychodynamic perspective, his cultural relativity was not well received by Freud.

During the same period, Indian philosopher and yogi Sri Aurobindo directly attacked psychoanalysis.[14] Aurobindo didn't deny that the subconscious could be a potential source of psychiatric disorders but argued that an overemphasis on suppressed sexuality risked prompting dark, sexual preoccupations.

Instead, Aurobindo held that the physical body was at greater risk of depression and other emotional disorders when stressful situations arose. The suggestive power of negative thoughts in such situations was seen as the primary cause of pathology. Defects, and by extension mental disorders, were seen as the body's response to the pull of unhealthy material pleasures.

Psychoanalytic approaches to the psychopathology found in other cultures came under increasing criticism in the 1960s. Two forces contributed to this. One was the gradual weakening of psychoanalysis as the dominant paradigm in psychology and psychiatry. The other was an increasing belief that psychodynamic assumptions were inescapably rooted in Western ways of thought.

Those who continued to attempt to catalogue indigenous attitudes towards psychiatric disorders increasingly attempted to do so from an atheoretical perspective. For example, L. Lewis Wall investigated indigenous Hausa medicine in his 1970s fieldwork in a northern Nigerian village.[15] Wall was able to identify several types of madness frequently mentioned by his informants, but strict typologies were absent. Laughing madness, for example, was marked by excessive laughter and emotional expression, while babbling madness involved rambling, meaningless speech. Parallels to Western diagnostic categories were not lost on Wall, who made obvious links to mania and delirium, among other disorders.

But Wall himself noted that what he was doing ended up seeming largely an intellectual exercise largely irrelevant to the practical lives of the people he was studying. Put in other words, Wall's attempt at defining a strict Hausa classification system of disorders was not an action done in the spirit of Hausa thought but rather a distinctly Western passion for categorization.

THE CREATION OF TRANSCULTURAL PSYCHIATRY

The universality of the Western diagnostic system was gently challenged in 1951 by Pow-Meng Yap, a psychiatrist practicing in Hong Kong. Yap wrote a journal article titled "Mental diseases peculiar to certain cultures: A survey of comparative psychiatry," in which he summarized the apparently regional disorders like running amok and *koro* that had fascinated Kraepelin fifty years earlier.[16] In doing so, Yap initiated a modern and psychologically more sensitive discussion of such disorders.

Half a world away, Eric Wittkower took note of this new line of research. Wittkower, a German Jew originally trained as a psychoanalyst, had immigrated first to England and then to Canada. Settling in at McGill University in Canada, in collaboration with an anthropologist named Jacob Fried, Wittkower established a program in 1955 in what he labeled transcultural psychiatry, a discipline that he believed should strive to be free of overriding theoretical biases. Wittkower then initiated an academic newsletter entitled *Transcultural Psychiatric Research Review* the following year. This provided a place where researchers from different countries could have a better chance at getting their cross-cultural research published. The newsletter morphed into a successful journal, simply titled *Transcultural Psychiatry*.

In 1957, his organizational skills once again in evidence, Wittkower brought together psychiatrists from 20 different countries to discuss matters of mutual interest in a mental health conference held in Zurich, Switzerland. Many of the most prominent international researchers received a powerful motivational boost from the meeting. Among those attending were Pow-Meng Yap;

Thomas Lambo, an indigenous Nigerian psychiatrist; G. Morris Carstairs from England; and Carlos Alberto Seguin from Peru.

As a result of their new global network, Wittkower and his colleagues attempted an ambitious, but ultimately flawed cross-cultural study of schizophrenia in 1960.[17] A questionnaire was sent to psychiatric hospitals around the world in the hopes of gathering atheoretical, descriptive data on patients with that diagnosis. Ultimately, 87 surveys were returned from a total of 25 countries. Given the relatively small sample, findings for black African, Arab, and Asian groups were unfortunately summarized together. Even so, some intriguing findings emerged. The research group noted that non-Christian patients with schizophrenia rarely had religious delusions. Visual and tactile hallucinations were relatively higher among Arab and African patients. The authors acknowledged that different regions appeared to have different constructs of schizophrenia. They also felt that limiting their sample to hospital patients did not allow them to explore how different types and levels of community support might impact the disorder.

Emerging from this zeitgeist was the important 1961 anthology, *Studying Personality Cross-Culturally*. G. Morris Carstairs was enlisted to write a chapter on cross-cultural psychiatric interviewing.[18] Carstairs suggested that when a patient from a non-Western country was interviewed in a psychiatrist's office, the patient was likely to present as more acculturated to European mores than he actually was. He noted that interviewing patients in their own language was essential for rapport. Fellow psychiatrists were cautioned against assuming that any paranoia they detected was unwarranted by actual situations in the patient's life. What's more, he advised his readers that norms regarding aggression could vary considerably between cultures. Finally, he believed—as many had before him—that indigenous patients adjusting to the different mores of Western cultures could result in the creation of an anxiety disorder.

Also featured in the anthology was Donald Kennedy's discussion of key cross-cultural issues to consider when engaged in practice or research in other countries.[19] Among the issues Kennedy raised were culture-specific definitions of health, the relative prevalence of psychiatric disorders (complicated by definitional concerns), and particular situations in specific cultures that might increase the risk of psychopathology. Kennedy also argued that cultural variations in psychiatric disorders might also suggest different causal factors. Witchcraft was cited as a perceived causal factor in African cultures worthy of further investigation. Kennedy also felt it would be important to identify what different modal personality types existed within cultures (which thus define the parameters of abnormality); how specific abnormal patterns develop within a given culture; and how families react to those disorders. Exploring these and other factors would provide a fertile opportunity for testing the validity of supposedly universal psychological theories.

Finally, Kennedy specifically asked a critical question that was rarely raised in American and European journals: How ethnocentric was the existing Western system of classifying mental disorders?

Other books soon appeared in the cross-cultural field. In the 1964 foreword to *Magic, Faith, and Healing,* American psychiatrist Jerome D. Frank wrote that "mental illnesses" were always contextual, dependent on a variety of individual and cultural factors.[20] Healers in any culture, be they shaman or psychotherapist, were effective only to the degree they successfully embodied the roles and functions of that culture. But regardless of the particular manifestation, Frank felt all mental illnesses created anxiety and self-doubt in the sufferer and negatively impacted his relationship with those around him.

By 1968, Wittkower attempted to definitively identify the goals of the new discipline.[21] As regarded mental illnesses in different cultures, such research should identify

1. similarities and differences in manifestation;
2. cultural factors that predispose one to mental illness (or health);
3. the impact of such factors on rate of incidence and manifestation;
4. forms of treatment utilized in different cultures;
5. beliefs regarding etiology; and
6. culturally specific attitudes towards the mentally ill.

Wittkower saw the collaboration between psychiatrists, anthropologists, and epidemiologists as critical.

During the 1960s, what would come to be called an essentialist understanding of mental illness (i.e., there are common biological underpinnings to all disorders despite cultural variations) held sway among most writers on the topic. In the coming decades, a social constructionistic perspective, emphasizing cultural relativity, would become increasingly dominant. It was also in the 1960s that Pow-Meng Yap began to regularly utilize the term "culture-bound syndromes" in his writings. Others soon took up the term, which reached its zenith as an organizing concept in the 1990s.

THOMAS LAMBO AND THE FIRST AFRICAN PSYCHIATRISTS

Coinciding with the birth of transcultural psychiatry in the 1950s was the entry into the field of the first African-born psychiatrists. According to medical historian Alexander Boroffka, Thomas Adeoye Lambo was among the first ethnically African physicians to specialize in the treatment of mental disorders.[22] Trained in London in 1954, Lambo was placed in charge of a new psychiatric facility in his home country of Nigeria. Lambo began immediately to write about paranoid schizophrenia among the Yoruba, who represented the majority of the hospitalized patients under his care. Dissatisfied with traditional European approaches, Lambo implemented a new model of treatment, transforming the institution from a locked facility to one of open community whenever possible. In this more community-oriented model, Lambo insisted that patients be accompanied to the treatment facility by a family member who cooked for them, washed their clothes, and otherwise provided support. In this way, their cultural milieu was not as severely disrupted. Lambo also saw to it that cultural beliefs were not ignored. Notwithstanding these culturally-based adjustments, based on his observations, Lambo placed himself firmly in the cross-cultural psychiatric tradition, asserting an essential similarity between psychiatric disorders found in Nigeria and the rest of the world.

In 1961, Lambo also helped organize the *First Pan-African Psychiatric Conference* in the Nigerian city of Abeokuta. Raymond Prince, a psychiatric associate from Canada who had first begun to practice in Nigeria in 1957, described Lambo as having "immense personal charm" and a "genius for interesting the 'right people'" in his projects. A total of 85 psychiatric professionals attended from 13 different African nations, mostly male psychiatrists and female nurses and social workers. There were no psychologists present, not beginning to be trained on the continent until the 1979s.

Among the attendees and speakers at the conference was Tigani el Mahi, who has been identified as the first black African trained in psychiatry. A Sudanese practicing in Egypt, el Mahi wrote as early as 1956 about the history of mental health issues in North Africa. He was one of the first psychiatrists to offer a psychological perspective on *zar*, a dissociative state in which an individual is thought to be possessed by a spirit. Relatedly, el Mahi posited the regional relativity of concepts of health and stated explicitly that he believed that definitions of *mental* health were dependent on cultural values.

Also in attendance was Henri Collomb, a French psychiatrist who had in the 1950s identified an indigenous disorder he called *bouffée délirante*, an acute reaction characterized by disorientation, agitation, and aggression. Collomb went on to establish the journal *Psychopathologie Africaine* in 1965. It would provide a French language outlet for works in comparative psychiatry in West Africa in particular.

Conference notables also included Alexander Boroffka, the German psychiatrist to whose account of the history of psychiatry in Nigeria this section is indebted; John C. Carothers of England, whose less than progressive perspectives have already been discussed; and of course, the ever present Eric Wittkower.

Bouffée délirante and *zar* would both later be identified as so-called culture-bound syndromes. Though it is worth noting that while French psychologists observed and diagnosed *bouffée délirante* in both North and West Africa, Anglo-Saxon-trained English practitioners typically did not.[23] It would appear that culture-bound syndromes may be "bound" both by the culture in which the disorder occurs *and* the culture in which the diagnosis originated.

ACCULTURATION STRESS SEEN AS A SOURCE OF PATHOLOGY

Only a year prior to the 1961 conference, Lambo's associate Raymond Prince had identified a syndrome he attributed to the stress of Nigerian children adapting to Western culture.[24] Symptoms included headaches, lack of comprehension of lectures or readings, reduced concentration, and memory loss. Prince called this cluster of symptoms *brain fag* syndrome, a term derived from the then current slang of "fagged out" for someone who was exhausted. Prince noted that this phenomenon was widespread amongst Nigerian students attending secondary school or universities. Prince hypothesized that the imposition of European teaching approaches, with their emphasis on individual effort, personal responsibility, discipline, and written assignments, were inconsistent with the Nigerian student's upbringing, which placed an emphasis on group activities, oral communication, and a general permissiveness. Later writers suggested the syndrome wasn't just limited to schools. Implications of intellectual inferiority were still in evidence, though the blatant racism of earlier writers was generally absent.

Lambo continued to be the preeminent researcher in Africa during this period.[25] By 1962 he had begun to write with an increasingly clear perspective about the mental health problems created for Africans by the loss of traditional values and practices as many adapted to a new and unfamiliar urban environment. Lambo didn't see such struggles as inevitable but rather felt they arose out of a lack of compensatory cultural supports. The lack of such supports, Lambo believed, led variously to symptoms of depression, anxiety, malaise, and irrational outbursts of anger.

In 1965, building on this perspective, Lambo suggested a new diagnostic category he labeled *malignant anxiety*; by this, he meant individuals whose aggressive criminal acts were preceded by a period of severe, acute anxiety. This was not unlike Carothers's and Collomb's earlier concepts of frenzied anxiety and *bouffée délirante*, respectively. Lambo theorized that the behavior of those suffering from malignant anxiety was not the result of psychosis or mental deficiency but rather of changing cultural and societal conditions, among other factors. At the time of his article, he had documented 29 such cases in Nigeria.

Lambo felt that these changes in cultural setting resulted in numerous disorders not typically seen in traditional, non-urban African settings. He noted that same year that the use of barbiturates and amphetamines was now occurring in male students, young migrant workers, male bachelors, and polygamous men. Two years later, Lambo further observed that uprooted adolescents brought up in traditional village settings were now presenting with a greater frequency of mental health problems, psychosomatic disorders, and behavior problems such as aggression, delinquency, and prostitution in major urban centers across the continent. Lambo felt the loss of traditional hierarchies and transitional rituals without any new supportive social structures were likely the cause. He later wrote of his belief that many male migrant workers had also started engaging in atypical homosexual behavior due to similar cultural dislocations.

John Dawson, a Scottish psychologist, explored some of these same issues in a study in the West African nation of Sierre Leone in 1962.[26] Members of different ethnic groups in the country could choose five characteristics out of 21 to describe their people. Three of the most common self-ratings of the Temne ethnic group were "always want to fight," "strong-minded," and "hot tempered." In contrast, the most common self-ratings of the neighboring Mende group were "very friendly," "hard workers," and "good farmers." Then, in a survey of the country's lone mental hospital, Dawson determined that even though the more even-tempered Mende were the largest ethnic group in the country, they only constituted 17 percent of those hospitalized. In contrast, while the Temne represented a smaller part of the total population, they represented 29 percent of those hospitalized. Dawson hypothesized that the self-identity of the Temne was inconsistent with the demands of urban life and that their values of aggressive masculinity were grounded in the tribal past. He felt the Mende, in contrast, had either adjusted better to the transition or were intrinsically more amenable to modern urban life. While a more nuanced writer than many of his contemporaries, Dawson did not address the impact of Sierra Leone's colonial history and the related demands on both the Temne and Mende to be politically and socially acquiescent to the English.

In 1972, Henry Murphy, Wittkower's key partner in the discipline of transcultural psychiatry, summarized what he saw as several key developments in the field.[27] First among them, Murphy felt, was an increasing recognition that depression, initially thought to be rare in Asia and Africa, was indeed fairly common. The difference, Murphy argued, was an increasing recognition that depression in Asia and Africa was not typically characterized by self-blame but rather had prominent psychosomatic elements and the projection of blame onto other people or supernatural elements.

Murphy also noted an increased understanding that delusional symptoms could actually assist the patient in relating to his environment and that this positive function in some cultures needed to be recognized. Similarly, trance or dissociative states, while typically dysfunctional in Western societies, often served a positive adaptive function in non-Western ones. Cross-cultural studies of suicide, in Murphy's view, were also showing that the act had different triggers and meanings in different regions, more often related to a threat to social ties in non-Western cultures. This, of course, would be consistent with distinctions that are now commonly summarized as individualistic versus collectivistic functions. Finally, common elements between traditional healing in non-Western cultures and psychotherapy in Western ones were increasingly being identified.

Transcultural psychiatry in the 1960s proved to be a culturally more sensitive enterprise in studying mental illness across the globe than its predecessors had been. The lens through which it looked at these psychiatric disorders, however, remained a decidedly European/American one. In his summary of developments in the field, Murphy had failed to highlight the increasing realization of many researchers, namely, that a clash of cultures appeared to be at the center of many contemporary disorders. The precise nature of that clash remained open to dispute.

COLONIAL OPPRESSION SEEN AS A SOURCE OF PATHOLOGY

Meanwhile, a growing discourse about the psychological impact of colonial domination on indigenous peoples was just beginning to catch fire. Albert Memmi, a philosopher and social scientist of joint Jewish and Tunisian background, wrote the highly influential *The Colonizer and the Colonized*, which was first published in French in 1957.[28] Memmi argued that the colonized internalize the negative image that the colonizer has of them. They attempt to become like the colonizer, but only end up becoming alienated from their true self at the same time as they increasingly despise that self. Memmi likened this phenomenon to the internalized racism many black men and women experienced or the anti-Semitism many Jews held for themselves. Memmi indicted colonial psychiatry for promoting the notion that the Arab was predisposed to psychological disorder and therefore unsuited for self-government—a narrative that served colonial interests very well.

Working along similar lines, Frantz Fanon—a black psychiatrist from Martinique—developed a theory of the pathogenic quality of the colonial experience in his classic *The Wretched of the Earth*, first published in French in 1961.[29] While Fanon accepted the common perception of Arabs being more prone to violence than Europeans, he attributed that physical aggressiveness to the various indignities of living under colonial rule. Unlike earlier psychiatrists,

Fanon also felt the Arab experiencing colonial oppression also suffered from symptoms of self-doubt and hypersensitivity.

The liberation psychology movement in Latin America travelled similar intellectual territory in the early 1970s.[30] Paolo Fiere and Ignacio Martin-Baro drew from the writings of Fanon and Memmi, as well as from the emerging liberation theology movement within the Roman Catholic Church. They characterized individual unhappiness and dissatisfaction among the working or peasant class as resulting from disparaging self-narratives pressed upon them by the ruling class consciously or unconsciously seeking to insure their position of privilege. In their view, only by becoming aware of this process of psychic diminishment might workers regain the pride and grounding of their indigenous traditions.

In the work of all of these writers, there was an underlying premise that most psychopathology in non-dominant populations was not determined by an underlying biological process but rather was culturally constructed by the experience of being subjected to economic, political, and psychological oppression. This was also one of the main thrusts of Michel Foucault's contemporaneous *Madness and Civilization*. The rhetoric of Foucault's social constructionism was appealing to indigenous psychologists and psychiatrists practicing in countries just then emerging from colonial rule.

This new way of understanding allowed previously described "culture-bound" syndromes to be reassessed. For example, *pibloktoq*, or "arctic hysteria," was a dissociative syndrome observed by Europeans primarily in Inuit women, in which they acted bizarrely, tearing off their clothes and/or acting violently, later suffering from a seizure and lack of memory of the preceding events. In a new look at the historical manifestations of the disorder, a psychologist named Lyle Dick suggested that *pibloktoq* might not be an "exotic" aspect of Inuit culture as originally thought, but rather the traumatic result of European merchants sending Inuit husbands away on dangerous missions and then all too often procuring their wives for sexual services without any regard for preexisting relationships.[31] An open question for all of these writers seemed to be, what happens to justifiable frustration and anger when an entire class of people cannot safely express it directly?

THE NEW INDIGENOUS PSYCHOLOGIES

The rise of indigenous psychologies was inseparably linked to the movement towards political freedom from European rule that most "colonies" experienced between 1945 and 1970. For example, India became self-governing or independent in 1947, Indonesia in 1949, Tunisia in 1956, Nigeria in 1960, Algeria in 1962, and Kenya in 1963. With independence, increased opportunities for higher education in the fields of psychology and psychiatry followed, as well as exposure to the ideas of Fanon, Memmi, Foucault, and others.

The development of indigenous psychologies began in earnest in non-Western cultures beginning in the late 1970s and early 1980s.[32] The movement appeared to be motivated by three factors:

1. anti-colonial feelings prompting negative attitudes towards Western influences, including Western psychology;
2. the constructs of Western psychology not proving particularly helpful in addressing local social problems;
3. growing pride in indigenous cultural constructs and a sense that they might prove more easily applicable to indigenous dilemmas.

Indigenous concepts of health and wellness were articulated with increasing clarity by professionals within those cultural traditions. From the perspective of the indigenous psychologies movement, Western psychology was understood as an indigenous rather than a universal psychology, grounded as it was in European and American cultural concepts. As such, it was seen as appropriate for application in Europe and the United States, but not in a wholesale way for other cultures. Early important figures in the movement were Kuo-Shu Yang from Taiwan, Virgilio Enriquez from the Philippines, and Durgannand Sinha from India.

Perhaps not surprisingly, these indigenous researchers have been more interested in reclaiming, in psychological terms, what is normal and healthy in their cultural traditions rather than what is pathological. This tendency can be understood as a necessary corrective to earlier psychiatric narratives in which entire cultures were deemed childlike, primitive, and in some cases even pathological. Collectivistic cultural values, in contrast to the more individualistic values of Western cultures, are often stressed.

A. Bame Nsamenang, a psychologist from Cameroon, has written extensively since 1983 on how parenting and early childhood development differ in Central Africa compared to Europe and the United States.[33] He observes that more childhood socialization in Cameroon occurs through interaction with other children, and the Western ideal of the emotionally engaged father is not the rule there. Nsamenang conceives of the father's role in Cameroon as liaison with the wider community and as less hands-on. At the same time, he argues that a totally absent father can result in pathology in the child. One senses the tension between Western and African ideals in his writing.

Some indigenous psychologists have also discussed how these differing social values might also result in alternative ways of organizing psychopathology. For example, N. Esther Nzewi, writing about the Ibo people of Nigeria in 1989, classified psychiatric disorders in psychosocial terms.[34] She identified five such patterns: inability to engage in beneficial reciprocity in social relationships; lack of displays of shame after wrongful behavior; non-directional or excessive speech and behavior; inappropriate emotional displays; and symptoms that interfere with fulfilling family obligations. Causes of these disorders could include possession by malevolent spirits or, more mundanely, personality disorder.

Still more authors attempted to meld indigenous and traditional European attitudes towards psychiatric disorders and their treatment. Jean Masamba ma Mpolo, a Baptist minister from the Democratic Republic of the Congo, is regarded by some as the father of African pastoral counseling.[35] Masamba has been recognized in the African Christian community for integrating traditional Western psychological concepts with both a Christian and an indigenous African perspective. Given the widespread influence of Christianity in Africa, his theory of African pastoral counseling is worth referencing.

Masamba wrote in 1984 of a young woman who was experiencing acute anxiety over a divorce. Masamba learned she was having recurring dreams of her dead grandfather telling her that she should sacrifice a goat to appease her uncles, who had never approved of the marriage in the first place. In addition to endorsing the intervention proposed by her grandfather in her dream, Masamba also negotiated an agreement between the woman and the family of her ex-husband. While suggesting that the counselor should not encourage superstition, Masamba also wrote of the need to meet people "in their culture." Other relevant examples of indigenous psychologies' understanding of mental disorders can be found across Latin America and Asia.

CULTURE-BOUND SYNDROMES AND DSM-IV

Pow Meng Yap, writing out of Hong Kong, had set the stage for the study of culture-bound syndromes. By 1965, Yap had broadened his focus, discussing how depression and other affective disorders manifested differently in China than other cultures.[36] Arthur Kleinman, an American psychiatrist working in Taiwan, became familiar with Yap's work and proceeded to expand on his notions of how culture impacted the form of psychiatric disorders.

Kleinman agreed with Yap that depression in China was more likely to manifest itself in somatic symptoms than emotional ones. This perspective was first fully expressed in his 1986 book *Social origins of distress and disease*.[37] Kleinman was also one of the first mental health professionals to systematically describe the impact of the severe measures enacted in China during the so-called Cultural Revolution. His interest in cultural variations in psychological disorders led him to cofound a journal devoted to the topic, *Culture, Medicine, and Psychiatry* in 1976.

In his work, Kleinman made a clear argument about some of the problems of trying to establish the universality of a psychiatric disorder. Such an enterprise encounters the difficulty in establishing assessment questions that don't suffer from translation into another language and that adequately tap into differing cultural contexts. Asking traditional East Africans if they personally blame themselves for mistakes (a question intended to assess depression) may not be effective because there may be a cultural belief in other people's use of witchcraft as the cause of personal difficulties. Similarly, Kleinman argued, the assumption that Western terminology for mental illnesses is the de facto starting point of such investigations carries its own risks. What if someone from South Asia, where a dysfunctional belief in semen loss, or *dhat*, commonly causes distress in men, looked for symptoms associated with semen loss (weight loss, physical weakness, and sexual preoccupation) in the United States? She might very well conclude that semen loss syndrome exists there but is just largely unrecognized. As such, Kleinman's thinking and that of others like him were part of the impetus to recognize culture-bound syndromes as their own entities in formal diagnostic classification systems.

An increasing number of psychiatric syndromes that appeared to be specific to a given culture fueled discussions of this sort. Such discussion ultimately led in 1994 to the *Diagnostic and Statistical Manual of Mental Disorders, Fourth Edition* (DSM-IV) devoting a section to 25 brief descriptions of culture-bound syndromes.[38] The American Psychiatric Association defined such syndromes as "recurrent, locality-specific patterns of aberrant behavior and troubling experience that may or may not be linked to a particular DSM-IV diagnosis," explicitly sidestepping the universality question. Among those disorders included in the list of culture-bound syndromes were *amok, bouffée délirante*, brain fag, *dhat, koro, pibloktoq* and *zar*.

This recognition of culturally specific syndromes corresponds with a more general push for indigenously constructed psychologies to address the problems of a specific culture. But the concept of culture bound–disorders still raises fundamental questions of whether there is an essential foundation to most mental illness or whether all or most mental illness is culturally constructed and thus relative.

The inclusion of the culture-bound syndrome section prompted a vigorous and productive debate. Multiple voices soon suggested that *all* psychiatric disorders are impacted by culture and are to some degree "culture-bound." More modern explorations of disorders such as *amok, dhat*, and *koro* suggest that such disorders are nowhere nearly as culturally circumscribed as first thought. Further, to the extent that some mental health disorders *are* limited to specific regions, it isn't only in Africa and Asia that they occur. Some have suggested, for example, that disorders such as anorexia, bulimia, and dissociative identity disorder are in essence American/European culture–bound disorders.

Most compellingly, several researchers have noted that all disorders are by necessity culturally situated if not actually "bound."[39] As such, phenomena like *dhat* are not so much discrete disorders in their own right, but rather reflect more universally distributed disorders expressed in "a culturally specific idiom." As such, there is no reasonable reason to sequester some disorders from others on that basis. W. S. Tseng, in his 2001 *Handbook of Cultural Psychiatry*, argues that we must begin to move past simply stating that culture impacts pathology and get better at describing at *how* it impacts that pathology.[40] Tseng notes that cultural factors may alternatively generate a dysfunctional strategy, influence which type of dysfunctional coping strategy is selected, modify that strategy, build on it, facilitate its strength, or foster specific societal reactions to a dysfunctional strategy. Individual and familial influences should not be discounted either.

Not all psychologists and psychiatrists, however, have rejected the notion of culture-bound syndromes. Some, in fact, have utilized the notion of culturally determined disorders in some creative ways to condemn what they see as an excessive and destructive influence by Western values.

HOMOSEXUALITY: A CULTURE-BOUND DISORDER?

Support for indigenous constructions of abnormality is generally applauded by progressive psychologists. The freedom of previously non-dominant peoples to define for themselves what is normal and what is abnormal has clear parallels in feminist, African-American, and queer empowerment movements within American psychology. It would be easy to suggest a simplistic narrative of "progress" in psychological paradigms that have moved from patronizing and patriarchal colonial perspectives to affirming and universally more constructive indigenous ones.

But what constitutes indigenous perspectives and what may represent unhealthy colonial remnants are not always so clear-cut in practice. Nowhere is this more apparent than in a cultural debate over homosexuality that has been spreading across Africa for the past decade. While political and religious leaders on the one hand and human rights activists on the other have been the primary speakers in this debate, African psychologists, psychiatrists, and social workers have been far from silent.

In academic circles, it has been argued that homosexuality and gender variance such as cross-dressing and transgender identities were historically common. Reports of positive roles for such figures date back to 1732 and persist into the 20th century, via anthropological reports.[41] With the arrival of European colonial powers and American missionaries, homosexuality and transgendered behavior were increasingly condemned as abnormal by both colonial authorities and the indigenous peoples they colonized. Homosexual and transgendered behavior necessarily became more discreet. But with the emergence of a Euro-American-inspired gay and lesbian rights movement in the 1990s, the reaction of politicians and religious leaders (both Christian and Muslim) in Africa was almost entirely hostile. Persecution of homosexuals as either morally depraved or psychologically disordered became common in the region.

An example of these attitudes can be seen in the statements made by Akwasi Osei, chief psychiatrist of the Ghana Health Service, as recently as 2011.[42] Osei considers homosexuality a reflection of decadent societies and a psychological aberration, though he recognizes that this is not the official professional stance in Europe and the United States. Osei argues that, given that homosexuality is not accepted as psychologically healthy in most of Africa, it should be considered a culture-bound syndrome. As such, Osei concludes that considering homosexuality as a mental disorder is solidly grounded in indigenous African values.

But it is informative to examine some of the pillars on which Osei rests his argument for homosexuality being considered a disorder, namely Christian theological objections and the psychoanalytic notion that repression of certain impulses is necessary for the maintenance of a healthy society. The sources of evidence that allow Osei to cast homosexuality as a psychological disorder have largely Western origins but have become a pervasive part of Ghanian academic and political culture.

Not all African mental health professionals agree with Osei, but many do. Several questions are raised by his intellectual argument. At what point do cultural influences and perspectives from other regions have sufficient longevity to be legitimately considered indigenous? Have indigenous perspectives become the final arbiter, the new orthodoxy of what is ethical practice? If a mental health construct is genuinely indigenous, is it automatically positive and therefore should be embraced? Advocates for sexual minorities in Ghana and elsewhere in Africa would argue not. And who gets to define what is healthy and what is abnormal anyway?

Other behavioral and attitudinal patterns that vary across cultures could easily substitute for the issue of homosexuality. For example, what is the appropriate response to an argument sometimes put forth by the indigenous practitioners of clitorectomy (deemed abusive genital mutilation in the wider global community) that the procedure is necessary for women in that culture to fit in and have self-esteem? What if some of the defenders of the practice are women? The conundrum of what constitutes universal human rights, regardless of the values of a dominant culture, and what are individual cultural values that need to be respected remains a dilemma for psychologists who practice across cultures.

SUMMARY

Colonial psychiatrists speculated freely on the mental disorders they encountered in lands and languages not their own. Early accounts seem clearly rooted in racist assumptions. But the cultural biases of the Personality and Culture movement, though more subtle, could almost be as damaging. Instead of being intellectually inferior, the objects of such psychodynamic studies were often seen as primitive and childlike. Entire cultures could display what seemed to Western eyes aberrant behaviors but that to only a few in any culture would be considered "deviant."

With political independence, and increased indigenous awareness of the full impact of the colonial process, came efforts in those cultures at a self-aware reconstruction of what is meant by mental health. The inclusion of culture-bound syndromes into the academic dialogue appeared as an imperfect transitional step in recognizing how much culture plays a role in the manifestation of those disorders.

Finally, it seems very much the case that merely recognizing the key role of culture in defining what is normal and abnormal for any culture doesn't settle the matter entirely. European and American constructs of individual human rights may make an entirely relativistic notion of the abnormal morally unpalatable. In any event, considering pathology through a cross-cultural lens remains a marvelous corrective for culture-bound perspectives that are ultimately limiting to all concerned.

REFERENCES

1. Mahone, S. (2006). Psychiatry in the East African colonies: A background to confinement. *International Review of Psychiatry, 18*(4), 327–332.
2. Saint Martin, M. L. (1999). Running amok: A modern perspective on a culture-bound syndrome. *Primary Care Companion to the Journal of Clinical Psychiatry, 1*(3), 66–70.
3. Chowdhury, A. N. (1998). Hundred years of koro: The history of a culture-bound syndrome. *International Journal of Social Psychiatry, 44*(3), 181–188.
4. Pols, H. (2006). The development of psychiatry in Indonesia: From colonial to modern times. *International Review of Psychiatry, 18*(4), 363–370.
5. Kirmayer, L. J. (2011). Cultural psychiatry in historical perspective. In D. Bhugra & K. Bhui (Eds.), *Textbook of Cultural Psychiatry*. Cambridge: Cambridge University Press.
6. Jilek, W. G. (1995). Emil Kraepelin and comparative sociocultural psychiatry. *European Archives for Psychiatry and Clinical Neurosciences, 245,* 231–238.
7. Pols, H. (2007). Psychological knowledge in a colonial context: Theories on the nature of the "native mind" in the former Dutch East Indies. *History of Psychology, 10*(2), 111–131.

8. Keller, R. K. (2007). *Colonial madness: Psychiatry in French North Africa*. Chicago: University of Chicago Press.
9. Carothers, J. C. (1953). *The African mind in health and disease: A study in ethnopsychiatry*. Geneva: World Health Organization.
10. Mahone, ibid., pp. 327, 330.
11. Cooper, J. M. (1934). Mental disease situations in certain cultures—a new field for research. *Journal of Abnormal and Social Psychology, 29*(1), 10–17.
12. Singer, M. (1961). A survey of culture and personality theory and research. In B. Kaplan (Ed.), *Studying personality cross-culturally* (pp. 9–90). New York: Harper & Row.
13. Bhatia, S. (2002). Orientalism in Euro-American and Indian psychology: Historical representations of "natives" in colonial and post-colonial contexts. *History of Psychology, 5*(4), 376–398.
14. Aurobindo, S. (1993). *The Integral Yoga: Sri Aurobindo's Teaching and Method of Practice*. Pondicherry, India: Sri Aurobindo Ashram, p. 265.
15. Wall, L. L. (1988). *Hausa medicine: Illness and well-being in a West African culture*. Durham, NC: Duke University Press.
16. Saint Martin, ibid.
17. Boroffka, A. (2006). *"Psychiatry in Nigeria": (A partly annotated bibliography)*. Kiel: Brunswiker Universitätsbuchhandlung.
18. Carstairs, G. M. (1961). Cross-cultural psychiatric interviewing. In B. Kaplan (Ed.), *Studying personality cross-culturally* (pp. 533–548). New York: Harper & Row.
19. Kennedy, D. (1961). Key issues in the cross-cultural study of mental disorders. In B. Kaplan (Ed.), *Studying personality cross-culturally* (pp. 405–425). New York: Harper & Row.
20. Frank, J. D. (1964). Foreword. In J. D. Frank (Ed.), *Magic, Faith and Healing: Studies in Primitive Psychiatry Today* (vii–xiv). New York: The Free Press.
21. Boroffka, ibid.
22. Boroffka, ibid.
23. Al-Issa, I. (1990). Culture and mental illness in Algeria. *International Journal of Social Psychiatry, 36*(3), 230–240.
24. Prince, R. (1960). The "brain fag syndrome" in Nigerian students. *Journal of Mental Science, 106*, 559–570.
25. Boroffka, ibid.
26. Dawson, J. (1964). Urbanization and mental health in a West African community. In A Kiev (Ed.), *Magic, faith and healing* (pp. 305–342). New York: Macmillan Publishing.
27. Murphy, H. B. M. (1973). Current trends in transcultural psychiatry. *Proceedings of the Royal Society of Medicine, 66*, 19–24.
28. Memmi, A. (1965). *The colonizer and the colonized* (tr. H. Greenfield). Boston: Beacon Press.
29. Fanon, F. (1963). *The wretched of the earth* (tr. C. Farrington). New York: Grove.

30. Burton, M. (2002). Liberation psychology: Learning from Latin America. Retrieved from http://www.liberationtheology.org/library/liberation-psychology-article-by-mark=burton.pdf

31. Kirmayer, L. J. (2011). Cultural psychiatry in historical perspective. In D. Bhugra & K. Bhui (Eds.), *Textbook of cultural psychiatry* (pp. 3–19). Cambridge: Cambridge University Press.

32. Allwood, C. M., & Berry, J. W. (2006). Origins and development of indigenous psychologies: An international analysis. *International Journal of Psychology, 41*(4), 243–268.

33. Nsamenang, A. B. (2000). Fathers, families, & child well-being in Cameroon: A review of the literature. Philadelphia, National Center on Fathers and Families.

34. Idemudia, E. S. (2004). Mental health and psychotherapy 'through' the eyes of culture: Lessons for African psychotherapy. Retrieved from http://inst.at/trans/15 Nr/02_7/idemudia15.htm

35. Lagerwerf, L. (1987). *Witchcraft, sorcery and spirit possession: Pastoral responses in Africa*. Harare: Mambo Press.

36. Yap, P. M. (1965). Phenomenology of affective disorders in Chinese and other cultures. In A. V. S. DeReuck and R. Porter (Eds.), *Transcultural psychiatry* (pp. 86–114). Boston: Little Brown.

37. Kleinman, A. (1986). *Social origins of distress and disease: Depression, neurasthenia, and pain in modern China*. New Haven, CT: Yale University Press.

38. American Psychiatric Association (1994). *Diagnostic and statistical manual of mental disorders*, fourth edition. Washington, DC: American Psychiatric Association.

39. Sumathipala, A., Sirbaddana, S. H., & Bhugra, D. (2004). Culture-bound syndromes: The story of dhat syndrome. *The British Journal of Psychiatry, 184*(3), 200–209.

40. Sumathipala, et al., ibid.

41. Murray, S. O., & Roscoe, W. (Eds.). *Boy-wives and female husbands: Studies of African homosexualities*. New York: St. Martin's Press.

42. MacDougall, C. (2011). "Homosexuality is un-African," says Ghanian psychiatrist. *North of Nowhere*, par. 10. Retrieved from http://crossingtheatlantic.blogspot.com/2011/04/homosexuality-is-un-african-says.html on 1/2/2012.

Chapter 5

The Rise of Abnormal Psychology during the Progressive Era: Reflections from an American Scientific Periodical

D. Brett King, Anne Bliss Niess, Alexandra
Elisabeth Maddi, and Layne S. Perkins

The story of abnormal psychology during the 19th century is one of bold transformation. In previous centuries, people with mental disorders were perceived as less than human, more in league with animals or even demons. According to the thinking of the day, lunacy was a mysterious or supernatural affliction caused by the influence of the moon. The Age of Reason, however, taught a more existential lesson, one that challenged conventional ideas about madness. From this new perspective, mental illness was seen as rooted in a divorce from one's reason. At the dawn of the 19th century, American physicians in the field referred to themselves as "alienists," a term signifying the patients' alienation from their sense of reason, making them strangers to the world in which they lived.

THE GILDED AGE OF PSYCHIATRY

In one gradual advance after another, alienists of the early 19th century advocated reform for individuals with psychiatric disorders.[17] Revolutionary in its scope, humanitarian reform introduced sweeping changes, often in the name of "moral therapy." A select group of doctors promoted treatments that drew upon recreation, diet, and music as well as more dramatic therapies such as bloodletting, purging, and blistering. In time, pockets of reform emerged throughout Europe and the United States. For more than four decades, an ambitious Boston reformer named Dorothea Dix conducted tireless research on the appalling conditions of the "insane poor" and campaigned state and federal officials to provide humane treatment. Inspired by her work, state-sponsored treatment of the mentally ill became a priority. American mental institutions proliferated, numbering more than 25 at mid-century.

Around this time, a Quaker alienist named Thomas Kirkbride introduced a scheme for constructing asylums. Known as the "Kirkbride Plan," his asylums encouraged environments with natural light and fresh air. His model stood in contrast with London's notorious Bethlehem Royal Hospital; better known as "Bedlam," it offered squalid and inhumane standards, wherein patients were whipped and chained to walls.

In 1844, Amariah Brigham founded the *American Journal of Insanity*. That same year, Kirkbride joined twelve colleagues to found the Association of Medical Superintendents of American Institutions for the Insane; 77 years later, the organization changed its name to the American Psychiatric Association. Such developments signaled an evolution from a scattered handful of reformers and alienists to a more organized profession. No longer esoteric, psychiatry had gained a new luster.

During this period, the American satirist Mark Twain and fellow novelist Charles Dudley Warner wrote *The Gilded Age*. Their 1873 novel offered a biting commentary on American society during the three decades following the Civil War, an era of unparalleled economic progress. Industry and technology flourished from coast to coast and birthed demand for transcontinental railroads, steel mills, and factories while captains of industry and robber barons amassed vast fortunes. As Twain and Warner pointed out, the gilt veneer didn't long hide the turmoil lurking among immigrants and other destitute families. In New York City, the mansions crowding Fifth Avenue's "Millionaire's Row" couldn't shadow unrest in congested tenements, where violence roiled in neighborhoods like Hell's Kitchen and Five Points. The Gilded Age cast a blind eye toward hardscrabble conditions and did little to temper social injustice until riots and strikes raged toward century's end.

In the same way, psychiatry enjoyed success with government support and growing status as a new branch of medicine. For all the triumph, however, a disturbing underbelly became visible. Seeking treatment, individuals who once languished in prisons and poorhouses swelled the population of psychiatric institutions. The trend proved overwhelming for asylum staff. Williams, Bellis, and Wellington[32] note that

> Increasingly, the major task of the asylum staff became the control of what was seen as deviant and dangerous behavior. The humane authoritarianism of moral treatment was transformed into rigid authoritarian control of people of whom little was understood or expected. Within a few years of their founding, the public asylums had become repositories for the custodial care of the poor and immigrant classes.

Before long, the demand for care began to eclipse gains made on the humanitarian front. Innovation gave way to institutionalization, creating a hospital model that taxed the energy of both staff and patients. The movement seemed lost and beleaguered, a victim of its own heady success.

To complicate matters, a drought of private and public resources withered further hope for a solution. It all signaled a collapse. Adding to the desperation, many earlier treatments that seemed promising now seemed anemic, faltering in contrast with other branches of medical science. As Pickren and Rutherford[22] observed:

> The discovery of germ theory in mainstream medicine in the second half of the 19th century, with its ability to explain cholera, typhoid, and other deadly diseases, placed mental medicine or psychiatry, as it was beginning to be called, even further from the medical mainstream. Although many theories of the etiology and treatment of mental disorder were proposed by alienists in this period, few had any major impact, leading historians of psychiatry to refer to this time as an era of therapeutic nihilism, or absence of belief in the possibility of developing effective treatment.

The acid of "therapeutic nihilism" was spilled at an 1894 meeting of medical superintendents. S. Weir Mitchell, America's first neurologist, had been invited to address the conference, but his unforgiving speech became more of an assault. Mitchell accused the superintendents of unprofessional conduct and cited a lack of rigor in their investigations, medical records, and training programs. Such haphazard work, he argued, had distanced them from more laudable colleagues in the medical community.

Besieged on all fronts, it seemed, psychiatrists began looking for answers. "It was in this atmosphere," Pickren and Rutherford[22] noted, when psychiatrists "turned to other disciplines for help, including psychology."

ABNORMAL PSYCHOLOGY DURING THE PROGRESSIVE ERA

As the Gilded Age faded, a new social activism came to prominence in the United States during the mid-1890s. The Progressive Era was a period of vigorous reform built on the distressed hopes of the Gilded Age.[24] Teeming with optimism, the country witnessed dramatic changes in workplace safety, social justice, corporate regulation, and political reform. Progressive causes inspired four constitutional amendments and fueled the political careers of Theodore Roosevelt and Woodrow Wilson. Far from unified, progressive advocates composed a diverse group with a variety of agendas.[12]

Many progressives believed that science and technology could transform society. They witnessed breathtaking inventions including the electric trolley, phonograph, long-distance radio transmission, electric light bulb, and motion pictures. They rejoiced at the triumph of the Wright Brothers piloting an airplane above a wind-swept beach and mourned the tragedy of the *Titanic* colliding with an iceberg in chill Atlantic waters.

During this time, social sciences prospered at universities in the United States and, before long, psychology found its place among them. Born toward the end of the Gilded Age, fresh from university laboratories at Leipzig and Harvard, the new science came of age during the Progressive Era. A generation later, abnormal psychology, or psychotherapeutics, as it was known at the time, came into existence in the 1890s.[29] Independent of psychiatry, psychotherapeutics spanned a period of time between the work of the French neurologist Jean-Martin Charcot and the psychoanalysis of Sigmund Freud. Taylor[29] observed that, "contrary to the prevailing assumption that psychotherapeutics originated within psychiatry, in America it had its origins in a confluence of such seemingly disparate sources as physiological psychology, neurology, and psychical research."

The venerable Harvard psychologist William James provided inspiration for a movement known as the Boston School of Abnormal Psychology. As the epicenter for psychotherapeutics, it attracted like-minded thinkers from different fields who practiced psychotherapy in addition to conventional specialty areas.[29] Also known as the Boston School of Psychotherapy, it became the foremost authority on scientific psychotherapy. Thereafter, Lightner Witmer founded the first American psychological clinic at the University of Pennsylvania in 1896 and created the journal *Psychological Clinic* in 1907.

Following the period from James to Witmer, abnormal psychology began to find momentum during the first two decades of the 20th century. In 1917, a handful of clinicians formed the American Association of Clinical Psychologists. The organization was short-lived, but the AACP stimulated professional changes, leading to the creation of the Clinical Section of the American Psychological Association in 1919.

Still, it was a hard road. As the Progressive Era came to a close, experimental psychology continued to dominate the discipline. Among the 200 American psychologists in 1909, only a handful counted themselves as clinicians. A decade later, only 15 of 375 APA members listed clinical psychology as an interest. As their modest professions grew, both psychiatrists and psychologists understood the value of educating the American public about psychopathology.

The year after William James's seminal book *The Principles of Psychology* was published in 1890, only two scholarly journals were dedicated to the new discipline. By 1913, psychology could boast only a meager 16 journals. Unlike psychology journals, however, American cultural and popular magazines proliferated during the 19th century.

During the period from 1885 through the First World War, a drop in publication expenses escalated the publication of mass-circulation magazines.[19] Between 1885 and 1905, over 7,500 periodicals were created and a powerful industry emerged. Driven by an insatiable readership, mass-circulation magazines like *Cosmopolitan, Harper's Weekly, The Nation,* and *Popular Science Monthly* became household names. Piott[24] noted that, "by focusing on popular content and attracting advertisers, which helped keep the magazine's price low, sales soared." In promoting social causes, advocates of the Progressive movement found inspiration from popular magazines of the period.[13] The middle class had emerged during the 19th century and progressives understood the power of popular magazines to reach that audience. Like progressive reformers, early psychopathologists tapped into public support. Psychology became a popular topic in mass-circulation magazines, and readers were enthusiastic about the area.[16]

POPULAR SCIENCE MONTHLY

Perhaps more than any other magazine of the era, *Popular Science Monthly* featured articles on abnormal psychology from a scholarly perspective. Founded in 1872 by Edward Livingston Youmans, an American science writer, it was conceived as a monthly compendium of articles that summarized advances in science and technology. Youmans was versed in social causes, dating back to his father's work as an early New York abolitionist. His interest in psychology began in 1856 when he read a book on the subject by Herbert Spencer, later to become a close friend.

From the beginning, *Popular Science Monthly* was designed to appeal to educated readers. It shared scientific articles authored by such trailblazers as Alexander Graham Bell, Franz Boas, John Dewey, Havelock Ellis, Francis Galton, Ernst Haeckel, Thomas Henry Huxley, William James, Lord Kelvin, Emil Kraepelin, James Clerk Maxwell, Louis Pasteur, Charles Sanders Peirce, Spencer, Edward Bradford Titchener, Edward L. Thorndike, Alfred Russel Wallace, and Wilhelm Wundt. Youmans edited the periodical until his death when his brother and co-founder, William Jay Youmans, took over editorial chores. Trained as a physician, the younger Youmans served as editor-in-chief for thirteen years.

In 1900, the American psychologist James McKeen Cattell assumed responsibilities as editor-in-chief and then publisher. After studying with Wundt in Germany, Cattell had returned to the United States to teach at the University of Pennsylvania before moving to Columbia University in 1891. He became president of the American Psychological Association four years later and played a visible role as a promoter of psychological science and practice.

Cattell was already a distinguished editor and publisher when he took over *Popular Science Monthly*. Together with James Mark Baldwin, he had founded the journal *Psychological Review* in 1894. He also purchased publishing rights for *Science*, founded by Thomas Edison and Alexander Graham Bell in 1880. Despite its promise, *Science* was not a financial success and had ceased publication in 1894. Cattell struck a deal to make *Science* the official journal of the American Association for the Advancement of Science (AAAS). He engineered the deal with AAAS in 1900, the same year he purchased *Popular Science Monthly*. Near the end of the Progressive Era, Cattell sold the magazine's name and founded another title, *Scientific Monthly*, to replace it.

ABNORMAL PSYCHOLOGY AS PORTRAYED IN *POPULAR SCIENCE MONTHLY*

Popular Science Monthly straddled the Gilded Age and the Progressive Era during a time that was critical in laying the foundation for abnormal psychology. Intelligent discussions of psychopathology were found in its pages, sprinkled alongside curiosities from a different age, including articles on "The problem of a flying machine," "How spelling damages the mind," "What is electricity?" and "What keeps the bicycler upright?" We will focus on a few themes that played a role in establishing the identity of abnormal psychology in the American imagination.

MORBID PSYCHOLOGY: HYSTERIA AND NEURASTHENIA

Taylor[29] claimed that hysteria and neurasthenia were the most prevalent illnesses of the 19th century, a notion supported in the pages of *Popular Science Monthly*. Both disorders were understood as a condition of their time, specifically that modern life and its collateral stresses had made Americans— especially women—susceptible to nervous disease.

With a heritage rooted in antiquity, hysteria could be revealed in an assortment of symptoms, including headaches, melancholy, fatigue, severe cramps, wild and pained cries, minor paralysis, emotional instability, aggression, and "brain-fever." A woman's reproductive system was suspected as the primary culprit. The hysterical woman was believed to show faltering control over her emotions and could be gripped, without warning, by seizures and emotional outbursts or even unconscious trances. In *Popular Science Monthly*, Noble laureate Charles Richet challenged the idea that hysteria was an "erotic disease."

He concluded this brand of "morbid psychology" was a "nervous disease, which has no more to do with sexual passion than other nervous diseases."[25]

Not everyone agreed with Richet's assessment.

At the time, attending doctors would make house calls, treating a hysterical patient with pelvic massages until she experienced a clinical orgasm or "hysterical paroxysm." Select homes featured "fainting rooms" for comfort during home treatments and led to the popularity of the fainting couch and the chaise longue. Competing treatments for hysterical illness included prolonged bed rest, a water massage known as "hydrotherapy," and the use of vibrators. More dramatic measures involved bleeding and even oophorectomy, surgery to remove the ovaries. Certain metals were applied to the skin as a treatment for hysterical paralyses, neuralgias, a loss of sensation, and headaches. With the glow of confidence, Richet[26] reported that the "application of pieces of gold or silver or other metal upon the insensible region is sufficient to produce a complete restoration of sensibility in the course of a few hours. Some patients are cured with gold, others with silver, others with zinc or copper. This process of treatment, which consists in the application of pieces of metal to the skin, is called metallotherapy."

Hypnosis was lauded as another treatment for hysteria going back to the older tradition of mesmerism and animal magnetism.[27] In one article, Newbold[20] described how hypnotic trances could induce a state of ecstasy. A friend of Darwin, psychologist George John Romanes[28] dismissed myths revolving around hypnotism and promoted the work of Rudolf Heidenhain[14] at the University of Breslau. Heidenhain studied the cortical inhibition of hypnosis, research that had an impact on his student, Ivan Pavlov. Psychoanalysis was also promoted as a viable treatment method (Freud and Jung had given a series of lectures at an American psychology conference in 1909, and James McKeen Cattell had attended their lectures). Later to become president of the University of North Carolina, Harry Woodburn Chase[8] reported on the revolutionary promise of psychoanalysis for treating hysteria. It all signaled progress from older treatments. In fact, Richet enthused how "grave hysteria," once condemned as demonic possession, could now be understood as a critical disorder of the mind, proving the "innocence of the miserable sufferers from these diseases who were formerly consigned to the stake."[27]

It was believed that the disorder was linked to other afflictions such as somnambulism[27] and "double personality."[21] Hysteria's closest psychiatric cousin, however, was the disorder known as neurasthenia. A short time after the Civil War, the American neurologist George Miller Beard[4] coined the term to describe the nervous exhaustion brought on by the rigors of urbanization and the workplace. The hurried pace of modern life was said to have a destructive effect on "tired nerves," an effect that depleted nervous energy. One physician warned that

Neurasthenia and hysteria spread wider and wider, like a devastating epidemic, attacking not merely the lower classes but also the 'upper ten thousand.' It is educated society which is threatened with total overthrow by utter derangement of the nerves. 'Whither is this to lead, and how is it to end?' lament some solicitous prophets who already see yawning before them the gulf by which the enervated human race is about to be swallowed up.[15]

Among that population, the United States offered a number of the susceptible, leading William James to re-christen neurasthenia as "Americanitis." James himself had been diagnosed, along with other high-profile figures including Theodore Roosevelt and Jane Addams.

Beard also found evidence of neurasthenia in French-Canadian lumberjacks, reputed for their exaggerated startle reflex and excitability. He discovered curious symptoms while profiling the "jumpers" from the Moosehead Lake region of northern Maine:

These Jumpers have been known to strike their fists against a red-hot stove; they have been known to jump into the fire, as well as into water; indeed, no painfulness or peril of position has any effect on them; they are as powerless as apoplectics or hysterics, if not more so . . . they must do as they are told, though it kill them, or though it kill others.[4]

Beard's research on the jumpers of Maine stimulated subsequent research by French neurologist Georges Gilles de la Tourette.

An entire industry came to life in response to the threat of neurasthenia, giving rise to a carnival of consumerism for potions and bitters and elixirs. Certain brands of "brain and nerve food" promised to restore vigor with ingredients such as cannabis or cocaine. Neurologist S. Weir Mitchell pioneered the "rest cure" along with sponge baths, massage, and a diet consisting of eggs and milk. Thomas Clifford Allbutt, a British physician who had invented the clinical thermometer, worried about "brain-forcing" patients:

We do not realize how long a time the exhausted brain takes to recover itself! A young physician may boldly tell the overtaxed merchant or student to take three months' rest; but probably three months must be added to that, and even six months again to the sum, before any degree of stability is regained. It is nearly always true that a case of brain-exhaustion needs what may seem a disproportionate time to get well. Repair in so delicate an organ is slow.[1]

Scottish physician Thomas Lauder Brunton[5] warned that indigestion could cause nervous depression and encouraged a regulation of exercise and diet for the "exhausted brain-worker" while advising the use of purgative medicines to clear out the liver and remove waste products.

Not all bought the idea that society was the problem. As early as 1878, alienist Daniel Hack Tuke had advised caution about drawing a link between the stresses of modern civilization and mental illness. In searching for "hard facts" on the matter, he acknowledged difficulty in attempting to "connect the social evils of the present day with the statistics of lunacy."[30] As the Great Depression waited a decade after the Progressive Era, the diagnosis of neurasthenia began to vanish, rendering it a lost relic of its time.

STEREOTYPES AND PUBLIC FEARS

Like other forms of media, popular magazines reinforced stereotypes as well as challenged their prevalence. Articles in *Popular Science Monthly* provided stereotypical accounts of women and people of different ethnicities. At times, however, an attempt was made to confront stereotypes about abnormal psychology and to address public fears about madness.

Like many of his day, Baker argued that mental disorders were hereditary in origin, inherited from a stream of unhealthy, uneducated, and poorly functional family members from generations past. In a more contemporary light, however, he brought to light an unhealthy bias associated with such disorders: "Many times families are loath to reveal things which might indicate such a basis of the dreaded disease."[2] Such stereotypes, he warned, prevented the mental health field from advancing unless "the public shall have come to look upon insanity as merely an unfortunate disease instead of a stigmatized disgrace."[2]

A growing concern about alcohol also ignited public apprehension. In 1784 psychiatrist Benjamin Rush had discussed the dangers of alcoholism. In the years afterward, the temperance movement had arisen with calls to reduce or prohibit liquor. In response, the issue found its way into several *Popular Science Monthly* articles. As a Quaker and a psychiatrist, Tuke[30] shared apprehension about the "mental evil exerted by drink." Crothers[9] regarded inebriety as a disease but one that was preventable and curable. Some saw alcoholism, like hysteria and neurasthenia, as an epidemic. That kind of thinking was consistent with the public fear that mental illness was a form of group lunacy.

Mass hysteria was an idea that dated back to the dance manias of the medieval period, but it returned during the Progressive Era. Motion pictures took off in popularity during this time. At the center of the craze, nickelodeons charged a nickel admission to attend single-reel movies. By 1910, 26 million people, a full one-fourth of the American population, attended movies every week. It was a troubling development for some. Piott[24] noted that "guardians of public morality took a dim view of the new medium. Some saw the popularity of movies as a form of mass delirium they called 'nickel madness.'"

But could insanity be contagious? It was a real public fear at the time.

Charles Pilgrim, later to become state commissioner of the insane hospitals in New York, explored a phenomenon that French alienists were calling *folie à deux* or *folie imposée*. He wrote in response to a number of cases of "communicated insanity" that had gained publicity in New York, Buffalo, and Philadelphia. He argued that the "fact that an insane person can, under certain conditions, produce the same form of insanity in another previously sane, or infect him as it were, is indisputable."[23] Although he believed the threat was slight under ordinary circumstances—citing the immunity of doctors and nurses in asylums—he found examples of the contagious nature of insanity among his patients, especially the women. As a precaution, he encouraged the "early removal of the patient from the influence of home and friends" but shared,

> I would not for a moment subscribe to the doctrine that insanity is contagious and communicated from one to another, as, for instance, smallpox is, and I altogether repudiate the common idea that it is easy to become a lunatic when compelled to associate with and listen constantly to the ravings of madmen.[23]

Despite his belief in catching insanity through association, the author challenged the idea that sending a patient to state hospitals would worsen their condition.

SURVIVAL OF THE UNFIT: EUGENICS AND SOCIAL CONTROL

During the Progressive Era, there was a growing concern that "lower and more degraded types" of people might hold back the cause of social advancement. Famed naturalist Alfred Russel Wallace[31] shared with readers of *Popular Science Monthly*, "In one of my latest conversations with Darwin, he expressed himself very gloomily on the future of humanity, on the ground that in our modern civilization natural selection had no play, and the fittest did not survive." For some, the idea was that the focus should shift from reform to prevention. Wallace added, "What we want is, not a higher standard of perfection in the few, but a higher average, and this can best be produced by the elimination of the lowest of all and a free intermingling of the rest."[31] He shared the words of a progressive who claimed, "we need less of the weak and the bad. This weeding-out system has been the method of natural selection by which the animal and vegetable worlds have been improved and developed. The survival of the fittest is really the extinction of the unfit."[31]

The call for extreme action settled on the idea that a number of societal problems could be solved with eugenics.[18] Although the notion can be traced back to antiquity, eugenics found a vigorous advocate in Victorian scholar Francis Galton. Inspired by the work of his cousin, Charles Darwin, Galton[10] defined it as "the science which deals with all influences that improve the inborn qualities of a race; also with those that develop them to the utmost advantage." In the ideal world of Progressive thinkers, eugenics would be a broad-based movement that would advance society through the mechanism of social breeding. Indeed, Galton[11] suggested that the "first object" of eugenics "is to check the birth rate of the unfit instead of allowing them to come into being."

In 1901, sociologist Edward A. Ross popularized the expression "social control" to refer to eugenics as a means of protecting and preserving Anglo-Saxon civilization. He sensed a shift taking place, one in which the fertility of the white middle class was diminishing, compared with higher birth rates among inferior groups. A popular term at the time put it more bluntly, insisting that white America was committing "race suicide." Reform-minded thinkers saw legitimacy in the ideals of social control. Once again, it was critical to bring the idea to the public.

In 1910, Galton had written a novel about eugenics in the hope of bringing his message to a broader audience. *Kantsaywhere* described a utopian society based on eugenic principles wherein the unfit were banished from their communities. Piott[24] observed, "College textbooks and popular magazines presented eugenics to an even wider audience, prompting one historian to note that more articles on the topic of eugenics appeared in print between 1910 and 1914 than on slums and poverty."

The idea took root. Inventor of the corn flake breakfast cereal, Michigan physician John Harvey Kellogg was a co-founder of the Race Betterment Foundation in 1906, an organization dedicated to eugenics and social control. Even prominent figures in the woman's movement endorsed eugenics, including Charlotte Perkins Gilman and Margaret Sanger. An admirer of Galton, James McKeen Cattell was also an enthusiastic supporter of eugenics (in a popular bit of legend, he promised his children $1,000 each if they agreed to marry the son or daughter of a college professor). Before becoming editor of *Popular Science Monthly*, Cattell[6] wrote in its pages, "as things go at present, the thoughtless and criminal are apt to have offspring early, while the reliant and mentally endowed postpone marriage until a long course of education is accomplished and a social position is secured."

The intersection between abnormal psychology and eugenics came when authorities insisted that people with mental disorders posed a threat to society. "What is society to do with its horde of defectives?" American physician and social reformer Henry Dwight Chapin asked in an article titled "Survival of the Unfit." He concluded,

> Unfortunately, it does practically nothing to check their production. The sources of the muddy stream are left untouched, while larger and larger reservoirs are being constantly built to collect and conserve the contaminated flow. One can not help noticing how this humanitarian age is abundantly equipped

with asylums, almshouses, reformatories, and hospitals of all kinds. If the good accomplished by such agencies could be measured solely by relief of suffering and cure of disease, the results would be nothing but gratifying. A collateral danger is in keeping alive sickly and defective classes, who are often as prolific as they are inefficient. In our civilization these institutions have become a necessity, but their abuse should be carefully guarded against.[7]

In his mind, the social sciences should "devote its principal energies to avoiding the production of the unfit, and then see to it that they do not survive beyond one generation. Here lies the only solution of this difficult problem"—"first prevention, next permanent isolation."[7]

In that spirit, Barr[3] warned that, based on his work with "mental defectives," they were an "enemy that attacks not our frontiers but our hearthstones." He supported social legislation in Connecticut that made it illegal for any "imbecile or feeble-minded" person to marry or else risk a minimum three-year sentence in prison. Any person aiding and abetting such a union was also liable. Barr[3] concluded that "laws preventing the marriage of defectives and of their immediate descendants would go far to stem the tide of harmful heredity." This kind of social control would prohibit them from overtaking society and standing in the way of natural selection, making artificial selection a necessity. Barr[3] encouraged his readers to act "heroically" to support such action because the "hope of the legislation is to keep down degenerate families." But what about Americans who already suffered from mental disorders? He championed the development of farm colonies where people with mental disorders would be supervised and guarded. More effective than a prison, such "noble" compounds would provide a "national colony for this race."[3]

In that spirit, the Virginia State Colony for Epileptics and Feebleminded was founded in 1910. From that time until 1917, legislation was passed in 17 states that encouraged the sterilization of unfit individuals. While at the Virginia Colony, a patient named Carrie Buck became the first person to be sterilized under the Racial Integrity Act of 1924, advocating compulsory sterilization for people diagnosed as feeble-minded, imbeciles, or epileptics. Buck also became a plaintiff in *Buck v. Bell* when the issue of her sterilization went to the Supreme Court. Justice Oliver Wendell Holmes Jr. wrote the decision to uphold the practice. The Court's decision legitimized sterilization laws and opened the door to new legislation in dozens of states until the sobering actions of the Nazi regime cast disgrace on the practice. Leonard[18] concluded, "The hubris of Progressive Era eugenics was twofold. First, the naïve faith that science would prove a cure-all for social ills, which led to overreaching by eugenicists and those social scientists who appealed to their authority, and second, the naïve faith that the state, as guided by experts, would prove to be the best guarantor of human biological progress."

CONCLUSION

Psychopathology came of age during a time of unprecedented reform. At the beginning of the 19th century, humanitarian reform and moral therapy offered new insights into the study of mental disorders, casting out antiquated notions of demonic possession—where no decisive treatment was believed possible—while promoting humane care. Psychiatry cultivated that promise into a legitimate branch of medical science and came to prominence during the age of the asylum but faced nagging conflicts regarding treatment and custodialism.

Later in the century, abnormal psychology transformed into a credible discipline as the United States transformed into a more progressive society. From the start, abnormal psychology appeared in articles in mass-circulation magazines and, facing a poverty of scientific journals, experts used popular magazines to educate the American public about psychopathology. Although written for a non-scientific audience, the ideas expressed in periodicals such as *Popular Science Monthly* reflected an enthusiastic public appetite for information on abnormal psychology. A host of scholars shared opinions on and research about mental illness, including ideas about symptomology, etiology, and treatment. Straddling the Gilded Age and the Progressive Era, such writings reflected public perceptions ranging from the contagious nature of insanity to precipitating stressors in modern living to issues relating to the social control of madness. Although rudimentary, such efforts contributed to abnormal psychology's subsistence during the first decades of its existence and, at the same time, laid the groundwork for publicizing the rise of the new science.

REFERENCES

1. Allbutt, T. C. (1878). On brain-forcing. *Popular Science Monthly, 13,* 217–230.
2. Baker, S. (1899). Causes and prevention of insanity. *Popular Science Monthly, 55,* 102–113.
3. Barr, M. W. (1899). Mental defectives and the social welfare. *Popular Science Monthly, 54,* 746–759.
4. Beard, G. M. (1880). Experiments with the "jumpers" of Maine. *Popular Science Monthly, 18,* 170–178.
5. Brunton, T. L. (1881). Indigestion as a cause of nervous depression. *Popular Science Monthly, 18,* 374–384.
6. Cattell, J. M. (1893). The progress of psychology. *Popular Science Monthly, 43,* 779–785.
7. Chapin, H. D. (1892). The survival of the unfit. *Popular Science Monthly, 41,* 182–187.
8. Chase, H. W. (1911). Freud's theories of the unconscious. *Popular Science Monthly, 78,* 355–363.

9. Crothers, T. D. (1884). Alcoholic trance. *Popular Science Monthly, 26*, 187–194.

10. Galton, F. (1904). Eugenics: Its definition, scope, and aims. *The American Journal of Sociology, 10*, 1–25.

11. Galton, F. (1908). *Memoirs of my life.* London: Methuen.

12. Gendzel, G. (2011). What the progressives had in common. *The Journal of the Gilded Age and Progressive Era, 10*, 331–339.

13. Hart, P. S. (2012). Little magazines and little wanderers: Building advocate networks for adoption during the Progressive era. *American Journalism, 29*, 32–59.

14. Heidenhain, R. (1881). Artificial hypnotism. *Popular Science Monthly, 18*, 362–367.

15. Hirsch, W. (1896). *Popular Science Monthly, 49*, 544–549.

16. King, D. B., Raymond, B. L., & Simon-Thomas, J. A. (1995). History of sport psychology in cultural magazines of the Victorian era. *The Sport Psychologist, 9*, 376–390.

17. King, D. B., Viney, W., & Woody, W. D. (2009). *A history of psychology: Ideas and context.* Boston: Pearson.

18. Leonard, T. C. (2005). Eugenics and economics in the Progressive Era. *Journal of Economic Perspectives, 19*, 207–224.

19. Mott, F. L. (1957). *A history of American magazines.* Cambridge, MA: Harvard University Press.

20. Newbold, W. R. (1896a). Hypnotic states, trance, and ecstasy. *Popular Science Monthly, 48*, 804–815.

21. Newbold, W. R. (1896b). Double personality. *Popular Science Monthly, 50*, 67–70.

22. Pickren, W. E., & Rutherford, A. (2010). *A history of modern psychology in context.* New York: Wiley.

23. Pilgrim, C. W. (1895). Communicated insanity. *Popular Science Monthly, 46*, 828–833.

24. Piott, S. L. (2011). *Daily life in the Progressive Era.* Santa Barbara, CA: Greenwood.

25. Richet, C. (1880a). Hysteria and demonism: A study in morbid psychology I. *Popular Science Monthly, 17*, 86–93.

26. Richet, C. (1880b). Hysteria and demonism: A study in morbid psychology II. *Popular Science Monthly, 17*, 155–165.

27. Richet, C. (1880c). Hysteria and demonism: A study in morbid psychology III. *Popular Science Monthly, 17*, 376–385.

28. Romanes, G. J. (1888). Hypnotism. *Popular Science Monthly, 18*, 108–113.

29. Taylor, E. (2000). Psychotherapeutics and the problematic origins of clinical psychology in America. *American Psychologist, 55*, 1029–1033.

30. Tuke, D. H. (1878). Modern life and insanity. *Popular Science Monthly, 12*, 432–445.

31. Wallace, A. R. (1890). Human selection. *Popular Science Monthly, 38*, 93–106.

32. Williams, D. H., Bellis, E. C., & Wellington, S. W. (1980). Deinstitutionalization and social policy: Historical perspectives and present dilemmas. *American Journal of Orthopsychiatry, 50*, 54–64.

Chapter 6

The Ascent of Psychiatry and Psychology in 1800–1945: Multiple Dimensions of Mental Conditions Emerge

Eva D. Papiasvili and Linda A. Mayers

The Romantic spirit of the 19th century, "bent toward exploration and discovery, at whatever risk of error or failure"[1] (p. 491), provided fertile ground for the intensification of scientific inquiry into the human condition in all its normal and abnormal dimensions.

Within the increasingly specialized sciences and professions, there arose at least three distinct areas that explicitly concerned themselves with the abnormal mental conditions. In medicine, psychiatry emerged as a specialty at the turn of the 18th and 19th century. Within the young field of psychology, the applied field of experimentally based clinical psychology and the theoretical field of dynamically based abnormal psychology established themselves in the last decades of the 19th century and at the beginning of the 20th century, respectively. The multidimensionality of modern thought about abnormal mental conditions starts here.

After defining the three fields as to their different and converging perspectives, this chapter will trace major themes on the path to modernity: recognition of severe mental conditions as illnesses in need of treatment, triggering both the humanitarian reforms of asylums and the biological discoveries of a link between the brain and mental disorders and the first biological treatments; the development of the first comprehensive classification system of mental disorders; the development of the dynamic theory of the psychological basis of mental disorders; and the evolution of the psychological research tradition, which forms a basis for increasingly sophisticated and multidimensional psychometrics.

These themes, together with the integrative aspirations of the field of abnormal psychology, establish a basis from which the multidimensional dynamic picture of the human mind and behavior with its normative and abnormal characteristics can begin to emerge.

PSYCHIATRY, CLINICAL PSYCHOLOGY, AND ABNORMAL PSYCHOLOGY

When, during the 18th-century Enlightenment era, it became increasingly clear that confinement in an institution could be curative, a new field of medicine was born. The term "psychiatry" was coined in 1808 by Johann Christian Reil.[2] The Greek origin of the word designates this medical specialty as "the healing of the mind." Over time, psychiatry evolved to focus on the research, assessment, and treatment of mental disorders, deficiencies, and abnormalities, through biological and psychological means.

Whereas psychiatry emerged as a branch of medicine, the object of which is the healing of illness, clinical psychology emerged as a branch of psychology, the object of which is the understanding of the functioning of the normal mind. If "psychology" translates from Ancient Greek as "the study of the mind," then "clinical psychology" studies the mind afflicted with clinical conditions. When clinical psychology first emerged as an applied specialty, the experimental science of psychology was only 20 years old. Its previous life as a branch of philosophy had begun 2,500 years prior, in Ancient Greece. The term "Psichologia," or "Psychologia," dates to the Renaissance, but its popular usage waited for the Enlightenment and Denis Diderot's *Encyclopedia* of 1751, which referenced Christian Wolf's earlier publication of *Psychologia Empirica et Psychologia Rationalis*. In England, the term "psychology" overtook "mental philosophy" in the mid-19th century before emerging in Germany as an independent, experimentally based discipline. In 1896, the formal beginning of the field of clinical psychology was heralded by the founding, at the University of Pennsylvania, of the first psychological clinic.[3] Its founder, Leightner Witmer, defined his field as the application of experimental psychology to psychopathology.

Prompted by the increased societal interest in human development and education, clinical psychology initially concerned itself with the diagnostic testing of children, working to identify those with special educational needs and those with intellectual "subnormalities." The field evolved as a science and profession applying psychological means to the assessment and treatment of psychological conditions and mental disorders of individuals of all ages.

The major transitional figures Wilhelm Wundt and Jean Martin Charcot personified the initially permeable boundary between the two clinical fields. Neither psychiatrists nor clinical psychologists, their students defined psychiatry and clinical psychology for 70 years to come. Each field defined and redefined itself in dynamic interaction with the other, competing and cooperating, both locked in reciprocal interaction with their mother fields, the culture at large, and the progress of technology.

In 1906 the inaugural issue of the *Journal of Abnormal Psychology* marked the formal beginning of a dynamically synthetic, theoretical field. It is no accident that the field of abnormal psychology appeared after the two clinical disciplines had attained their initial major advances, even as it predates its clinical cousins as an area of scholarly interest. In comparison, its scope is wider: abnormal psychology studies unusual patterns of behavior, emotion, and thought that may or may not be understood as precipitating a mental disorder.[4] Abnormal psychology identifies multiple causes of various conditions, employing diverse theories from the fields of psychology, psychiatry, and related areas of medicine, anthropology, sociology, and others. Its knowledge base, in turn, may form the basis for the work of clinical psychologists and psychiatrists.[5]

As the clinical fields evolved in relation to each other, abnormal psychology evolved in relation to both, from mostly dynamically rooted syntheses towards experimental integrative models of abnormal mental conditions. It was here, between these fields, that the multiple dimensions of the human mind emerged.

EARLY DEVELOPMENTS IN PSYCHIATRY

From the outset, psychiatry was torn between two conceptualizations of mental illness: the biological and the psychosocial. While the psychosocial approach concerned itself with righting the incorrect, "alienated" thinking of afflicted individuals, the biological approach was rooted in experimental investigations modeled on the natural sciences: physics, biology, chemistry, anatomy, and physiology. Both, however, originated in the great expansion of the experimental sciences of the 18th-century Enlightenment.

As the 19th century dawned, so too did the Romantic cultural movement of the "Mind and Heart,"[1] and the psychosocial approach to psychiatry was sometimes dubbed "Romantic Psychology." The Romantic practitioners attributed their patients' symptoms to dilemmas of morality and the passions. Meanwhile, biological psychiatrists came to see psychic distress as originating in the cerebral cortex, although "the real notion of how brain biology was implicated, was [considered] unknown"[2] (p. 28).

In practice, the social and biological approaches sometimes overlapped. Practitioners of the psychosocial tradition may have subscribed to organic, biological, or hereditary aspects of mental affliction, just as those who practiced biological psychiatry may have perceived the participation of social factors. An example of such intermediary practices is the concept of "tired nerves" and a curative spa treatment. The beginnings of multidimensional thought about mental abnormalities can be traced to such intermediary practices.

SOCIAL TRADITION AND HUMANITARIAN REFORMS

In England and continental Europe, early custodial asylums predated the birth of psychiatry by several centuries. What led to the ascent of psychiatry as a separate discipline, however, was the realization that confinement in an institution with a "right-thinking therapeutic philosophy"[2] (p. 9) could be curative.

Following William Battie of England and Vincenzio Chiarugi of Italy, who maintained that asylums should not merely segregate mental patients but heal them,[2] it was Philippe Pinel in revolutionary France who unchained the mentally ill and became the "hero" of psychiatric hospital reform. In his 1801 textbook *Traité medico-philosophique sur l'alienation mentale*, Pinel put particular stress on two aspects of asylum life. The first was the setting itself. Asylums, asserted Pinel, should be calm and quiet places where therapeutic self-control could be learned. The asylum's routine was designed to encouraged limit setting, self-mastery, and a communal spirit. The curative propensities of the doctor-patient relationship added a Romantic aspect. This special psychological relationship between psychiatrist and patient was referred to as "Moral Therapy."

In 1825 Jean-Etienne Dominique Esquirol developed a prototype therapeutic community where patients and physicians lived together in a psychiatric setting, adjoined with a hospital. Esquirol believed that isolation from family and friends would divert the patient from the unhealthy passions that had ruled his or her life.[2]

Even before Esquirol, Moral Therapy had found a home in England at the independent York Retreat, founded in 1796 by the Quaker tea merchant William Tuke. Modeled on the ideal of bourgeois family life, Tuke's private asylum represented another prototypic therapeutic community. Patients and staff lived and labored side-by-side, with the restoration of self-control as their therapeutic goal.

The father of American psychiatry, Benjamin Rush, despite his country's lack of an asylum tradition, worked for the humane treatment of the mentally ill, and his efforts were felt at the Pennsylvania Hospital from 1783 on. In his first systematic treatise on psychiatry in the United States, *Medical Inquiries and Observations upon the Diseases of the Mind*, 1812, Rush explicated his version of Moral Therapy. Referred to as Moral Management in America, it focused on the patient's social, individual, and occupational needs[6] (p. 44).

These seeds grew rapidly, and by the late 1830s, a spate of psychiatric asylums had been founded across Continental Europe, Britain, and the United

States in what came to be called the Great Confinement. This approach rested on the calming environment of the asylum, the curative factors of the doctor-patient relationship, and the management of time, with the goals of restoring self-control and alleviating "mental alienations" caused by disorders of the brain. The Industrial Revolution ushered in the sometimes mistaken "bigger is better" credo. As psychiatric facilities grew in size, and as their proliferation outpaced the training of qualified staff, their conditions progressively deteriorated.

Dorothea Dix, a Boston schoolteacher, made humanitarian care a public and political concern in the United States. From 1841 to 1881, Dix campaigned for reform before state legislatures and the United States Congress. Her work garnered new laws and government funding for improvement in patients' treatment and physical conditions. Dix personally helped found 32 state hospitals, all intended for the practice of what was later called Mental Hygiene.[7]

When practiced by well-trained staff at smaller institutions, both Moral Management and the Mental Hygiene movement matched high rates of recovery with shortened periods of hospitalization. These conditions were frequently met in the initial stages of their broad implementation, but problems grew as standards sank towards the last decades of the 19th century. Overcrowding, severe money and staffing shortages, inadequate staff training, and the lack of a real treatment methodology were just some of the many emerging troubles.[6] Paradoxically, progress in biological psychiatric research helped bring about the stagnation and decline of the mental hospital. The decisive biological breakthrough was anticipated to come any day; in the meantime, patients were to be kept safe and comfortable and little else. By the early 20th century, public hospitals were again providing only custodial care, and long-term hospitalization became the norm once again.[8]

Worsening conditions would finally bring the state of mental health care back under public scrutiny in 1908, spurred by the autobiographical publication of former mental patient Clifford Beers, *A Mind That Found Itself*. Picking up where Dix left off, Beers "stirred up a mental hygiene chain reaction, . . . of national and international concern"[3] (p. 131). Soon after, Beers joined William James in founding the National Committee for Mental Hygiene to publicize the necessity of the treatment and prevention of mental illness.

BEGINNINGS OF THE INTERMEDIARY SOCIAL-BIOLOGICAL TRADITION

The multidimensional socio-biological tradition in psychiatry dawned in the middle decades of the nineteenth century with the study of "Nerves"—a euphemism for mental illness. In the latter part of the century, European middle-class patients not suffering from acute psychotic conditions began to join the similarly afflicted elite in seeking treatment at spas likes Bath in England, Evian in France, and Baden-Baden in Germany. Hydrotherapy became one of the choice methods for the treatment of "Nerves." A new diagnostic category, coined by American psychiatry, Neurasthenia— "Tired Nerves"—became a prototype of functional neurotic diseases, with symptoms involving mood, cognition, and soft physiological symptoms, like palpitation and sweating.[2]

As the patient's nerves were tired, they needed rest, and so various "rest cures" were implemented. The most famous rest cure, initiated by Weir Mitchell in the 1880s, consisted of forced seclusion, bed rest, a mild diet, electrical treatments, and massage. What soon became apparent was that the essence of the Weir Mitchell cure consisted of listening to the doctor's voice. The finding that certain psychiatric illnesses could be impacted by the "healing power of the human voice" opened the way for psychotherapy, where the doctor could now treat the mind and brain by psychological means in the context of a one-on-one relationship with the patient.[2]

THE FIRST PHASE OF BIOLOGICAL PSYCHIATRY: MID-19TH CENTURY TO MID-20TH CENTURY

From the first half of the 19th century, attempts were being made to understand the relationship between mental conditions and brain anatomy and physiology through systematic research in universities and laboratories, the testing of experimental drugs, and the post-mortem examination of the human brain.

Progress toward determining the mind/brain connection was gradual. Clinical conditions served as a major catalyst because the 19th century saw a massive increase in the number of asylum patients afflicted with neurosyphilis and alcohol psychosis.

In its later clinical stages, the syphilitic infiltration of the central nervous system was often found to manifest itself in the form of psychiatric symptoms, with dementia, delusions, and paralysis most prevalent among them. By 1826 Antoine-Laurent Bayle had demonstrated that syphilitic patients' paralysis and delusions of grandeur resulted from a chronic inflammation of the meninges.[9]

In 1887, the Russian physician Sergei Korsakov described how excessive alcohol consumption could cause hallucinations, while alcohol withdrawal could produce tremors and the hallucination of small crawling animals, called delirium tremens. The complete syndrome was later called Korsakoff Syndrome.[9]

German and Austrian researchers raced to expand on these discoveries. In the mid-19th century, Hermann von Helmholtz, Paul Broca, Carl Wernicke, and others refined existing connections between dysfunction and localized lesions in various organic diseases indirectly associated with mental conditions. The first modern department of psychiatry was established in 1865 by Wilhelm Griesinger, who dedicated the Berlin institution to teaching and research. In the department's assessment of brain pathology, Griesinger emphasized its applicability to clinical findings. Other universities followed: in Paris, Jean-Martin Charcot, the father of modern neurology, identified multiple sclerosis; in Prague, Alois Pick identified Pick's Senile Dementia; Sergei Korsakoff's research spurred funding for Bechterev's institute in St. Petersburg; and Alois Alzheimer of Vienna and Heidelberg identified the microplaques that cause the disease now bearing his name. These efforts and many others allowed Vienna University's Paul Fleschig to lay down the basic map of cerebral localization in 1888.[5,9]

In spite of all this progress, the state of psychiatry was cause for general frustration in the last two decades of the 19th century, for there was still no effective biological treatment for any severe mental conditions or abnormalities.

The long-awaited breakthrough finally arrived in Vienna in 1917, when Julius von Wagner-Jauregg found that injecting patients with the fever-inducing malaria virus cured neurosyphilitic paresis and its accompanying psychotic symptoms. His fever cure triggered intensified effort to find biological treatments for psychotic conditions. Among schizophrenia treatments, barbiturate-induced sleep therapies became popular in the 1920s, as did insulin-induced comas in the 1930s. Shock treatments of many kinds were used after World War I to treat shell shock, among other disorders.

In Budapest, Ladislaw von Medina noted that epileptiform seizures naturally produced improvement in schizophrenics. He developed a shock treatment in which a camphor-like drug produced "therapeutic" convulsions. In 1938, Ugo Cerlutti began to use electric shock (ECT) in Genoa to alleviate severe depression. By 1959, ECT was widely used for major depressive illness and major depression episodes. It was more effective than any other physical therapy of the time, though it counted irreversible memory loss among its negative side effects.[2]

In the 1930s, the Portuguese neurologist Egas Monitz started to use psychosurgery, the surgical severing of the connections linking the frontal lobes with the rest of the brain, to improve severe obsessive and depressive symptoms as well as aggressive behaviors. In the United States a more limited version, trans-orbital lobotomy, was performed by neurologist Walter Freeman and neurosurgeon James Watts. The procedure tranquilized agitated patients presenting management problems, but it also lowered their judgment and social skills. With the advent of neuroleptics in the 1950s, the lobotomy gradually faded away[2] (p. 227).

THE FIRST CLASSIFICATION SYSTEMS
OF PSYCHIATRIC DISORDERS: 1880s–1940s
PSYCHIATRIC NOMENCLATURE

While the state of psychiatry in the late 19th century was the cause for general frustration among physicians and patients alike, the field's practitioners were simultaneously grappling with its underlying causes. Psychiatry was deficient in several factors essential to clinical science, including effective communication and an information structure facilitating assessments and treatments.

In 1888, German psychiatrist Karl L. Kahlbaum called for the meaningful classification of mental illnesses according to their course. He noted that counting only overt symptoms was useless because the same symptoms might accompany different diseases and vice versa. As an example, he cited the high co-occurrence of mania and depression/melancholia, suggesting that they might be two complementary manifestations of the same underlying illness.[10]

Emil Kraepelin answered Kahlbaum's call. He was encouraged by his teacher Wilhelm Wundt, founder of Leipzig's Psycho-Physiological Laboratory. Between the years 1883 and 1926, Kraepelin authored nine editions of his influential classification system of mental diseases, sorting them according to their cause, symptomatology, and course, as well as the anatomical findings of the time. Most notably, he established the clinical picture of dementia praecox (today's schizophrenia) and manic-depressive psychosis (today's bipolar disorder).[10]

With the term dementia praecox, Kraepelin primarily depicted a thought disorder. It translates literally from Latin as "early onset dementia," while Eugen Bleuler's later term, schizophrenia, translates as "deep split of personality."[3] Both remain core characteristics of the diagnosis. Kraepelin characterized the illness as manifesting three forms. Hebephrenia was a clinical picture of exaggerated adolescence; in catatonia, muscular rigidity contributed to bizarre movements and postures; and in paranoid schizophrenia, the clinical picture is dominated by persecutory hallucinations, mostly auditory in character, as well as persecutory delusions with bizarre content (e.g., a third party puts thoughts into the patient's head or eats her intestines, etc.). Over the normal course of life, the patient's personality deteriorates. There are periods of "remission" in which the most debilitating symptoms are relatively absent.[10] Etiologically, hereditary metabolic dysfunction was considered the primary factor.

According to Kraepelin, a manic episode of manic-depressive psychosis would center on metabolic hyper-production, evidenced by the expansion of self-importance and elevation of mood, during which thought and speech would increase in rapidity at the expense of quality and coherence. During a depressive episode, metabolic hypo-production dominated the clinical picture. In between were periods of full health, known as intermissions.

The seventh edition of Kraepelin's classification included milder disturbances (neuroses): hysteria, fright-anxiety, and neurasthenia. Kraepelin conceded that they may have a psychogenic origin. He also identified the category of excitable personality, which corresponds to today's borderline personality.[10] With inclusion in Kraepelin's psychiatric nomenclature, neuroses gained "official" status as part of "minor psychiatry," whose symptoms could often be treated in a doctor's office or a spa, while psychotic illnesses were part of "major psychiatry" and may have required hospitalizations, especially during acute states. This division between "major" and "minor" psychiatry is still used in European psychiatry. The nomenclature of Kraepelin's seventh, eighth, and ninth editions was widely used until the aftermath of World War II, with minimal alteration. Subsequent to advances in psychological testing and the assessment of children, mental retardation and various child psychiatric illnesses were gradually added through the first three decades of the 20th century.[3]

In 1921 the psychologist Ernst Kretchmer began to investigate the relationship between physical type and temperament, an undertaking with considerably more history and meaning in Europe than in the United States. Using precision biometrics and advanced mathematical formulas, this student of Kraepelin's arrived at three basic physical types—asthenic, pyknic, and athletic. He related these to temperaments and the prevailing tendencies to specific mental disorders; for example, the pyknic type was said to have an affinity for manic-depressive illness, the asthenic for schizophrenia. He also identified intermediary types of personality disorders and neurotic tendencies, according to the relative presence of each tendency.[3]

THE PSYCHOANALYTIC REVOLUTION, 1890s–1950: THE PSYCHOLOGICAL BASIS OF MENTAL DISORDERS

Like Kraepelin's classification system, psychoanalysis emerged in response to great frustration with the state of psychiatry in the last decades of the 19th century. Psychoanalysis would come to make a major contribution towards the understanding of the psychological basis of mental illness, mental abnormality, and human behavior. Sigmund Freud (1856–1939), a Viennese neurologist and the founder of psychoanalysis, initiated the far-reaching study of man as a dynamic striving organism. Sometimes referred to as the dynamic psychology movement,[3] this intellectual trend dominated "the mind field from 1900 to 1950."[1] While Kraepelin concentrated on psychoses, Freud focused on neuroses and personality disorders.

After studying with such luminaries in the fields of biological psychiatry and neurology as Theodore Meynert and Ernst Wilhem von Brücke, Freud became increasingly frustrated with the ineffectiveness of biologically based treatments and sought a new frontier. He found it in Paris, where he studied with the famed father of modern neurology, Jean-Martin Charcot.[11] Charcot, the chair of neuropathology at Paris's Salpêtrière, was one of the leading figures of the French school of neuropathology. Among the school's adherents were Ambroise-Auguste Liebeault and Hippolyte Bernheim, both of Nancy, as well as Pierre Janet of Paris, Charcot's former student. Charcot and his colleagues picked up where Franz A. Mesmer and Pierre Briquet had left off, studying the etiology of hysteria, a nervous disease with peculiar, diffuse physical symptoms, like paresis with no anatomical findings. Their attempts to treat hysteria with hypnosis demonstrated the existence of unconscious phenomena and Janet's postulate of "disassociation," notable in posttraumatic states as well as hysteria.

Absorbing the findings of Nancy and Paris, Freud returned to Vienna convinced that powerful mental processes which participated in the development of mental disorders could remain hidden from consciousness.

Upon his return to Vienna, Freud started to systematically build the complex psychoanalytic theory of personality and development, the clinical theory of psychopathology, and the psychoanalytic technique of assessment and treatment.

In the late 1880s, Freud teamed up with another Viennese physician, Josef Breuer. Just as the American functionalistic psychologist William James was concluding that "the mind is first of all a stream,"[1] Freud and Breuer were employing a modified form of Charcot's clinical method. They asked their hypnotized patients to speak freely about their problems. Patients usually displayed strong affects while in the hypnotic state and, upon awakening, felt emotional release or "catharsis" accompanied by symptom relief. They remained unaware, however, of the potential relationship between their problems reported under hypnosis and their hysterical symptoms. Freud soon dispensed with hypnosis altogether and formalized the method of "free association" (saying anything that comes to mind without regard to logic or propriety), which often led the patients to remember long-forgotten traumatic origins of their problems. During this pre-analytic Cathartic Trauma Stage of his work (1893–1895), Freud theorized that conflict arose between the affects associated with traumatic events and the moral prohibitions of society.[12]

As Freud proceeded with his self-analysis,[13] using his friend Wilhelm Fliess as a sounding board, he increasingly came to view conflict as primarily internal. In his conceptualization of unconscious internal conflict, he replaced affect with sexual and aggressive instincts and postulated internal prohibitive forces. Conflict came to be conceptualized as an instinctual drive versus a defense (repression). This first stage of psychoanalytic theory was based on the mental topography of conscious, pre-conscious, and unconscious strata, hence its name: the Topographic Theory (1900–1920). During this stage of the theory's development, anxiety was viewed as resulting from repression. The psychosexual stages of early development—oral, anal, and phallic-oedipal—were here identified,[14] as were the two mental processes: the primary, driven by wish fulfillment, and the secondary, oriented in reality.[13]

The next stage of the theory's development was presented in 1923. This "Structural Theory" was a systematic exposition of a proposed tripartite personality structure, consisting of the Id, Ego, and Superego.[15] The signal theory of anxiety, triggering the psychic conflict between the structures of the mind, came in 1926. Here, anxiety was a trigger for, not a result of, repression.[16] Psychoneurotic symptoms and abnormal behaviors were viewed as compromise formations, born out of conflict between instincts (id) and defenses (unconscious elements of ego), with internalized moral imperatives (superego) and external pressures participating.

As the concept of conflict became more stratified, the analyst's technical armamentarium became more complex. As the analyst interpreted the patient's conflict, the patient came to understand how his past influenced his present. In the process of transference, the patient unconsciously displaced his or her childhood wishes onto the analyst and behaved as though the analyst were a parental figure from the past. Unless interpreted, it would constitute a resistance to free association and treatment. The analyst's position was defined as neutral and abstinent—the analyst did not have a preference for what the patient should be talking about and how the patient would be talking about it and abstained from directing the session's course or advising the patient to action. The analyst was to be a relatively blank screen onto which the patient could displace and project his wishes, fears, and other emotions. This requirement was originally implemented in response to the rather authoritative manner of Victorian-era physicians, which promoted dependency and passivity on the part of the patients. Freud's patients came to his office five times a week for analytic sessions, each lasting 50 minutes. The overall course of analysis rarely exceeded two years.

By 1926, it was clear to Freud that unconscious conflict had two dimensions, one being the defended content (i.e., sex and aggression), the other the defense processes (i.e., repression). While Freud concentrated more on defended content, his daughter Anna Freud elevated defense processes to equal status in the genesis of conflict.[17] Heinz Hartmann, Ernst Kris, David Rapaport, and Erik H. Erikson further elaborated the wider adaptive functions of the ego. Their work became known as Ego Psychology.[12]

Early psychoanalytic outcome studies were conducted in the 1930s by Otto Fenichel in Germany, Ernest Jones in England, and Franz Alexander in the United States, with the impressive results averaging 83 percent improvement.[18]

The philosophy behind this improvement was that insight into unconscious early-life conflicts led to the lasting alleviation of symptoms and troublesome personality traits.

Freud's views were formally introduced to American scientists in 1909, when he was invited to deliver a series of lectures at Clark University by its president, the psychologist G. Stanley Hall. Freud traveled with Sandor Ferenczi and Carl Jung, both of whom later developed alternative modes of dynamic thinking. Besides taking a walk with William James, Freud met with a circle of enthusiastic physicians who included Morton Prince, Ernest Jones, James Putnam and others, who organized the psychoanalytic movement and its institutes and journals in the United States and Great Britain.[19]

Freud's views attracted a devoted following and passionate dissent in his lifetime, and both continued after his death in London in 1939. Early on, Jung, Alfred Adler, Harry Stack Sullivan, Karen Horney, and others launched "spin-off" dynamic theories with their own respective followers. Some, like Melanie Klein, working with children, developed certain aspects of the theory further, bordering on dissent while remaining within the larger mainstream frame. Tensions within the mainstream led some to branch out into separate psychoanalytic or psychodynamic schools later in the 20th century. These following generations of theorists and clinicians would give rise to British and American object relations and self-psychology, which took their place beside ego psychology and the modern Freudian/classical core.[19] Plurality joined integrationist tendencies in shaping further development as psychoanalysis came of age in the second half of the 20th century, when it would face comparison with other psychotherapies and the psychopharmacological revolution of the 1950s.

Dynamic thought and psychoanalysis contributed directly or indirectly to the further development of other psychotherapeutic methodologies, group and family therapies and counseling. One example is the development of the expressive group technique of psychodrama by Jacob Moreno in Vienna during the first years of the psychoanalytic movement.[20] From experimentation with a drama support group for street people and prostitutes, Moreno developed the psychodrama technique of "playing out internal conflicts on the stage," first called "An Invitation to Encounter." As used for psychotherapeutic purposes, the psychodrama technique has a complex structure, with a director, director's assistants (usually staff), and patients. The protagonist (identified patient) re-enacts his/her problems on the stage, externalizing and projecting internal conflicting tendencies, personified by others on the stage. Moreno's philosophy that a curative power lies in spontaneity expressively engaged in an accepting interpersonal atmosphere underlies the psychotherapeutic use of this group technique. While psychodrama focuses on the individual and his problems,

Moreno's group techniques of sociometry and sociodrama focus on the group as a whole. Moreno immigrated to the United States in 1925 and staged his psychodrama performance at Carnegie Hall in New York. He is commonly credited with the advent of group psychotherapy and expressive active therapeutic methodology. He is also considered a forefather of the humanistic movement in group and individual psychotherapy, as well as much development in sociology.[19]

Psychoanalysis proliferated in culture at large in various ways. It provided further transfiguration of the traditional image of man: like Darwin before him, Freud "dethroned the human race from its fictitious position of rational supremacy and undermined narcissistic illusions by his disclosure of unconscious (and irrational) motivation in human conduct"[20] (p. 25). The modernist movement in 20th-century art, literature, literary criticism, sociology, and philosophy had to take into account the irrational, the unconscious, and the primitive as parts of the complex picture of human motivation ever since.

THE ASCENT OF CLINICAL PSYCHOLOGY

The beginnings of clinical psychology were encompassed by Lightner Witmer's 1896 vision, to "establish the tradition of clinical psychology as a field that exemplifies the application of experimental psychology to the study of psychopathology."[3] Rooted in the rigorous experimental methodologies of Gustav Theodore Fechner and Wilhelm Wundt, prompted by blossoming social interest in progress, development, and education, clinical psychology found its first contribution to the study of abnormal conditions in developmental psychometrics.

Following, in the 1860s, Gustav Theodore Fechner's experimental work in psycho-physics, the psycho-physiological laboratory of Wilhelm Wundt laid the foundation for the experimental method in psychology. Founded in 1879, Wundt's laboratory correlated objective physiological measures with the systematic introspection of mental events (perception, sensation), the awareness of which was the subject matter of psychology. Two of Wundt's students, James McKeen Cattell and Lightner Witmer, incorporated his experimental method and its underlying theory in their psychometric, experimental, and clinical activities in the U.S.

Cattell introduced the term "mental test" in his 1890 text, *Mental Tests and Measurements*, his focus on individual differences serving as an essential precursor of psychometrics.[21]

In 1896 Lightner Witmer presented "The Clinical Method of Psychology and the Diagnostic Method of Teaching," formally establishing the field of clinical psychology. The lecture developed a seminal clinical method out of the case of the "bad speller," a child with learning problems. Witmer's Laboratory of Psychology at the University of Pennsylvania, the first institution of its kind, encompassed a teaching hospital where children were systematically observed for a period of time. Only after such a period of observation could a child's cognitive problems be understood and modified. Witmer's clinical work emphasized intellectual subnormality, sensory and educational difficulties, speech problems, and college and vocational counseling. Other cognitively focused psychological clinics followed, and by 1914 the United States counted over 20.[3]

In contrast, the Child Guidance Movement, a part of the National Committee for Mental Hygiene's preventative effort, was dynamically oriented and focused on a variety of non-cognitive behavioral and emotional aspects of personality. In 1909 the Juvenile Psychopathic Institute, later known as the Institute for Juvenile Research, was founded in Chicago to work with delinquent children. William Healy, its first director, was a psychiatrist and a student of William James. The professional staff initially consisted of Dr. Healy and Dr. Grace Fernald, a psychologist. In 1917 Healy moved to Boston to organize and direct what came to be known as the Judge Baker Guidance Center. Although early clinics were greatly concerned with delinquency, they gradually enlarged their scope of activity to include a wide variety of behavioral problems in children.[3]

While the first psychological clinics and child guidance centers used time-consuming observation to identify children's problems, a more efficient method was being developed by the French psychologist Alfred Binet. With the government mandate to identify children with special learning needs on a national scale, Binet collaborated with Theodore Simon to develop the first intelligence test between 1905 and 1908.[21] In 1910, Henry Goddard translated and re-standardized the test for the U.S. population. Goddard's activities on behalf of the cognitively impaired went beyond academia and the laboratory. In 1911, he helped write the first U.S. law requiring that blind, deaf, and mentally retarded children be provided special education within the public school system. Three years later, Goddard testified in court that subnormal intelligence should limit the criminal responsibility of the accused, becoming the first American psychologist to do so.[3] The greatest impact on both testing and clinical work, however, can be attributed to Lewis Terman's revision and re-standardization of Binet's test at Stanford University. After its 1916 introduction, the Stanford-Binet version became so popular for testing children that it was adopted to develop the Army Alpha and Army Beta tests, which assessed the leadership potential of recruits as the United States prepared to enter World War I. This widened use of testing furthered its utility, and by the 1920s and 1930s the use of testing to determine cognitive subnormality was widespread.[3,21]

Concomitantly with these efforts, a distinct strand of psychological experimentation focused on complex cognitive processes. Following Hermann Ebbinghaus's introspective investigation of memory, Edward Thorndike was the first to investigate the complex process of learning. In his 1898 *Law of Effect*, Thorndike departed from the mainstream introspective experimental method and recorded objectively observable animal learning behaviors.[3] Following Thorndike, John B. Watson issued the positivistic "Behaviorist's Manifesto" in 1913, which defined the object of psychology as observable, "objectively measurable" behavior, rather than subjective introspection.[22] Watson extended Ivan P. Pavlov's concept of classical conditioning into the realm of neurotic human fears. Whereas Pavlov had conditioned a dog to salivate in response to a formerly neutral stimulus, Watson conditioned a fear response to rats in a boy named "Little Albert," a reference to Freud's report on the dynamic treatment of Little Hans's phobia of horses. Clark Hull and B. F. Skinner originated another conditioning paradigm, operant conditioning, in which a rat or a person looks for reinforcement via the active learning of a new response to an originally neutral stimulus. Out of both conditioning paradigms, various versions of behavioral and cognitive therapies developed later in the 20th century, such as Hans J. Eysenck's re-training of new responses to habit-forming stimuli, Aaron Y. Beck's cognitive therapy of depression, Josef Wolpe's systematic desensitization for the treatment of phobias, and others.[19]

In the meantime, psychometrics was enriched by the construction of projective personality tests, such as Rorschach's 1924 Inkblot test, in which a person assigns meaning to various inkblots, and Henry Murray's Thematic Apperception Test of 1935, in which a person takes a picture as inspiration to make up a story, based on a dynamic notion of the projection of unconscious motivation onto the ambiguous test material. Clinical psychologists administered these together with the Stanford-Binet in psychological clinics, child guidance centers, state hospitals, and the court system.[3]

During World War II the noted psychoanalyst and psychologist David Rapaport introduced the Comprehensive Psychological Test Battery into the diagnostic evaluation of patients. Rapaport's contribution was the development of a theoretical framework for the interpretation of test patterns as a means of more fully understanding personality dynamics and psychopathology of the patient.[3] In 1939 David Wechsler had produced the first adult intelligence scale and called attention to its diagnostic possibilities. In addition, personality inventories were now included in the test battery, among them the Minnesota Multiphasic Personality Inventory, which was standardized for the hospital population. The use of a psychological test battery was a complex clinical diagnostic activity.

As they constructed increasingly complex batteries of psychological tests, clinical psychologists were becoming more and more aware that the normality-abnormality spectrum presented a multidimensional picture (a diagnostic profile), and a better, more refined, and accurate system of classification was needed[2] to reflect this reality. This concern was only addressed in 1952, when the new *Diagnostic and Statistical Manual of Mental Disorders* was introduced.[23]

During wartime, clinical psychologists started working as therapists. In 1942 Carl Rogers published "Counseling and Psychotherapy," with a focus on "Client Centered non-directive interview," making clinical use of Abraham Maslow's Hierarchy of Needs, a humanistic personality theory. The Humanistic Movement envisioned itself as the "third revolution in therapy,"[19] referring to psychoanalysis and behaviorism. It highlighted the personal aspirations and growth potential of the individual, corresponding to the existential philosophy of the day. In the group therapy modality, the mixture of the humanistic and dynamic orientation dated back to Moreno's psychodrama, and it now continued with verbal interaction groups. Group, family, and couple therapies and counseling were on the rise, and clinical psychologists stood at the movement's front lines.[24]

In the postwar era, traumatized veterans needed psychiatric hospitalization and extensive outpatient care. First established in England by Maxwell Jones to meet this need, therapeutic communities later spread throughout the European continent. These communities frequently utilized clinical psychologists in positions of leadership, especially those clinicians eschewing biological treatment. The dominant theoretical orientations were the dynamic, the humanistic, and the eclectic combination of both.[12,19]

World War II and its aftermath also brought progress in the identification and classification of organic brain syndromes, which are abnormalities in behavior, emotion, and cognitive functioning associated to specific sites of brain trauma. Beginning in the 1940s, the dynamically informed Russian psychologist Alexander Luria worked with war veterans and analyzed the specific connections between their traumatic brain lesions and the corresponding mental functions, such as written and spoken language, thought, and action.[3] He also developed a remediation program for specific traumatic syndromes. Luria's work was acclaimed internationally, and the new subspecialty of neuropsychology was born.

THE EARLY YEARS OF THE FIELD OF ABNORMAL PSYCHOLOGY

The field of abnormal psychology evinced a multidimensional view from its inception in 1906, as evidenced by early issues of the *Journal of Abnormal Psychology*.

The journal began as the official publication of the emerging American Psychoanalytic Association, yet it asserted its independence through its editorial practices. Contradictory theoretical models sometimes sat side-by-side in its pages as the journal practiced the dynamic belief that overt contradictions may depict different facets of the normality-abnormality spectrum or another different developing knowledge base. The wide range of topics covered in the early years of the journal reflected an awareness of the importance of genetic, biological, psychological, behavioral, societal, and cultural factors. Such an approach translated into articles on classification of both clinical psychopathology and the psychopathology of "everyday life." Volumes covered mental retardation, character, delusions, dream analysis, human motivation, hystero-epilepsy, nightmares, laughter, perception and illusions, posttraumatic stress, psychoneuroses in indigenous population, studies of symbolism in indigenous population, psychobiology, educational psychology and learning paradigms, sexual tendencies in monkeys, and social psychology.[25]

Thus, abnormal psychology addressed biological, psychodynamic, behavioral, comparative, and cultural-anthropological paradigms even in its earliest models of mental life, its norms, and its abnormalities. As all were conceptualized dynamically interacting in their contributions to the developing knowledge base, these early models pioneered an unruly experiment in the emerging multidimensionality of the mental processes.

REFERENCES

1. Barzun, J. (2000). *From dawn to decadence: 500 years of western cultural life.* New York, NY: Harper Collins.
2. Shorter, E. (1997). *A history of psychiatry: From the era of the asylum to the age of prozac.* New York, NY: John Wiley and Sons.
3. Wolman, B. (1965). *Handbook of clinical psychology.* New York, NY: McGraw Hill.
4. Hansel, J., & Darmour, L. (2005). *Abnormal psychology.* New York, NY: Von Hoffman Press.
5. Bennett, P. (2003). *Abnormal and clinical psychology.* New York, NY: Open Universities Press.
6. Carson, R. C., Butcher, J. V., & Mineka, S. (2000). *Abnormal psychology and everyday life*, 11th edition. Boston, MA: Allyn and Bacon.
7. Zilboorg, G., & Henry, G. W. (1941). *History of medical psychology.* New York, NY: Norton.
8. Comer, R. J. (2011). *Fundamentals of abnormal psychology*, 6th edition. New York, NY: Worth Publishers.
9. Andreasen, N. (2001). *Brave new brain: Conquering mental illness in the era of the genome.* New York, NY: Oxford University Press.

10. Burgmair, W., Engstrom, E. J., & Weber M. (2000–2008). *Making Kraepelin history*, vols. 1–8. Munich, Germany: Belleville.

11. Freud, S. (1956). Report on my studies in Paris and Berlin (1886) carried out with the assistance of a traveling bursary granted from the University Jubilee Fund (October 1885–End of March, 1886). *International Journal of Psycho-Analysis, 37,* 2–7.

12. Papiasvili, E. D. (1995). Conflict in psychoanalysis and in life. *International Forum of Psychoanalysis, 4,* 215–220.

13. Freud, S. (1900/1953). *Interpretation of dreams*, standard edition, vols. IV and V. London: Hogarth Press.

14. Freud, S. (1909/1955). *Two case histories ('Little Hans' and the 'Rat Man')*, standard edition, vol. X. London: Hogarth Press.

15. Freud, S. (1923/1961). *The ego and the id*, standard edition, vol. XIX. London: Hogarth Press.

16. Freud, S. (1926/1959). *Inhibitions, symptoms and anxiety*, standard edition, vol. XX. London: Hogarth Press.

17. Freud, A. (1936/1971). *Ego and the mechanisms of defense.* New York, NY: International Universities Press.

18. Bergin, A. E., & Garfield, S. L. (Eds.) (1971/1994). *Handbook of psychotherapy and behavior change*, 1st and 4th editions. New York, NY: John Wiley and Sons.

19. Kratochvil, S. (1987). *Zaklady psychoterapie.* Prague: Avicenum.

20. Schick, A. (1978). The pluralism of psychiatry in Vienna. *Psychoanalytic Review, 65,* 14–37.

21. Anastasi , A. (1976). *Psychological testing.* New York, NY: Macmillan.

22. Watson, J. B. (1919). *Psychology from the standpoint of a behaviorist.* Philadephia, PA: Lippincott.

23. American Psychiatric Association (1974). *Diagnostic and statistical manual of mental disorders* (DSM I). Washington, DC: American Psychiatric Press.

24. Wolberg, L. R., & Aronson, M. L. (1981). *Group and family therapy.* New York, NY: Brunner/Mazel.

25. Prince, M., Putnam, J., and Jones, E. (Eds.) (1916). *Journal of Abnormal Psychology*, vol. X: 436 pp. Boston, MA: The Gorham Press.

Chapter 7

Continuing Explorations of the Multiple Dimensions of the Human Mind: 1950–2000

Eva D. Papiasvili and Linda A. Mayers

As the battlefields of World War II fell silent, mental illness was still to be conquered.

This chapter will track a succession of achievements, frustrations, and failures which only led to further discovery. The pharmacological revolution of the 1950s transformed the landscape of mental health, but it also bred unforeseen consequences and side effects, both literally and figuratively. The initial success of psychotropic medication prompted a growing need for new generations of biological treatments, as well as new classifications of mental illnesses and abnormalities. This in turn prompted a growing plurality within each of the three main branches of psychological therapy: the dynamic, the humanistic and the behavioral. With this increasing stratification came a rise in multimodal therapeutic approaches, combining traditionally separate therapies to match the needs of the individual patient. This plurality in the clinic was reflected in the essential interdisciplinary character of modern neuroscience as it emerged in the last two decades of the 20th century. Simultaneously, the adaptational view of the relationship between mental illness and creativity enriched the picture further. Throughout, increasingly sophisticated statistical and methodological tools were developed to evaluate the effectiveness (or ineffectiveness) of the battle against mental illness, now waged on many fronts in both the laboratory and the clinic.

By the end of the 20th century, the field of abnormal psychology came to conceptualize biological and psychological traditions, perspectives, and viewpoints as dynamically interrelated dimensions of the human mind.

THE PSYCHOPHARMACOLOGICAL REVOLUTION: 1950–2000

Initially popular, the biological treatments of psychoses of the pre–World War II era did not effect any substantial change in the most severely ill patients and came to, therefore, be seen as failures. For those less severely ill, psychoanalysis and variously modified psychodynamic treatments dominated the scene.

The long-awaited breakthrough that would change the frustrating status quo came from an unlikely place: in 1951, Henri Laborit, a French surgeon, discovered a new antipsychotic drug, chlorpromazine, originally used in his practice as a "potentiator" for anesthetics.[1] In 1952, French psychiatrists Jean Delay and Pierre Deniker began to administer chlorpromazine, the first neuroleptic/antipsychotic medication, to their schizophrenic patients, with excellent results.[1]

Chlorpromazine and other first-generation antipsychotic medications diminished the acute, positive symptoms of psychosis (exaggeration of normal function), like bizarre hallucinations, delusions, and disorganized thought and behavior. As the use of the first-generation antipsychotics continued, however, it became apparent that the negative symptoms of psychosis (loss of normal function), such as flatness of affect, abulia (lack of will), and social withdrawal, were not alleviated and sometimes even increased. Patients looked like zombies, staring motionlessly into space for hours on end. Further, patients began to develop troublesome extra pyramidal side effects, including facial tics and an involuntary movement of the limbs, called tardive dyskinesia. It took decades of brain-chemistry research to develop the second generation of "atypical" antipsychotic medications, such as Clozapine and Reserpine, which manage negative symptoms and side effects while minimizing positive symptoms. Outpatient treatment remained problematic, however, for patients taking the new medications required frequent monitoring for adverse changes in blood levels. Discovered at the close of the 20th century, third-generation antipsychotic medications like Xyprexa do not require frequent blood tests and are therefore more suitable for self-administration on an outpatient basis.[2]

The search for effective mood disorder medication proceeded on a parallel path. In 1949 John Cade, an Australian psychiatrist, discovered Lithium, a medication for manic depression (bipolar disorder). Cade found that Lithium provided relief from manic symptoms as long as the medication was taken regularly. It was not until 1970 that Lithium was approved by the Food and Drug Administration (FDA) in the United States.

The early 1950s saw the development of imipramine (Tofranil), the first tricyclic medication to act specifically against depression, followed shortly by rival tricyclic drugs such as Elavil. In addition to their primary function, the most recent class of anti-depressive medications, SSRIs (Prozac or Zoloft) among them, have been found to alleviate anxiety.[2]

By the 1960s the most widely prescribed medications around the world were the benzodiazepines used to treat anxiety and mild depression, the most popular among them being the tranquilizer Valium. Because of their fast action, benzodiazepines were found to be addictive, and attempts at discontinuation were often followed by withdrawal and the sometimes long-term intensification of the original symptoms. New anti-anxiety medications without these addictive properties were subsequently developed, such as BuSpar. If depression was present, Paxil or Prozac was often prescribed instead.[2]

In general, all psychotropic medications developed during the latter part of the 20th century operated on the level of brain chemistry, specifically the process of neurotransmission. Various hypotheses and models of mental illnesses, such as the Dopamine Model of Schizophrenia and the Serotonin Model of Depression, were advanced, according to which abnormal neurotransmission agents and mechanisms were believed to be involved.

DEINSTITUTIONALIZATION AND ANTI-PSYCHIATRY: "SOCIAL SIDE EFFECTS"

Coupled with complex social and cultural conditions in Western Europe and the United States, two trends developed as unwitting consequences of the antipsychotic medication revolution. One was deinstitutionalization—the other, the anti-psychiatry movement.

In the United States, the National Institute for Mental Health was created in 1946. Its objective was to administer the community mental health centers that had been established to treat deinstitutionalized patients. After the FDA licensed chlorpromazine in 1954, it was possible to calm agitated patients and mitigate psychosis with drugs. In theory, patients could live in the general community again, as long as they were given consistent follow-up treatment.

In practice, however, few administrative arrangements were made to service the acutely ill patients who had been prematurely discharged from mental hospitals. On their own, such patients were often unable to continue using their medications as prescribed. Without effective follow-up, deinstitutionalization failed the seriously disturbed. Subsequent studies found that a third of the homeless on the streets were, in fact, mentally ill, unable to organize their lives to find shelter and work. Others drifted into the criminal justice system.[1]

Meanwhile, a series of influential publications in the 1960s and 1970s heralded the rise of a vocal anti-psychiatry movement. The basic argument of the movement was that mental illness was not an illness but a social, political, and legal phenomenon, a socially constructed myth which should be considered "scientifically worthless and socially harmful"[3,4] (p. xii). In his book *Asylums*, published in 1961, Erving Goffman (1961) argued that every psychiatric facility was a closed system and that, on admission, the patient "begins a series of abasements, degradations, humiliations, and profanations of self"[5] (p. 67). Ken Kesey's 1962 novel *One Flew over the Cuckoo's Nest*, later adapted for the screen, effectively argued that psychiatric patients were not ill but merely deviant, and therefore should not face discrimination or be locked up and medicated. In his 1960 book *The Divided Self*, the British anti-psychiatry writer Ronald D. Laing charged that mental illness represented a sane response to a mad society.[1]

In 1973 the psychologist David Rosenhan published a study questioning the validity of psychiatric diagnoses.[6] In his experiment, eight non-psychotic volunteers, specially instructed to simulate schizophrenia or bipolar disorder, were admitted to a psychiatric hospital and kept there for between 7 and 52 days. Later, the staff of a different hospital was led to believe that pseudopatients might be sent to the hospital, but none were sent. Nevertheless, at least one staff member considered a sizable portion of the admitted patients to be actors. Rosenhan's conclusion was that individuals who suffered from psychiatric disorders were indistinguishable from those who did not. Robert Spitzer, a prominent psychiatrist who later chaired the American Psychiatric Association's DSM-III team, criticized the validity of the study but conceded that the classification of psychiatric disorders needed improvement in validity and reliability.[6]

By the 1980s, the deinstitutionalization experiment and the antipsychiatry movement had run their course, and both general hospitals and private facilities resumed admitting an increasing number of psychiatric patients.

Although it was pronounced a failure, the positive outcomes of deinstitutionalization included a diversification of mental health services with the addition of many new modalities less restrictive than full hospitalization, such as social-rehabilitation clinics, halfway houses, and day hospitals, together with an increase in private and community outpatient facilities. Patients were engaged in a variety of adjunctive treatments, such as art therapy, occupational therapy, and various mental health and self-care educational activities.

In the same vein, the anti-psychiatry movement contributed indirectly to the construction of the DSM-III.

NEW CLASSIFICATIONS: 1950s–2000

In 1952, the first *Diagnostic and Statistical Manual* (DSM-I) was published in the United States, a variant of the Mental Disorders section of the International Classification of Disorders (ICD). It contained several categories of psychoses and psychoneuroses, as well as disorders of character, behavior and intellect.[7] Throughout, the term "reaction" was used in place of "disorder" or "illness," due to the influence of Adolf Meyers' bio-psychological theory that mental disorders were reactions to psychological, social, and biological factors. The DSM-II eliminated the word "reaction" but kept most of the DSM-I's categories.[8]

In 1970 American psychiatry, much like the psychiatry Kraepelin had faced in the 1880s, was in a state of crisis. At the height of the anti-psychiatry movement, a decade of research grant cutbacks at the National Institute of Mental Health (NIMH) made conditions even less favorable to the credibility of diagnostic classifications. Under the leadership of Robert L. Spitzer, a group of prominent psychiatrists created a new classification of mental disorders for the DSM-III.[9] The DSM-III's diagnostic criteria for schizophrenia, paranoia, affective disorders (in the psychotic and neurotic range), and anxiety disorders proved to have much higher inter-rater reliability and validity. The multi-axial diagnostic system, introduced in the DSM-III,[9] reflecting a shift toward multi-dimensional thinking in both the field and society at large,[10] was added. The multi-axial diagnostic system has been incorporated in all of the following U.S. diagnostic systems. In the century's final edition, the DSM-IV, the axes are as follows:[11]

Axis I: Clinical Disorder or Other Conditions that may be a focus of Clinical Attention (Disorders diagnosed in Infancy and Childhood; Cognitive Disorders; Schizophrenia and Other Psychotic Disorders; Mood Disorders, i.e., Depressive, Bipolar Disorders; Anxiety Disorders)
Axis II: Personality Disorder or Mental Retardation
Axis III: General Medical Condition
Axis IV: Psychosocial and Environmental Problems and Stressors
Axis V: Global Assessment of Functioning Scale (GAF), with a scale of 1–100

The ICD's "Mental Disorders" section is not multi-axial, as it primarily serves epidemiological purposes, statistically evaluating frequencies of mental disorders and abnormalities across the world.[11]

THE POLITICAL ABUSE OF PSYCHIATRY

Psychiatry possesses a built-in capacity for abuse due to its close relationship with cultural definitions of behavioral norms and abnormalities. The diagnosis of mental disease can serve as a proxy for the designation of social dissent, allowing the state to hold persons against their will and to prescribe treatments to effect conformity. In an authoritarian or dictatorial political system, psychiatry can be used to bypass standard legal procedures. The period from the 1960s to 1986, for example, saw the systematic, documented political abuse of psychiatry in the Soviet Union.[12] Although some Soviet psychiatrists of the Stalin era saved dissidents from torture in the Gulags of Siberia, under Khrushchev and Brezhnev psychiatry was used to diagnose and incarcerate dissenters.

Diagnosed with asymptomatic "sluggish schizophrenia," which only specially instructed psychiatrists could recognize, dissidents were held indefinitely in a "Special Psychiatric Hospital," undergoing "treatment," using heavy doses of antipsychotic medication. After release, individuals diagnosed with sluggish schizophrenia were stripped of their credibility, civic rights, and employability.[12] The 1977 World Psychiatric Congress in Honolulu voted to dismiss the Soviet Psychiatric Association from the world body on the basis of confirmed systematic abuse, while also establishing firm ethical guidelines for member societies. Similar guidelines were soon implemented in clinical psychology and other mental health fields.[12]

The relationship between the antipsychiatry movement and the systematic abuse of psychiatry is worth mentioning. On one hand, they stand opposite to each other: the basic tenet of the antipsychiatry movement is that mental illness is not an illness but a social, political, and legal phenomenon,[3] while the essential characteristic of the systematic abuse of psychiatry is that social, political, or legal phenomena are diagnosed as illnesses. On the other hand, they converge when the systemic abuse of psychiatry is the policy of a monolithic state: in the Soviet Union, dissent was pronounced a psychotic illness and diagnosed as "sluggish schizophrenia." Under such extreme circumstances, dissent (so diagnosed) may, in fact, be the sane response to an insane society, which is in agreement with Laing's antipsychiatry motto.[1]

PSYCHOTHERAPIES: 1950–2000

The most precise classification and diagnostic assessment will never fully capture the individual's personal battle with her mental anguish, which can be addressed only in the context of psychotherapy. Only there is the unique subjective experience of suffering from mental affliction given voice.

Once more effective anti-psychotic medication was introduced, psychotherapy was applied primarily to non-psychotic conditions. People suffering from various anxieties, depressions, phobias, and posttraumatic states received psychotherapy in doctors' private offices and outpatient clinics. So did those with personality disorders, who suffered from interpersonal problems, self-defeating habits, as well as highly distressing attitudes and behaviors that diminished their quality of life. During this time, multi-modal treatments, in which medication was used conjointly with psychotherapy, became more common. So, too, did eclectic combinations of various types of psychotherapies.[13]

Within the dynamic therapies, psychoanalysis proper (four sessions per week for several years, aiming at lasting reconstructive changes of personality) endured on a progressively smaller scale. Increasingly more common was psychodynamic or psychoanalytic psychotherapy, which refers to a range of treatments based on psychoanalytic concepts and methods that involved less frequent sessions and a sometimes shorter duration of treatment. The essence of psychodynamic therapy was the exploration of the unknown aspects of the self, especially as they were manifested in and influenced by the therapeutic relationship.[14]

In the latter half of the 20th century, the classical Freudian orientation, sometimes called Ego Psychology, was joined by Otto Kernberg's Object Relations school, focusing on the "split" in borderline personalities, and Hans Kohut's Self-Psychology school, which focused on "Self-Object" undifferentiated states in narcissistic personality disorders. In the meantime, the classical Freudian orientation was extended by Charles Brenner, Jacob Arlow, Leo Rangel, Harold Blum, and others. Among other dynamically oriented schools were Harry Stack Sullivan's Interpersonal school, which focused on the conflict between primary physiological needs and the need for safety, as primarily applicable to psychotic individuals.[15]

Rooted in the learning theories of Edward Thorndike and Clark Hull, various cognitive and behavioral therapies were developed to apply Ivan P. Pavlov's and John Watson's Classical Conditioning models and Skinner's Operant Conditioning clinically. Examples of such clinical applications include the habit-altering behavioral training of Hans J. Eysenck, Josef Wolpe's systematic desensitization of phobias, aversion therapies for alcoholism practiced in Russia, and Albert Bandura's modeling-based social learning system.[15] Cognitive therapies and Cognitive Behavioral therapies include Aaron T. Beck's Cognitive Model for the Treatment of Depression; Albert Ellis's Rational Emotive Therapy, characterized by the close tracking of unproductive thoughts and emotions; and Donald Meichenbaum's Cognitive-Behavioral Therapy (CBT), with its emphasis on the re-learning of dysfunctional personal constructs.[15]

Under the wide umbrella of the Humanistic and Existential Movement, Carl Rogers's Client-Centered therapy was gaining ground in the 1960s alongside the Gestalt school of Fritz Perls. Based on Abraham Maslow's principles of personal growth and self-realization, the movement also included Leon Binswanger's and Rollo May's Existential schools, with their focus on fulfilling one's unique being-in-the-world in regard to questions of death, freedom and responsibility, being alone, and life's meaning.[16]

In addition, discrete techniques like hypnotic therapies, emotional abreaction with cathartic effect, and various relaxation techniques were also used for specific problems, for example, acute posttraumatic states, life-threatening lifestyles, etc.

Group and family therapies mushroomed after the 1950s. There were three psychoanalytic schools of group therapy. Samuel R. Slavson's orientation aimed at the analysis of the individual within the group. On the other end of the spectrum was Wilfred Bion's approach: analyzing the group as a whole. In between was Sigmund H. Foulkes's orientation, according to which the individual's participation in the group dynamic was analyzed. This orientation was practiced and developed further by Henrietta Glatzer, Helen Durkin, and others in the United States.[17]

Therapeutic communities, originally developed within the dynamic tradition by Maxwell Jones for World War II veterans in Great Britain, were further developed within an eclectic dynamic-humanistic framework by Stanislav Kratochvil, Alexander Lapinski, and others in Central and Eastern Europe. Meanwhile, Ferdinand Knobloch founded therapeutic communities along the lines of the integrated-dynamic orientation in Central and Eastern Europe and Canada.[15]

Family therapy has a long tradition in the United States, with psychoanalysts like Nathan W. Ackerman leading the way, initiating the dynamic systems approach for treating the family as a whole.[18] In the second half of the 20th century, Murray Bowen's Bethesda team worked with schizophrenic parents and their children to develop an alternative family-system-dynamic approach, aimed at strengthening the child's internal separation-individuation before the detrimental identification with the afflicted parent would take place.[15]

CLINICAL STUDIES OF THE EFFECTIVENESS OF PSYCHOTHERAPY

In a classic 1952 study, Eysenck found an alarming lack of positive effect in the published outcome studies of psychoanalytic and eclectic therapies, as compared with spontaneous recovery (44 percent average improvement after therapy versus 72 percent spontaneous recovery). This stirred up the need to study the effectiveness of psychotherapy. In the 1960s, Allen Bergin[19] subjected Eysenck's research to rigorous methodological review and came up with very different numbers, in favor of psychotherapy (83 percent improved after psychotherapy versus 52 percent spontaneous recovery).[19] Together with the insurance industry's pressure for evidence-based treatments, this debate led to a fruitful array of studies and meta-studies on the effectiveness of all the main modalities of psychotherapeutic treatments that reported quantifiable results. In 1970, Julian Meltzoff and Melvin Kornreich calculated overall improvement in 100 published outcome studies of dynamic, humanistic, eclectic, and behavioral-cognitive therapies and found an 80–84 percent average improvement.[20] While specific outcomes varied according to the particular issue studied and differing criteria for improvement, the consensus at the end of the 20th century was that behavioral and cognitive behavioral therapies were, in the short term, effective mainly against discrete symptoms (phobias, discrete depressive symptoms, thoughts) and behaviors (addictive habits), while dynamic therapy was effective with personality disorders, longer-term patterns of maladaptive interpersonal attitudes and behaviors, and more complex symptomatologies of anxiety and various depressions.[19,21] Eclectic dynamic therapies tended to be effective with both over a longer term.[13] With the advent of neuro-imaging methodology at the turn of the 21st century, new studies traced the effect of various psychotherapies on brain chemistry. Interestingly, the therapies so tested were found to be increasingly more, not less, effective.[2,14] As both psychotherapies and psychotropic medications seem to affect our plastic brain, the two methods seem to enhance each other's effects, as some end-of-the-century studies were finding.[22,23]

In 1997 Mary Lee Smith and collaborators[21] constructed a new measure of psychotherapy's effect. Referred to as "Effect Size," it was especially applicable to the meta-analyses of multiple outcome studies. Effect size was calculated by measuring the difference between the average improvement of the patients who received psychotherapy and the average spontaneous improvement of those who did not, divided by the standard deviation (standard deviation—SD—being a statistical measure of how the individual results are distributed/how they "deviate" relative to the average result within each group) of both groups. After subjecting 475 outcome studies to their meta-analysis, they came up with an effect size of 0.85 units of SD, which they interpreted as follows: the average patient after psychotherapy was better off than 80 percent of those who did not receive psychotherapy.[21] The relevant context is provided by the FDA's approval standards, which hold an effect size of 35–40 percent to be suitably significant for most medications.

Using the same statistical procedure, Jonathan Shedler[14] compared studies of medication therapy with those of behavioral therapies and psychodynamic-psychoanalytic therapies for individuals with depressions, anxiety, panic, stress-related states, and personality disorders. The effect size for dynamic therapies was 0.8, which was comparable to, or slightly better than, the medication and behavioral therapies. Furthermore, patients treated with dynamic therapy showed continuing improvement after the therapy ended, while other patients did not.[14] Interestingly, this post-therapy improvement corresponds with the findings of a differently structured, late-1970's study by one of the authors of this chapter. Those patients who were rated high on "insight" at the end of time-limited dynamic psychotherapy, were found one year later to have continued to improve in their targeted symptoms, behavior, and attitudes. No such progressive improvement was found in patients who were rated low on insight at the end of psychotherapy.[13] Similar post-therapy improvement was consistently found in additional studies at the beginning of the 21st century.[14] The authors of these studies theorized that insight-oriented dynamic therapy might have set internal processes of ongoing recovery in motion.[14]

MODERN NEUROSCIENCE

In the later decades of the 20th century, the study of the brain, its anatomy, physiology, and chemistry, in relation to mental processes (cognition, emotions) and behavior, accumulated a vast body of knowledge, and the distinct interdisciplinary field of neuroscience emerged. The objective of its many branches became the explanation of mental processes and behaviors both normal and abnormal, in terms of the activities of the brain. Cognitive neuroscience studies the brain in relation to cognition; behavioral neuroscience (biological psychology) studies the brain in relation to behavior; affective neuroscience studies the neural mechanisms of emotions; and developmental neuroscience studies the brain in relation to development. In addition, the field of dynamic neuroscience, developing at the turn of the 21st century into the synthetic field of neuropsychoanalysis, studied unconscious motivational processes in relation to brain anatomy, physiology, and neural circuitry. There are intermediary areas and overlaps. A truly interdisciplinary field, modern neuroscience was formulated with the participation of clinical and research scientists with backgrounds in biology, genetics, chemistry, medicine, neurology, psychiatry, experimental and cognitive psychology, neuropsychology, and clinical psychology. Neuroscientific research proceeded from mapping "... the anatomical, chemical, and functional circuitry of the normal brain [towards] ... seeking out the sites of abnormality in the vast array of human mental illness"[2] (p. 320).

One of modern neuroscience's major findings is the concept of neuroplasticity, the brain's enormous ability to change and adapt, which is directly relevant to the etiology, therapy, and potential prevention of mental illness and clinically significant abnormalities.

During World War II, Alexander Luria, impressed by war veterans' adaptability to trauma, began his neuropsychological investigations of those brain lesions exerting influence on the higher cortical functions of speech and thought and proceeded with suggestions for remedial rehabilitative work. In 1949 Donald O. Hebb identified "cell assemblies," the reverberating functional circuits in the brain. His summary statement, "Neurons that fire together, wire together," has been widely cited as a definition of cellular neuroplasticity.[2] Further investigation refined the concept, finding out how nerve cells "talk to each other" through the study of neurotransmitters. This became a fruitful area for psychopharmacological therapy, aiming to balance problematic neurotransmission in psychoses and mood disorders. Different neuroscientific models of schizophrenia (the Dopamine hypothesis) and mood disorders (the Norepinephrine and Serotonin Hypotheses) were advanced. By the end of the 20th century, neuroscientists were studying neuroplasticity on the level of the gene, on the level of the cell, and in terms of the functional connections of established and newly formed circuits.

Molecular neuroscience and the Human Genome Project found polygenic patterns indicating polygenic causes for most mental conditions and behaviors, including mental illnesses and abnormalities. In identical-twins studies and studies of molecular biology and chemistry, genes were found to be even more plastic than previously thought.[2] The degree to which a genetic endowment (genotype) will be manifested (phenotype) is one such plastic characteristic, as is the gene's internal chemistry, which depends on environmental input and life experiences. Consistent with psychoanalytic-dynamic-developmental theories is the developmental neuroscientific finding of critical periods early in life, during which certain developmental influences have substantial impact on genetic expression and brain development. For example, secure emotional attachment during the first two years of life engenders greater resilience towards stress throughout life. The opposite is also true: problematic attachment early in life tends to predispose a person to mental illness, as do early infections and injuries. Intellectual development will also be facilitated or impeded, depending on early life experiences. Another critical period is adolescence, when the extent of neuronal growth and pruning seems to be paralleled only by the first two years of life. Thus, life experiences may either protect individuals from the expression of "ill genes" or predispose them towards their expression. The relative balance varies among different mental illnesses.[2]

The weight of the genetic component (heredity) in the development of mental illness was studied by following identical twins. Because identical twins have the same genotype, a concordance close to 100 percent would indicate a strong genetic determination. In reality, even in illnesses with high genetic loading such as schizophrenia and mood disorders, identical twins share the illness in less than 50 percent of cases. Neuroscientists have therefore concluded that non-hereditary factors play at least as great a role. Other predisposing factors are now being looked at for their etiological significance, among them infection, injury, and early psychosocial stress. Prospectively, with the mapping of the human genome for specific mental illnesses under way, early therapeutic intervention using a pharmacological and/or psychotherapeutic "head-start" could possibly manage, redirect, or prevent the manifestation of "ill genes."[2]

Dynamic affective neuroscience focuses on the brain's seats of dynamic unconscious and affective circuitry and their interplay with brain plasticity. It is historically rooted in James Papez's 1930's introduction of the limbic system's "Papez circuit," and the central role of the limbic system in affective responses to stress.

Multimodal research on depression from the last decades of the 20th century used neuro-imaging techniques to follow the action of the living brain in real time. As tracked by PET (Positron Emission Tomography) and fMRI (Functional Magnetic Resonance Imaging), the conscious subjective experience of depression reflected the interplay between the brain regions that register and interpret our current emotional experiences in light of past emotional experiences. The limbic system was confirmed in its role as a key region for unconscious emotional perception, unconscious memories, and the processing of emotions. The conscious subjective feeling of depressive affect was specifically registered in the orbitofrontal cortex, which came to be recognized as part of the extended limbic system by the end of the century. Neuroscientists dissected how these various distributed regions link together past memories and present experiences, underlying the unconscious attribution of the past feelings to the present situations. Joseph Le Doux explored how some limbic system structures (the amygdala and hippocampus) work together to produce built-in, unconscious memories that may come back to either help or harm us, without our being aware that this is happening.[24]

One of the leading neuroscientists of the turn of the 21st century, Nancy Andreasen noted that both behavioral therapies and psychoanalysis, each in its own way, may "re-build the memory traces in a plastic brain"[2] (p. 314). To the extent that these therapeutic techniques are effective, they tend to lead to changes in brain chemistry, circuitry, and structure; the "plastic brain" learns new ways to respond to emotionally charged events and adapt. This is then translated into changes in how the person feels, thinks, and behaves, which in turn solidify the changes in the brain. In this way, psychotherapy is as "biological" as the use of medication.

Another therapeutic relevance of the "reverberating" feature of neuroplasticity of the dynamic brain lies in the possibility that an adjustment to one site will have reverberating effects in other places and produce a therapeutic change[2] (p. 321). Just as the onset of illness can be triggered by a stressor, leading to a cascade of pathognomic changes that lead to mental symptomatology, so too, in reverse, we may trigger the cascade of adaptive changes that roll the illness back. This may be the case with both pharmacological and psychotherapeutic intervention alike.

At the end of the 20th century, neuroscience cast doubt on the dichotomies of brain versus mind, physical versus mental, biological versus psychological, anatomy versus physiology, and genes versus environment. As the appreciation for neuroplasticity on all levels grew, all such divisions began to appear to reflect different dimensions of the same adaptive interactive dynamic process.

ABNORMAL PSYCHOLOGY AS A FIELD IN THE LATTER PART OF THE 20TH CENTURY: SCOPE AND METHODOLOGY

As the methodological and statistical activities involved in experimental psychology, psychological test construction, and psychometrics became more sophisticated, abnormal psychology became more experimentally oriented. In its construction of models of mental illness and clinical abnormalities, it incorporated and further developed theoretical and methodological knowledge bases from biology, anthropology, ecology and sociology, and behavioral sciences, while staying in close contact with psychiatry, clinical psychology, and developing neuroscience. It postulated several concepts of abnormality: statistical abnormality, indicating behaviors and characteristics affecting a low percentage of the population, often used in epidemiological reports on prevalence or incidence (e.g., the prevalence of schizophrenia is 1.5 percent worldwide); psychometric abnormality, absorbed from the psychometric assessment of certain personality traits, abilities or aptitudes (e.g., an I.Q. of 135 is an example of the nonpathological abnormality of superior intellect, as the population's average is 100); and deviant behavior, deviating from the cultural-social norm and which may or may not indicate mental illness (i.e., the Olympic athlete whose socks never match). Traditional objective and subjective norms and abnormalities are now usually conceptualized in terms of clinical entities, used by clinicians who are assessing them according to specific criteria and procedures, for example, the psychiatric interview, psychological tests of personality attitudes, traits, and symptomatology, questionnaires, etc.

In its experimental or observational research and theory construction, abnormal psychology as a branch of psychology uses the standard statistical procedures and methodology of behavioral research:[19] formulating a research question—*hypothesis*; outlining the *research design for finding causality or correlation*; selecting *representative samples*; assigning subjects to varying conditions of *the independent variables* and following/measuring *dependent variables*; and using *statistical procedures* to maximize the *reliability and validity of the findings* and their *interpretation*. With increasingly sophisticated methodologies, many new factors could now be taken into consideration. Dynamic multifactorial experimental designs using multivariant analyses began to be used in the last decades of the 20th century to evaluate complex socio-ecological, developmental, and clinical conditions and processes, in relation to the multiple etiologies and therapeutic effects of various interventions.[19]

Drawing on its own research as well as on the knowledge bases of many related fields, abnormal psychology constructs etiological models of specific mental conditions and clinical abnormalities. One model was called the Diathesis-Stress Model, which describes the dynamic interaction between predisposing (diathetic) and precipitating (stress) etiological factors of a biological, genetic, psychological, and socio-environmental nature. Diathesis is defined here as a predisposition, based on hereditary, biological, or environmental factors. A specific example is the Neural Diathesis-Stress Model of Schizophrenia. Integrating psychosocial and biological findings on stress, with findings on the prenatal factors and brain abnormalities in schizophrenia, the model offers additional hypotheses about the neural mechanisms involved in the effects of stressors on diathesis, and it provides a framework for explaining some key features of schizophrenia's etiology.[25] Both the biological and behavioral data indicate that stress worsens symptoms and the diathesis is associated with a heightened response to stressors. The model proposes that the hypothalamic-pituitary axis (HPA—the site of the general response to stress) acts as a potentiating system effecting hyper-production of dopamine (DA), thus furthering DA receptor abnormality, which together with hippocampal damage, found in schizophrenia, renders the individual hypersensitive to stress.

A still more complex model from the end of the 20th century is the General Synthetic Model of mental illnesses, integrating the Diathesis-Stress Model with the latest findings in neuroscience and developmental and clinical research. In this model, mental illnesses arise from multiple interacting causes, ranging from genes and gene expression through the many non-genetic factors of cell metabolism, chemical circuits, and anatomical and functional circuits of the brain, all in interaction with the environmental factors and mental processes (cognitive, affective, conscious, and unconscious), in reciprocal interaction with both internal and external environment.[2]

One of the essential messages from such infinitely complex algorithms may be that there is no place for any "either-or" strict linear determinism, where the etiology of mental illness and abnormalities is concerned.

CREATIVITY AND MENTAL ILLNESS

Both mental illness and creativity are complex phenomena. The potential connection between them has been of interest to psychiatrists, psychologists, artists, and scholars for many years. An earlier example is Hans Prinzhorn's 1922 book *Bildnerei des Geisteskranken (Art of the Mentally Ill)*, based on a collection of artwork he had built at the psychiatric hospital in Heidelberg, which inspired such avant-garde artists of the period as Max Ernst, Paul Klee, and later Andre Breton and the Surrealists.[26] Recent studies [2,27] inquiring into a genetic link between creativity and mental illness seem to suggest a hereditary connection. Specifically, a link appears to exist between mood disorders and creative expression in the arts and humanities, while another is apparent between schizophrenia and creativity in math and science. Studying the mood disorder link, the researchers[2,27] found that as creative people are more intellectually adventuresome, curious, and generally more inventive, they are also more vulnerable to rebuffs and mood swings. Studying the link with schizophrenia, Nancy Andreasen and her colleagues at the University of Iowa observed a large number of adopted children of schizophrenic mothers, many of whom spontaneously pursued scientific interests either professionally or as hobbies. Researchers believe that these findings, in addition to the large number of prominent scientists and mathematicians who have been struck by schizophrenia or some related psychotic episode themselves (Isaac Newton, Nobel Laureate John F. Nash) or had schizophrenia in their family (Albert Einstein), present the possibility of a genetic link. Moreover, as schizophrenics do not usually marry or have children, and yet schizophrenia has persisted through the centuries at an equal rate throughout the world (1.5 percent), it is possible that "...'schizophrenic genes' may ... confer some evolutionary benefit. Having them may transmit some abilities that are useful to human beings [in a similar way] as Sickle-cell anemia persists in Africa because it protects against the development of malaria"[2] (p. 200).

Research into the adaptational and/or creative side of various mental illnesses is in its exploratory stage. We owe the law of gravity and the theory of relativity to the original minds of two people who seem to have carried "the schizophrenic tendency"—Newton and Einstein. The tendency to originality of both polarities—high creativity and mental illness—may be different sides of an unusual adaptational process. We still need to learn much more to be able to have any conclusive answers.

THE STATUS OF ABNORMAL PSYCHOLOGY
AFTER TWO CENTURIES OF DISCOVERY

The old mind/body and nature/nurture paradigms have now converged in the conceptualization of a multidimensional mind-brain dynamic and a psychobiological perpetually interactive system. The latest 20th-century findings from behavioral genetics, cognitive and affective neuroscience, neuropsychoanalysis, and the clinical sciences validate the connectivity and mutual influence of brain chemistry and psychological-emotional experiences. Based on late-20th-century neuroimaging studies in the context of research into the brain's neuroplasticity, it has been found that individually tailored psychotherapies, together with a new generation of narrowly targeted psychotropic medications, can alter dysfunctional brain chemistry and circuitry and work to prevent manifestations of abnormal gene architecture.

Throughout the 19th and 20th centuries, the sometimes cooperative, sometimes competing traditions of biological and psychological discovery comprise the multidimensional picture of the human mind. This multidimensionality is reflected in growing trends toward synthetic models of mental illness, and the pluralization and integration of therapeutic approaches to benefit the unique individual. It is both in the individual and in multidisciplinary scientific approaches that historical dichotomies present multiple sides of the dynamic interactive process at the dawn of the 21st century.

Over the course of the preceding 200 years, there were those who stubbornly insisted on divergence and specializations. They and their heirs accumulated a vast base of knowledge which ultimately formed the raw material of present-day integration and synthesis. Without them, the multidimensional mind would remain shrouded in darkness.

REFERENCES

1. Shorter, E. (1997). *A history of psychiatry: From the era of the asylum to the age of Prozac*. New York, NY: John Wiley and Sons.
2. Andreasen, N. (2001). *Brave new brain: Conquering mental illness in the era of the genome*. New York, NY: Oxford University Press.
3. Szasz, T. (1974). *The myth of mental illness*. New York, NY: Harper and Row.
4. Foucault, M. (1965). *Madness and civilization: A history of insanity in the age of reason*. New York, NY: Random House.
5. Goffman, E. (1961). *Asylums: Essays on the social situation of mental patients and other inmates*. New York, NY: Doubleday.
6. Rosenhan, D. (1973). On being sane in insane places. *Science, 179*, 250–258.
7. American Psychiatric Association (1952). *Diagnostic and statistical manual of mental disorders* (DSM-I). Washington, DC: Author.
8. American Psychiatric Association (1964). *Diagnostic and statistical manual of mental disorders* (DSM-II). Washington, DC: Author.
9. American Psychiatric Association (1974). *Diagnostic and statistical manual of mental disorders* (DSM-III). Washington, DC: Author.
10. Decker, H. S. (2010). *Tribute to Robert L. Spitzer*. Presentation on December 17, 2010, Psychiatric Institute of Columbia University, New York, NY.
11. American Psychiatric Association (1994). *Diagnostic and statistical manual of mental disorders* (DSM-IV). Washington, DC: Author.
12. Bloch, S., & Reddaway, P. (1977). *Russia's political hospitals*. London, UK: Victor Gollancz Ltd.
13. Papiasvili, E., & Papiasvili, A. (1983). Residential therapeutic community for neurotics. *International Journal of Group Psychotherapy, 33*(3): 387–395.

14. Shedler, J. (2010). The efficacy of psychodynamic psychotherapy. *American Psychologist, 65*(2), 98–109.

15. Kratochvil, S. (1987). *Zaklady Psychoterapie*. Prague: Avicenum.

16. Yalom, I. (1980). *Existential psychotherapy*. New York, NY: Basic Books.

17. Wolberg, L., & Aronson, M. (1980). *Group and family therapy*. New York, NY: Brunner/Mazel.

18. Ackerman, N. W. (1966). *Treating the troubled family*. New York, NY: Basic Books.

19. Bergin, A. E., & Garfield, S. L. (Eds.) (1971/1994). *Handbook of psychotherapy and behavior change* (1st and 4th editions). New York, NY: John Wiley and Sons.

20. Meltzoff, J., & Kornreich, M. (1970). *Researching psychotherapy*. New York, NY: Atherton Press.

21. Smith, M. L., Glass, G. V., & Miller, T. J. (1980). *Benefits of psychotherapy*. Baltimore, MD: Johns Hopkins University Press.

22. Eiser, N., West, C., Evans, S., Jeffers, A., & Quirk, F. (1997). Effects of psychotherapy in moderately severe COPD: A pilot study. *European Respiratory Journal, 10*, 1581–1584.

23. Keller, M. B., McCullough, J. P., Klein, D. N., Arnow, B., Dunner, D. L., Gelenberg, A. L., et al. (2000). A comparison of nefazodone, the cognitive behavioral analysis system of psychotherapy, and their combination for the treatment of chronic depression. *New England Journal of Medicine, 342*, 1462–1470.

24. Le Doux, J. (1999). Psychoanalytic theory: Clues from the brain. *Neuropsychoanalysis, 1*, 44–49.

25. Walker, E. F., & Diforio, D. (1997). Schizophrenia: A neural diathesis-stress model. *Psychological Review, 104* (4), 667–685.

26. Esman, A. H. (2004). Ernst Kris and the art of the mentally ill. *International Journal of Psycho-Analysis, 85*, 923–933.

27. Andreasen, N. C. (1987). Creativity and mental illness: Prevalence rate in writers and their first degree relatives. *American Journal of Psychiatry, 144*, 1288–1292.

Chapter 8

Reflections on Psychiatry in the Mid-20th Century

Enoch Callaway

Once upon a time, there were people who concerned themselves with issues of human dignity. They saw mentally ill patients exhibited like circus freaks. They saw them jailed along with common criminals. They recognized that the mentally ill needed care and treatment instead of incarceration. They used the term asylum for the new treatment facilities, which meant protection from arrest.

Almost a century later politicians, notably Ronald Reagan, supported by the arguments of Szasz,[1] decided that mental illness was a myth, and they put pressure on administrators of asylums to discharge patients into the community. There they were no longer protected from arrest. Although community treatment facilities were available, many psychotics couldn't take advantage of these clinics and "fell through the cracks." Many were returned to the prisons (with the enthusiastic approval of the Correctional Officers Association).

In retrospect, the cost-cutting Republicans and the cash-backed lobbying by correctional officers cannot be given all of the blame for the transition. There were misguided do-gooders who felt the asylums were inhumane. Then, too, perhaps mental health professionals oversold the advent of the pharmacological revolution. In any case, the states would soon find themselves confronted with overfilled prisons that put more of a burden on their budgets than asylums did.

The asylums were, of course, not perfect, but they had many advantages, both therapeutic and economic. For example, most of them were associated with farms which supplied the inmates with food and what was known as industrial therapy. The downside (and there always seems to be one in the treatment of the mentally ill) was lack of vitamin C in the winter with resultant scurvy. During the reign of Reagan, and under pressure from local businesses, the farms were shut down, and now most of the old state hospitals stand on many acres of rich fallow land.[2,3]

What follows is a chapter from a book I wrote,[4] recalling my days as a resident in a state hospital from 1950 to 1952. I included it here because it happens to be the best example I know of concerning the usefulness of farms and so-called industrial therapy for the management of schizophrenics.

PROMOTION TO JESUS

Knowing so little and having virtually no effective pharmacological tools, it's amazing that we still managed to help people. Small unpredictable rewards are remarkably effective in maintaining behavior and perhaps, as with Skinner's rats, those random reinforcements played a role in our devotion to our work. At any rate, in those days, the simple virtues of respectful concern and calm competence could be seen unclouded by the powerful chemicals psychiatrists have come to rely on these days. The case of a patient whom I will call Sam Turner (not his real name, of course) is illustrative.

I met Sam on a crisp fall evening. I had night duty on the male wings, and so after supper I was catching up on some charts when Miss Gurrey at the switchboard rang my office. I understood how Miss Gurrey knew everything the staff talked about on the phone. She eavesdropped on all our calls. But I never figured out how she knew where everyone was all the time. Was she psychic or hyperaware? She had blond bangs with tiny curls, and since the musical *Oklahoma!* was popular at the time, she was naturally known among the residents as "Gurrey with the fringe on top." When I picked up the phone, she said, "Noch, the state troopers are bringing in one at this very moment. Mary'll pick you up on her way to admissions."

Mrs. Mary O'Connell is another story in herself. As the night nurse supervisor on the male side, she was some sort of a hybrid between an earth mother and a Sherman tank. So with Mary at my side, I, weighing 160 pounds dripping wet and being quite devoted to my own safety, was quite concerned about taking a floridly psychotic patient off the hands of the state troopers.

Mary came by my office and I followed her out to the side door where the male admissions came in. Taking the big outdoor key, she opened the metal-clad door and welcomed the two husky state policemen and their prisoner into the asylum. The troopers flanked a black man of about 6'3", who was in handcuffs and leg irons. He was rail-thin with a stubble beard and was dressed in threadbare overalls that were most inadequate for the weather at the time. He emitted an odor that, even over the background emanations from a body long unwashed, was nevertheless easily identified as one of chronic schizophrenia's classic signs.

That smell has a sickly sweet quality and is not at all like the smell of stale healthy sweat, as, for example, one finds in sports locker rooms. The crushed leaves of the fetid iris give the closest match that I know. I cannot find the reference now, but I remember that around 1952 some research workers sterilized the skin of schizophrenics and normals, then collected sterile sweat by exercising them in plastic suits. The collected sweat showed that the schizophrenic sweat contained a smelly compound that normal sweat did not.

One of the troopers said Sam was out on the turnpike directing traffic. "Says he's God's chief of police on earth," he commented.

However, Mary spoke up. "You can take his handcuffs off. You can take them with you and call it a night." The younger officer looked dubious, but the older one had dealt with Mary before and reassured him. "They'll be all right." Turning to Mary, he said, "The papers are at the switchboard." Then the officers unshackled their ward, wished us good night, and departed. In that moment, the prisoner became patient. I probably took the miraculous transformation for granted since I was relatively new to the strange world of the state hospital and was so busy learning that nothing struck me as odd.

Mary turned to our new patient and said, "What's your name?"

"Sam Turner, ma'am," he answered politely.

"When was the last time you ate, Sam?"

"I'm not sure."

"Well, Sam, let's go back to get you a bath. Then after the doctor examines you, we'll get you some food."

"Thank you, ma'am!"

The three of us marched back through the two front wards to the rearmost one, where the most psychotic patients were housed. Then Mary left to go about her duties. The ward attendant led Sam to the shower while I opened the examining room and began putting together a chart. Soon Sam was delivered to me, dressed in a hospital bathrobe and smelling only of strong antiseptic soap. I examined him and couldn't find anything wrong physically other than malnutrition, scratches, and insect bites. I couldn't get him to tell me anything about his family, so I listened to his rambling account of how God spoke to him and how he advised God on improving the situation here on earth.

I was finishing my admission note when Sam's food arrived, so I turned him over to the attendant. Then I went back to my office, finished my charts, retired to bed in the resident's night room, and slept soundly, as usual. Later I learned that I had mild narcolepsy.

Sam settled into the routine of the Acute Back Ward. I chatted with him briefly every day in hopes of getting some usable history and finally came to the conclusion that he had neither family nor other social support system. Then one day, Sam told me with great enthusiasm that God had promoted him from police chief to Jesus. He elaborated on this in his usual disorganized way.

Sam was both vague and repetitive but said God was pleased with his work as police chief and pretty disappointed with everyone else in the world.

One of the occupational ladies told me that Sam had requested some yarn and a wooden hooking needle. The next time I saw him, Sam had embroidered the word "Jesus" on the back of his bathrobe.

Meanwhile he seemed to be putting on weight, becoming more physically active, and more actively psychotic. For example, at times he appeared to conversing out loud with his hallucinations.

One day we admitted a court case. An accused murderer had pled insanity and the court had committed him to the hospital for evaluation. Of course, we had to put him on the Back Ward with its maximum security. According to the attendant it was around midnight when Sam's pacing and muttering to himself were finally more than the accused murderer could stand.

"Jesus Christ," he exclaimed, "Shut up so I can get some sleep."

With sonorous and pompous tones reminiscent of a Baptist minister, Sam replied, "Since you address me by my proper name, I will!" And he did.

The next morning, the accused man asked if he could please be returned to jail, explaining, "There's really crazy people in here, and they scare me."

After about a month I presented Sam to Dr. Rothschild at rounds. Rothschild commented that the Acute Back Ward was probably just too stimulating for Sam and recommended that I transfer him to a quieter chronic ward. He also suggested that I see about getting Sam into industrial therapy on the state hospital farm. Sam was certainly looking more and more agitated, and, as usual, I took the chief's advice.

After Sam went to work on the farm, I no longer had regular contact and was so busy I didn't think much about him until about a month later, when the staff did their regular review of his case. Sam looked like a different person. He was now 20 pounds heavier, shaved, and wearing pressed overalls with a clean blue shirt. I reviewed his history. Then Mr. Interbitzen, the industrial therapist in charge of the dairy, gave his report.

He was a large, taciturn Norseman, who spoke with a faint lilting accent on the rare occasions when he made one of his laconic pronouncements. He reported, "Sam's doing well. Gets on good with the cows." Sam was sitting there listening and looking very pleased with himself until Mr. Interbitzen concluded, "We'll miss Sam if you discharge him." Sam's face fell and his eyes got as large as saucers.

Then he looked at Dr. Rothschild and said, "You can't discharge me. I'm crazy. I think I'm Jesus Christ!"

Rothschild replied, "Sam, we will not discharge you until you have some place to go that's better than this hospital. Now, you go along with Mr. Interbitzen, and don't you worry."

The study done after antipsychotics were in common use showed that low expressed emotionality around schizophrenics increased the duration of their remissions and reduced the probability of their readmission. In other words, patients do poorly in families that get upset about delusions and hallucinations and do better in families that seem more resigned to the symptoms of the schizophrenic.

At Worcester, everyone recognized that Mr. Interbitzen and his cows were natural therapists for schizophrenics. Looking back on the therapeutic farm, I suspect that Interbitzen and his cows were the ultimate in low expressed emotional responsiveness to psychotic behavior. I do not know what you could say to a cow that would upset her. Sad to say, such facilities no longer exist since almost all state hospital farming operations were shut down years ago. This was in part due to the misguided do-gooders that feared that the farms were exploiting mental patients as involuntary peons. I often wondered if the right-wing defenders of agribusiness profits also played a supporting role in shutting down the state hospital farms so that their constituents could make more money supplying the hospitals with the food they once produced for themselves.

Years later, I had the opportunity to ask the head of psychiatry at the woman's prison in Chowchilla, California, whether they had ever considered giving prisoners pet animals as cheaper and safer tranquilizers than the drugs they used. She told me that they had indeed used "Pet Therapy," and very successfully, until a prisoner had been bitten and sued the state.

WHAT CAN BE DONE WITHOUT MODERN DRUGS?

There were a variety of physical procedures in use before the "pharmacological revolution." One that continues to be particularly valuable even today is electric shock treatment (aka electroconvulsive therapy or ECT). It has been demonized in certain novels,[5] and because of that its use is often unreasonably delayed. Its beneficial effects have been demonstrated repeatedly. Particularly with depression in the elderly, where drug side effects are more common, it can be life-saving. If done by adequately trained personnel, the only adverse event is a potential lasting amnesia.

In the early 1940s, ECT was a rather crude procedure. The patient's temples were rubbed with a salt paste to improve conduction, a padded tongue depressor was put between the patient's teeth to prevent damage to teeth and tongue, then the electrodes were applied with wooden calipers (to insulate the operator), and a timer was set to turn the house current (60 cycles, 110 volts). Too little time and the patient would not have a full convulsion (missed shock), and there was no therapeutic effect, although there could be prolonged confusion and memory loss. With adequate time of the shocking power, there would be first a scream with a tonic convulsion, when the patient's back would arch rigidly. Too vigorous restraint could result in spinal fracture. This was followed by the clonic phase with its rhythmic jerking. After that, the patient would remain unconscious for a time, during which the patient would be laid on a padded floor (to avoid falling out of bed). To be effective, treatments were done three times a week for six or so treatments.

As time went on, the rather frightening procedure described above became more benign-appearing. More effective electrical wave shapes were used, and short-acting anesthetics were followed by curare-like muscle-paralyzing drugs so there was no apparent seizure. In some instances, an EEG was used to monitor the brain activity to make sure a seizure had taken place in the brain, since with muscles paralyzed, there was no outward seizure to be seen. Currently, studies are being done with trans-cranial electrical stimulation, which hopefully will have the therapeutic effects of ECT without the amnesic side effects.

Insulin coma has fallen out of fashion, largely because it is time-consuming and expensive in comparison to the antipsychotic drugs, although it was quite useful, particularly in the management of catatonic schizophrenics before antipsychotic drugs became available. Early in the morning, five times a week, the patient would skip breakfast and report to the insulin unit. There they would be put to bed and given enough insulin to produce a coma. This was allowed to continue for about four hours and was terminated by passing a nasogastric tube, checking with litmus paper to make sure the tube was in the stomach, and then administering a bolus of heavy sugar solution through the tube. Occasionally a patient would start to convulse, and then the heavy syrup had to be given intravenously. Sometimes later in the night a patient would lapse into coma again and would have to be resuscitated with intravenous sugar.

Since the usual course of treatment was four weeks, and since the insulin unit had to be staffed by expert nurses, the antipsychotic drugs were much more economical, and perhaps more effective. There were various other techniques used to calm overactive patients. A first-person account of cold packs can be found in Hanna Green's book.[6]

There was also a condition called catatonic excitement although I haven't seen a case in many years. But in those days schizophrenic patients could become so overactive that their body temperatures would reach a dangerous point. Over-activity and hypothermia occurred sometimes also in manic patients. In both manics and schizophrenics, ice packs could be literally life-saving and also really therapeutic, in that the patients would calm down to the point where you could converse with them.

The procedure involved putting the patients on a table and wrapping them in iced blankets. The therapist inserted a hand from time to time to make sure that the patient had not become overheated in struggling against the blankets. If this began to happen, fresh iced blankets would be applied.

This also has been superseded by drugs in the United States. However, in Germany, the science of treating people with iced blankets and baths persists, and many universities have endowed chairs of bainealogy. These are endowed professorships in the science of giving baths. Sulfur baths are relaxing, and seltzer baths (carbonated water) are stimulating. Some universities, embarrassed by that ancient term, now call themselves departments of Arbietsphysiology, or work medicine. The exhausted executive comes in and is given baths and hikes until he is rested and ready to resume work.

Lobotomy was a treatment of last resort in the hospital where I worked as a resident. Not only did it pose difficult ethical and clinical problems, but there were also economic issues, as it required bringing in a neurosurgeon from Boston who sectioned frontal tracts after a craniotomy (opening the skull). At about that same time, Dr. Walter Freeman developed what he called transorbital lobotomy. A knife called a lucatome was inserted above the eyeball and wiggled back and forth to section connections to the frontal cortex. Once I heard Freeman speak to a hostile audience. He reached down and picked up a box that was filled with Christmas cards from grateful patients, and he challenged his detractors to match him.

Lobotomy was particularly effective in obsessive-compulsive patients whose condition had reached psychotic proportions. One patient that I followed went on to become a very successful Boston politician. Another found that her family had closed ranks during her illness and she wasn't welcome at home anymore. She remained in the hospital as a non-patient working as a maid for senior staff. One of the side effects of lobotomy was a diminished self-control. She was working in the home of one of the senior staff members whose wife was preparing a lasagna feast for the house officers. The poor patient found when she tasted the lasagna, she couldn't stop eating it.

Of course, there were drugs used to affect the mind before the more specific antipsychotics became available. Barbiturates could be used effectively in acute post-traumatic reactions, where the drugs could be used to produce an abreaction in what was called narcosynthesis. The barbiturates were also sometimes referred to as truth serum, but in my one experience, they seemed to only produce more embellished lies.

Opium is an effective treatment for depression, and its use for that illness goes back into ancient history. Amphetamine was developed by Gordon Alles in the 1920s and was extensively used in World War II as an alertness enhancer.[7]

There were two other once-popular, centrally acting drugs that have almost disappeared. One was the bromides (dull stories were once called bromides for their soporific action), but they were found to have such adverse effects (e.g., thyroid cancer, hallucinations) that they were outlawed. The other was paraldehyde. This drug was excreted in the breath, thus avoiding interaction with the damaged livers of alcoholics, and is still in use in centers that deal with near-terminal alcoholics. Its respiratory excretion had one problem. The terrible odor of paraldehyde could pervade the whole ward and leave a lasting impression on staff.

In those days of limited therapeutic armamentaria, one fact stood out. Supportive compassion and calm acceptance of madness were powerful therapeutic tools. These were carried out both on a one-to-one basis and in what was somewhat optimistically called group psychotherapy.[8]

THE PROMISES OF PSYCHOTHERAPY

The histories of psychology and psychiatry are full of promises that have been only partially fulfilled. As we shall see, that seems to be a recurrent phenomenon in psychopharmacology, too. Good doctors have always talked to their patients with compassion. The fictional Dr. Stone[9] asks a group of students, "What very effective treatment is administered through the ears?" to which the hero answers, "Compassion."

In the 1940s, psychoanalysts were the royalty of psychiatry. It was like a closed guild, for only approved graduates could call themselves psychoanalysts, and instead of compassion, they spoke of arcane phenomena like transferences and counter-transferences, analyzing of the transference neuroses, etc.

My first analyst, Dr. Smith, was picked for me by Frieda Fromm-Reichman. She was of the "interpersonal school" and supposedly more supportive while Dr. Anderson, who was the head of the Baltimore Analytic Institute, was supposed to be so orthodox that he believed the developments in psychoanalysis ended with Chapter 5 of *The Dream Book*.[10]

For a year, five times a week I lay on Dr. Smith's couch, and all I ever heard, other than my own voice, was the sound when she scratched her girdle. When my money had run out, Dr. Anderson said he would see me on the cuff. I remember that supposedly ultra-orthodox analyst sitting on the foot of the couch, blowing pipe smoke in my face (I wasn't allowed to smoke), and practically shouting, "Jesus Christ, Noch, how stupid can you be?"

Pretty stupid, I recognize in retrospect, and I suspect analysis with Anderson could really have been therapeutic, but I was in the Navy Reserve and was called up for the Korean War because they were losing so many Army battalion surgeons.

I became involved in research and was admitted as a research trainee by the Baltimore Psychoanalytic Institute, although I had lost a little of my enthusiasm for analysis and had other priorities when I moved to Langley Porter in San Francisco. But fundamentally I still believed that psychoanalysis was the ultimate psychotherapy and so was pleased when I was invited to become a member of the Group for Advancement of Psychiatry.

Carl Menninger (of the Menninger Foundation) had organized the Group for Advancement of Psychiatry (GAP) to make the world safe for psychoanalysis and to fill department chairs with psychoanalysts. Not all members of Menninger's group were classic analysts. I had dropped out of analytic training to pursue my research interests, and at GAP I met Joe Wheelwright, the foremost Jungian analyst of his time.

By the time the GAP was in full swing, Frieda Fromm-Reichman had died.

She had once written a paper about trying to establish a relationship with a schizophrenic by sitting on the quiet room floor and smoking urine-soaked cigarettes with the patient. Frieda later visited our hospital and found that one of the residents had been trying to do what Frieda had done. I remember her saying, "We all make mistakes and that was a mistake. Sooner or later one gets tired of smoking urine-soaked cigarettes. In working with schizophrenics, you should not do or promise to do something unless you're willing to do it forever."

John Rosen was as flamboyant as Frieda was unassuming. A fellow resident once characterized his therapy as "an assault on the id from behind." I remember Rosen recounting a story of working with a patient whose delusion was that he was rich and famous. He took the patient to an expensive restaurant in New York and when the check came, Rosen said, "If you're rich and famous, then take care of the check." Of course the patient couldn't, so he and Rosen ended up washing dishes together. The late Jean Jacobson lived with Rosen's patients and said they showed dramatic short-term improvements. Subsequent follow-up studies, however, failed to show any durable therapeutic effect.[11]

Given the economic and technical problems with psychoanalysis and its offspring, a variety of different psychotherapeutic techniques made their appearance. First came a group of procedures that can be loosely categorized as behavior therapy and were based on concepts of reward and punishment, developed through animal research by B. F. Skinner[12] and translated to work with humans by Joseph Wolpe[13] and others.

The principal techniques are based on manipulating reward, punishment, and expectations. For example, severely retarded children will bang their heads to the point of producing life-threatening injuries. A behavioral therapist noticed that the head banging took place particularly when attendants were around. They would say, "Poor, poor Tommy. Don't do that," and put padding up around the child's head to lessen the damage.

So the therapist would come to visit the child, who would begin to bang his head. Then the therapist would say nice things and put a pillow under his head. She would repeat this for a week and then abruptly stop saying nice things to the patient or comforting him (i.e., stopped reinforcing the head banging). The therapist would stand with her arms folded. The patient would bang his head expectantly and then when he wasn't reinforced, he would stop. (If you won't do nice things when I bang my head, well, I'll quit banging my head.)

Behavioral therapies were just being developed in the 1940s, when investigators like Wolpe began to exploit the animal research of B. F. Skinner to treat humans. It was almost a decade later when Beck[14] described a combination of behavioral therapy and psychoanalysis that he called Cognitive Behavior Therapy or CBT. That has now been thoroughly evaluated with carefully designed and controlled experimental studies. Beck has written several books on CBT, so obviously I can't do justice in the space allowed. But I can give an illustration that shows something of his procedures.

Depressives feel miserable and often give themselves insurmountable tasks in hopes of restoring their self-esteem. But by definition, insurmountable tasks lead to failure, failure makes people feel more miserable, and so they feel that they must take on even more insurmountable tasks, which leads to more failure, and so on.

The answer to this is to have the patients schedule a series of tasks that they are bound to succeed at, and they must follow each success with a reward. The patients can choose their cycle times. For example, they might do 30-minute tasks alternating with 30-minute rewards.

In my experience, it is interesting that, at first, patients often find it very difficult to comply. The tasks are too easy, and they couldn't reward themselves for such an easy task. But with consistent admonitions from the therapist, this can usually be overcome. Then what had been a destructive cycle of failure and punishment is turned into cycles of success and reward, often with remarkable results.

Psychological therapies continue to develop, and a relatively recent one that has been carefully researched is EMDR[15] (Eye Movement Sensitization and Reintegration). There is an enormous literature on that subject, which must be left for the interested reader to pursue.

ELECTROENCEPHALOGRAMS (EEG) AND EVENT-RELATED POTENTIALS (ERP)

Hans Berger discovered the brain waves or EEG in the 1920s, but around 1940 they came into general use because of their clinical usefulness in cases of head injury and epilepsy and because of the availability of electronic recording equipment, based in large part on inventions in electronics produced during

World War II. Before that time, recordings of tiny potentials were made with "string galvanometers" that were hard to make and harder to maintain.

At Worcester we had one of the first fully electronic Grass EEG machines,[16] and since our patients included all sorts of organic conditions and head injuries, the EEG was of clear clinical value, and it was perfectly obvious that the EEG reflected things going on in the mind. So it was confidently studied in the belief that it would shed light on mental illness.

Since that didn't happen, averaging brain waves became all the rage as digital computers became readily available, and the study of event-related potentials (ERP) was pursued enthusiastically. No one was able to see changes with clear psychological correlates. Over the years, the Society for Psychophysiological Research has devoted itself largely to relationships between psychological process, EEGs, and ERPs. Some people would say I'm unduly pessimistic, but in my defense I will quote (I think) the late Charles Shagass. "We thought brain waves and evoked potentials were going to be windows on the mind, but they turned out to be peepholes into Halls of Mirrors."

Over the years, certain researchers have made extreme and unrepeatable claims for brain waves and evoked potentials. One man's work stands out from the rest for developing procedures that are exquisitely sensitive to drugs and other changes in brain function. Starting around 1955, he developed a mathematically sophisticated technique for combining behavioral and EEG measures. It has been shown to be sensitive to drug effects, sleep apnea, etc. This scientist is Alan Gevins.[17] He has achieved test-retest reliability on the order of $r = .9$ while most psychological testers consider reliabilities on the order of $r = .7$ to be adequate. I was very disappointed when by 2011 he could find no one that would take over the commercialization of his procedures. He is now closing his lab and writing a series of papers detailing exactly his procedures and results.

THE PSYCHOPHARMACOLOGICAL REVOLUTION

Today we have an impressive array of drugs and techniques that were almost unbelievable fifty years ago, yet the treatment of the mentally ill remains almost as much of a challenge and art as it was then. As we gain experience with each new drug, we find it is useful for some people while it has onerous side effects for others.

The psychopharmacological revolution began with the introduction of the first true antipsychotic: chlorpromazine. Initially, it seemed truly miraculous, but as time went on, the side effects became apparent. Obesity, tardive dyskinesia, parkinsonism, etc., made their appearance. But it still can reduce the symptoms of schizophrenia, although haloperidol (Haldol) and the long-acting, intramuscular haldoperidol deconoate have largely replaced the other "typical" antipsychotics.

A second wave of so-called atypical antipsychotics were introduced late in the 1950s. The first was clozaril, which began its evaluation in the 1950s. Atypicals were extensively studied before they came on the market. Besides apparently being effective, they had reduced side effects. Curiously, as time has passed, they appear to have become ineffective. Why this is the case, so far as I know, remains a mystery.

Lithium remains as effective in manic depressives as before. Its use goes back into antiquity, but its contemporary use dates to the studies by Cade[18] in 1945. Sadly, it reduces creativity to the point that some patients find intolerable. Some of these manics have found that atypical anti-epileptics better control their mania without the inhibition of creativity.

Dr. Kay Redfield Jamison[19,20] has described this inhibition of creativity by lithium, yet she has completed a number of excellent books while on lithium. On the other hand, one of my patients was a composer, and lithium totally stopped his creativity. We worked out a plan with his family and friends. When they detected the onset of mania, he agreed to go back on his lithium until the episode subsided.

One of the great unfulfilled promises is that of molecular biology. That should, by all rights, belong in a later chapter since Watson and Crick didn't discover the double helix until the 1990s. Shortly after that, one of the most respected researchers in this area confidently predicted that depression would be wiped out within a few years with advances in molecular biology. Such optimism should have been tempered by the knowledge that, even now, Huntington's disease still remains untreatable. Its genetic defect has been known for many years. It is a repeat of the DNA sequence CAG, which codes for glutamate; the longer the sequence, the earlier the onset. Today, Huntington's still remains a death sentence with a preceding dementia.

None of this is to say that the molecular biologists have given up. The new field of epigenetics deals with how the genome interacts with environmental and other factors. Take, for example, a flowering plant. The genes for the flowers exist in the winter and spring but only express themselves when temperature and humidity are optimal. Something like that must be going on with mental illness; otherwise, there would be 100 percent hereditability, and identical twins would always have the same mental illness (but they don't).

The hope is that more sophisticated genetic analysis can eventually serve to provide a biologically based diagnosis in place of the clinician-consensus-based diagnosis, as exemplified by the current Diagnosis and Statistical Manuals (DSM).[21] Such biological diagnoses should provide better guidance for the definition of diseases and for psychopharmacological interventions.

WHERE TO NEXT?

In spite of the fact that the future seems bright in many ways (although that is perhaps a necessary, shared delusion among researchers), all is not well in the psychiatric research establishment. Several years ago Greenberg wrote an article in which he said, "When the first new Ferrari appears on the campus, then all the rules change."

At first, that seemed to presage an era of cooperation between academia and industry. Instead it foretold the eventual dominance and corruption of the academy by industry, which, after all, has more money. For after the Nobel laureates formed their own companies, lesser lights began to see the drug companies as sources of money and to take that money for advertising their products.

Dr. Barry Blackwell recently (September 2011) wrote a letter to members of the American College of Neuropsychopharmacology (ACNP) that covers many of the more recent, unfortunate developments. As a retired professor, I have not been as immediately concerned with the current status of my former field as Dr. Blackwell.

He incidentally was three times chairman of psychiatry at the Milwaukee campus of the University of Wisconsin School of Medicine. Then the largest "not-for-profit" in the area bought the bankrupt city hospital and closed psychiatry because it could not make money from the Medicare population.

CONCLUSIONS

The decade from 1940 to 1950 was a time of great change in psychiatry. It saw a decline in the importance of psychoanalysis, with the beginnings of many other alternative psychological techniques, most notably behavioral techniques such as those Wolpe developed, based on B. F. Skinner's animal studies. Since then a host of newer psychotherapeutic techniques that combine insights from psychoanalysis with behavioral techniques have been found to be effective in well-controlled studies.

It also saw older physical treatments replaced by more effective pharmacological interventions. These new treatments included lithium for manic-depressive psychosis (which remained outlawed in the United States until 1979), the typical antipsychotics for schizophrenia, the antidepressants for a serious depression, Anafrinil for obsessive-compulsive disorder, and the atypical anti-epileptics for certain cases of manic-depressive psychosis. Antibuse was introduced for alcoholism, methadone for opiate addiction, and nicotine patches for smoking addiction. Later, the discovery of LSD-25 by Hoffman,[22] while of dubious clinical importance, lent increased credibility to the belief that mental illnesses have a biochemical basis.

Towards the end of the 1940s, society began ending the decriminalization of the mentally ill as sick people were returned to a society poorly equipped to handle them humanely, with the result that many ended up back in the criminal justice system.[23,24]

By 1950 the influx of money from pharmaceutical companies had begun with occasional wonderful meals, but over time researchers were simply being paid by pharmaceutical companies to recommend their drugs. The consequences of this properly belong in other chapters.

Once there was hope that the government would take over the funding of clinical psychopharmacological research, but with the cuts in federal funding and the enrichment of the pharmaceutical companies, drug evaluation has ended up being done by those who could not, by any stretch of the imagination, be considered unbiased. Basic research, funded by the federal government, continued with advances in brain imaging and genetics at the forefront. But just where the great advances will occur next, of course, remains to be seen. However, as a wise man once quipped, "Why can't we use what we already know?"

REFERENCES

1. Szasz, T. (1962). *The myth of mental illness: Foundations of a theory of personal conduct*. New York, NY: Hoeber-Harper.
2. Grob, G. N. (1966). *The state and the mentally ill: A history of Worcester State Hospital in Massachusetts, 1830–1920*. Chapel Hill, NC: University of North Carolina Press.
3. Morisey, P. J. (1980). *The enduring asylum: Cycles of institutional reforms at Worcester State Hospital*. New York, NY: Grune & Stratton, Inc.
4. Callaway, E. (2007). *Asylum: A mid century mad house and its lessons about our mentally ill today*. Westport, CT: Praeger.
5. Keesey, K. (1964). *One flew over the cuckoo's nest*. New York, NY: Viking.
6. Green, H. (pseudonym for Joanne Greenberg) (1964). *I never promised you a rose garden*. New York, NY: Holt, Rinehart and Winston.
7. Schultes, R. E. V. (*1995*). *Ethnobotany: Evolution of a discipline*. Retrieved on June 26, 2012 from http://books.google.com/books?id=90hLdfk8pGYC&dq=gordon+alles+date+of+birth&sitesec=reviews
8. Kanas, N. (1996). *Group therapy of schizophrenic patients*. Washington, DC: American Psychiatric Press.
9. Verghase, A. (2010). *Cutting for Stone*. New York, NY: Knopf.
10. Freud, S. (translation by J. Crick) (2008). *The interpretation of dreams*. New York, NY: Oxford University Press.
11. Bookhammer, R. S., et al. (1966). A five-year clinical follow-up study of schizophrenics treated by Rosen's "direct analysis" compared with controls. *American Journal of Psychiatry, 123*, 602–604.

12. Skinner, B. F. (1972). *Beyond freedom and dignity*. New York, NY: Vintage Books.

13. Wolpe, J. (1969). *The practice of behavior therapy*. New York, NY: Pergamon Press.

14. Beck, A. T., Emery, G., & Greenberg, R. L. (1985). *Anxiety disorders and phobias: A cognitive perspective*. New York, NY: Basic Books.

15. Shapiro, F. (2001). *Eye movement desensitization and reprocessing*. New York, NY: Guilford Press.

16. Hoagland, H. (1974). *The road to yesterday*. Worcester, MA: Author.

17. Gevins, A., & Smith, M. E. (2000). Neurophysiological measures of working memory and individual differences in cognitive ability and cognitive style. *Cerebral Cortex, 10*, 829–839.

18. Cade, J. F. J. (3 Sep. 1949). Lithium salts in the treatment of psychotic excitement. *Medical Journal of Australia, 2*, 349–352.

19. Jamison, K. R. (1940). *Touched with Fire: Manic-depressive illness and the artistic temperament*. New York, NY: Free Press.

20. Jamison, K. R. (1995). *The unquiet mind*. New York, NY: Knopf.

21. American Psychiatric Association (1994). *Diagnostic mental disorders*. Fourth edition. Washington, DC: Author.

22. Hoffmann, A. (1979). *LSD: My problem child*. Cited in Shulgin, THIKAL (p. 493). Berkeley, CA: Transform Press.

23. Isaac, R. J., & Armat, V. C. (1990). *Madness in the streets*. New York, NY: Macmillan.

24. Torrey, E. F. (1996). *Out of the shadows*. New York, NY: John Wiley & Sons.

Chapter 9

A Supernatural Perspective on Psychopathology

Phillip Brownell

If there are two psychology courses that epitomize the study of psychology at the undergraduate level, they are "Introduction to Psychology" and "Abnormal Psychology." This chapter continues the study of abnormal psychology through the ages by considering a supernatural understanding of psychopathology.

In 1940 Brown and Menninger described the relationship between a supernatural and a natural understanding of psychopathology by describing the developmental relationship among magic, religion, and science:

> We shall best understand the real significance of the modern viewpoint in psychopathology if we trace its slow development and see why this development had to be so slow. Magic, religion, and science are the three chief methods through which man has tried to understand his place in the cosmos and to better it. Sir J. G. Frazer writes in his *Golden Bough*, "The movement of higher thought has been from magic through religion to science." He goes on to point out that recorded history of man's intellectual production could be compared to a web woven of three differently colored threads, the black thread of magic, the red thread of religion, and the white thread of science. History thus represented would be a long rope beginning almost wholly with black, then changing to black and red with a single white strand or two. Gradually and very slowly we come to modern times, where the black has tapered off and the white becomes predominant. Even today, however, the black of magic is clearly discernible and the red of religion is very striking.[1] (p. 23)

That description came out of a thoroughly modern and more positivist philosophy of science than currently exists today. We live in a post-positivist era, and the assumptions of naturalism resident in the thinking of Brown and Menninger above (and in many others, even to this day) have been surpassed. In addressing philosophy of mind, one of the last bastions of an outdated 1950s philosophy of science, Steven Horst[2] addresses this point when he says, "...post-reductionist philosophy of science ought to occasion some serious re-thinking in philosophy of mind" (p. 5). I would add, not just in the philosophy of mind, but also in the approach to case conceptualization with regards to psychopathology. That is because today people do not assume that everything can be reduced to categories in the DSM or to physics, and scientists allow that some things are in separate categories of study. As will be seen by defining the three elements of naturalism, supernaturalism, and psychopathology, we are not on a simplistic ground, dealing with an anachronistic and primitive anthropology or a simplistic understanding of the supernatural.

DEFINITIONS

Three terms need to be understood: natural, supernatural, and psychopathology. They in turn give rise to considerations of the differences among such things as a natural attitude, a spiritual attitude, a supernatural attitude, and a scientific or psychological attitude.

Natura

The natural is what can be seen in nature. That is, the natural is what we can sense and/or measure in some way. In one way of thinking about this, it is what comes to a person "naturally." If I can touch it, see it, smell, it, taste it, or hear it—if I can measure it in some way—then it has meaning for me. But if I cannot, if I have to experience it as a thought—what phenomenologists call a categorial intentional object—then it might be a nice thought, but it has no scientific significance.

Naturalism is the philosophy of the naturalist perspective, and it stands behind the human science of psychology. K. A. Aho,[3] in the *Journal of Theoretical and Philosophical Psychology*, asserted that a human being is a "lived-body"—a dialogical way of being that is already engaged and embedded in a web of socio-historical meanings. That is, people are born embodied into a culture, thrown into it as the philosopher Martin Heidegger has said. Aho claimed that the job of the human sciences is not to explain existence but to understand how we interpret ourselves, how we make meaning out of our experience of being in this world. A background of meanings is always already in place informing the development and direction of a worldview. The background that informs the discipline of psychology is naturalism, but by contrast the background that informs the discipline of theology is anti-naturalism, and perhaps, for some, a more specific version of non- or anti-naturalism known as supernaturalism.

Philosophers regard naturalism to include everything that can be identified by the natural sciences, so naturalism is sometimes known as physicalism or materialism.[4] Dermot Moran,[5] in his *Introduction to Phenomenology*, wrote that naturalism "is the view that every phenomenon ultimately is encompassed within and explained by the laws of nature; everything real belongs to physical nature or is reducible to it" (p. 142). Laws and principles govern the events of nature. The naturalist takes for granted various beliefs about the world and how things operate in the world. Examples include objectivism, materialism, hedonism, atomism, universalism, determinism, a rational order, reductionism, and empiricism.[6]

Further, naturalism can be divided into subcategories. Ontological, or metaphysical naturalism, is concerned with reality—a commitment to the proposition that nothing exists outside of that which can be investigated empirically, while methodological naturalism is concerned with how to investigate reality—a commitment to certain methods for limited purposes, namely, the scientific method.[7]

> Under methodological naturalism, natural science methods are focused on uncovering physical facts and regularities without prejudging whether physical facts and regularities exhaust reality.... Furthermore, methodological naturalism carries no implication that everything in the world can be explained using natural science's method.... In contrast, metaphysical naturalism makes a substantive commitment to a picture of what really exists: namely, only matter, energy, and their interactions. In particular, metaphysical naturalism denies that there are divine beings, a spiritual reality, ultimate intelligent causes, and so forth.[8] (p. 108)

By contrast, non-naturalism, or anti-naturalism, is everything that goes beyond the physical world, and that has been termed the metaphysical. Thus for instance, phenomenology, which is a philosophy of subjective experience, is of the non-naturalistic perspective.[9] Classic, Husserlian phenomenology is a system designed to escape the natural attitude and one elevated into an all-encompassing theoretical outlook.[5] A naturalist theory cannot posit the existence of supernatural entities such as God or immaterial souls, even "mind," and it cannot adopt a metaphysical stance "in which the ontology of the natural sciences is not fundamental (e.g., transcendental idealism, pragmatism)"[2] (pp. 15–16). Thus, even among those who study the psychology of religion, if they follow a strictly naturalist philosophy of science, it puts them at odds with such things as mysticism and the paranormal.[10]

Supernatural

One of the most frightening movies to come out in the early 1970s was *The Exorcist,* a tale of demon possession and the terror that attended attempts to force demons out of a demon-possessed person. However, when the film was re-released in 2000, it did not evoke exactly the same reaction; many people laughed at it in places where previously they had recoiled, and the reason suggested was that society had, in the interim, lost its sensitivity to the numinous.[11]

The numinous is a type of experience. It is that which impacts a person and leaves the impression that one has encountered something wholly other. It is mysterious and unsettling. The numinous feels like a mystery from another dimension, another world. The mystery denotes

> that which is hidden and esoteric, that which is beyond conception or under-standing, extraordinary and unfamiliar ... that which is quite beyond the sphere of the usual, the intelligible, and the familiar, which therefore falls quite outside the limits of the "canny" and is contrasted with it, filling the mind with blank wonder and astonishment ... in a peculiar "moment" of consciousness, to wit, the *stupor* before something "wholly other" whether such an other be named "spirit" or "daemon" or "deva," or be left without any name.[12] (pp. 13, 26–27)

The Exorcist was one in a genre of supernatural horror stories that some might say belong to the fear of the unknown and the evil that potentially lurks in the dark. According to such a perspective, this kind of supernatural phenom-enon cannot find explanation by naturalistic means.[13]

A common way to understand the supernatural is to say that the super-natural involves what one believes while the natural refers to what one senses. However, if the supernatural is what a person believes, then it would include many things not usually considered to be supernatural. For instance, in cat-egorial intentionality a person holds in his or her mind a construct (such as "justice," "equity," "alterity," or "altruism"). While nobody can see, taste, smell, or measure these things by the senses, people believe they exist. People hold them in their minds as being real, and they do so by way of intentional faith.[14] Thus, phenomenology could be considered a supernatural system. Taking this one step further, when we perceive something by the senses, we believe that what we are sensing corresponds to something that is actually there, some-thing encountered in our lived body, and something the philosopher Maurice Merleau-Ponty termed "perceptual faith."[15] In fact, the naturalism behind the observational process in the scientific method relies on such faith. However, no one would call the scientific method a supernatural system.

More popularly, then, that which is supernatural is attributed to forces be-yond scientific understanding, the laws of nature, or the scientific method; it is above (super) nature and does not obey the laws of nature. With a supernatural attitude, one readily accepts such phenomena as spirits of the dead communicating with the living (spiritualism), and mediums and shamans being the service providers of choice.

In a study of supernatural belief, a curvilinear pattern was observed in which religious people believe in some kinds of supernatural phenomena but not others. People who have strong belief in the paranormal were found to display a broad spiritualist worldview, as opposed to those who are more materialist and narrow in their religious outlooks. Paranormal believers, on the other hand, show moderate levels of religious belief and practices with low levels of narrow ideology.[16] More conservative Evangelical and Pentecostal clergy tend to uphold a supernatural understanding of some mental illness, seeing it as demon possession, while other clergy in more mainstream denominations often have become "despiritualized" and are more comfortable with scientific explanations of mental illness.[17] It might also be said that conservative Christians believe in both the demonic and the scientific, allowing for a more complex understanding of psychological disorder than a reductionist polarity might suggest (i.e., demons versus science).

The supernatural, then, is the realm of ghosts, spirits, the occult, the paranormal, the gods, and angels. It is the realm of sickness and suffering attributed to such beings. Thus, naturalists believe that supernatural explanations for the etiology of psychological disorder refer to a primitive phase in the understanding of mental health.[18]

Psychopathology

Psychopathology is a compound term implying disease that is related to the mental processes. Psychopathology includes mental or emotional abnormality and dysfunction. There are thousands of articles and chapters in books about psychopathology, and this series of volumes is one example of how much can be written about it. I will leave it to other chapter contributors to make an exhaustive definition, and instead just briefly offer my impressions of three categories of psychopathology and my take on the Global Assessment of Function, which is a measure of psychopathology.

Global Assessment of Function

The Global Assessment of Function (GAF) consists of a set of numbers between one and one hundred that correspond to symptom descriptions in a range of increasing/decreasing severity. It has been shown to be a reasonably reliable means of ascertaining psychopathology.[19] The symptoms, in turn, are largely of two kinds: one kind of symptom descriptor lists examples of psychological and interpersonal suffering, and the other kind of symptom descriptor lists examples of individual and interpersonal functioning. I think of these two kinds of descriptors as subscales, such that as psychological pain goes up, functioning goes down. One hundred, in terms of pain, can put one at the utmost in suffering, while one hundred in terms of functioning can put one at the peak of accomplishment. Thus, psychopathology can be thought of as an inverse relationship between emotional or mental suffering and adaptive functioning. At roughly age 55 one could be hospitalized, and between ages 55 and 85 one could be treated in outpatient therapy.

Thought Disorders

Thought disorders represent a break with reality as reality is consensually understood. A thought disorder does not simply refer to a logical inconsistency in a person's constructions of meaning. It refers to one's sense of being in the world with other people, and more specifically it refers to great leaps in the way one perceives and connects incidents or associates concepts one with another. Another way of describing thought disorders is to realize that they come in basically two varieties, which either add something that most other people do not experience to one's subjective experience and understanding of what is real, or they take something away from a person's capacity to be in the world and function successfully with other people. Thus, a person with schizophrenia, for example, can add auditory hallucinations and a well-developed delusional system to the experience of being in the world, while a different person with schizophrenia can lose his or her ability to follow what other people are saying, hold thoughts in the mind, and construct meaningful sentences without degenerating into gibberish, and one's expression can become bland and monotonous. A person can be catatonic, disorganized, or paranoid. A person can experience erotomanic delusions, grandiosity, jealousy, persecutory delusions, or somatic delusions. Thought disorders include schizophrenia, delusional disorder, schizophreniform disorder, schizoaffective disorder, and psychotic disorders due to a medical condition.

Mood Disorders

Mood disorders largely involve the way a person feels, but in extreme forms they can develop features of psychoticism that resemble thought disorders. In general, one can be either up or down, and one can go up and down. Most mood disorders are cyclical. Using the metaphor of a weather front, mood is the barometric pressure associated with either a high or a low. With low pressure you get storms, wind, and a lot of rain. With high pressure you get fair skies, sunshine, and calm winds. The metaphor, like all metaphors, breaks down eventually.

Mood disorders include dysthymia (chronic depression), major depression, mania, bipolar of various kinds, and cyclothymic disorder. Clinicians have refined these categories over the years in recognition that there is no single way in which diverse people manifest mood disorders. In terms of cycling (going up and going down) for instance, people can cycle once in a year, four or more times in a year, or even in the course of a single day. In terms of depression, people lose the ability to experience pleasure, ruminate on self-critical thoughts or hopelessness, and often lose the ability to concentrate or remember things. They may become suicidal. Depressed people often isolate from others, because they lack the energy to cope with social demands.

Anxiety Disorders

Anxiety is worry that takes both a cognitive focus and a somatic expression. That is, people who worry are worried about something, and they are often overly concerned in proportion to what is going on. They might focus on their health, the quality of their friendships, money, or work. They may ruminate about how things in the future are going to turn out. This energy, generated in worry, finds somatic expression in muscle tension and aches, difficulty swallowing or breathing, agitation, perspiring, insomnia, rashes, and other bodily ailments. In generalized anxiety these symptoms persist for about six months or more.

Anxiety can take an extreme form called panic, and when panic becomes a disorder, then the person in question is often worried about experiencing repeating panic attacks. At that point fear of fear begins to rule their lives. A person can fear various specific things, such as being in an open, public place, or being in a closed, confined place. A person can fear heights. Specific fears like this are called phobias. One person I worked with was phobic about throwing up, and so she frequently experienced panic that she was going to become nauseated, and that caused her heart to beat fast, her body to perspire, her head to swim a bit, and ironically, her stomach to feel queasy, as if becoming nauseated.

All of these kinds of pathology involve some degree of psychological pain and functional decline. They can be quite debilitating. They involve all aspects of the whole person, from thinking, through feeling, to bodily actions.

A SUPERNATURAL UNDERSTANDING OF PSYCHOPATHOLOGY

That which is regarded to be supernatural spans primitive animistic and spiritualist perspectives as well as more mainline religious belief systems.

Animistic Perspective

Animism is the belief that spirit, spiritual beings, and/or a life force inhabits or is embodied in non-human forms. The philosophy stems from the thinking of Aristotle,[20] in his book titled *De Anima*, in which Aristotle explores the life force in various living bodies. Extending that thought, according to animists, there would be no separation between that which is spiritual and that which is physical. Some animists believe that the life force in colors conveys an energy and can affect an individual. Thus, spirits or souls exist in animals and also in rocks, trees, dirt, and even in ideas. Animistic constructs are found in some forms of Paganism, Buddhism, Hinduism, and Shinto. Thus, an animistic theory of pathology would involve a condition in which one was out of sync with the context of the life force in which one was located. That would be a kind of field approach—all things having effect in a sphere of influence.[21]

Spiritualist Perspective

Spiritualism (also known as spiritism) is the belief that people can communicate with the spirits of those who have died.[22] What is necessary for this is also the belief that people have an immaterial aspect to their essence and that it survives death. That immaterial aspect to human existence would be called one's spirit. In the religious practice of spiritualism, the person who is adept at communicating with these spirits is referred to as a medium. In the Bible, when King Saul had lost the comfort and support of the Holy Spirit of God, he became tormented by an unclean spirit, and he often felt terrified, fretful, peevish, and discontented. He often sought guidance from a medium. In a New Age version of mediumship, a person might claim to be "channeling" the spirit of someone departed, and the purpose would be to offer advice, consolation, or support, much the same as a life coach might do—to help a person function better with the perspective of one who has gone ahead. Thus, spiritualists believe in a growth theory of health and development in which each person is responsible for his or her own destiny.

Attitude

Attitude is the lens through which a person views the world. If the lens is green, then the person sees a green tint to everything. Put another way, attitude is the cradle of interest that rocks the baby of intent. If a person goes into a shopping mall in a designer's attitude, then that person will notice shops that coincide with his or her interest in color, shape, line, and composition. Other things will just not be noticed at all.

Thus, in the natural attitude, one takes for granted whatever comes his or her way in the world and does not question it. In a spiritual attitude one notices immaterial aspects to one's experience, is sensitive to the numinous, and is moved by the mystery of existence. In the supernatural attitude one stops at shops catering to the occult, and one entertains spirits regarded to have power over people. In the religious attitude one makes a point of attending mass, the synagogue, or the mosque. In the psychological attitude, one consults the *Diagnostic and Statistical Manual of Mental Disorders*[23] to locate categories of researched dysfunction and lists of symptomatology.

Speaking from the perspective of a naturalist philosophy of science and a scientific-psychological attitude, I see that people often regard religious and spiritual understandings to be in the category of supernatural experience, along with spiritualism, animism, the influence of the moon, and shamanic practices. This is partly because in previous ages what we now know to be medical conditions have been attributed to religious and supernatural causes. During the time of Hippocrates, for instance, various physical illnesses were regarded to be the result of demonic influence.[24] The example of epilepsy stands out as consistently attributed to supernatural forces, among them demons or even God:

> . . . for centuries the names given to this illness in medical terminology and in the vernacular throughout the various historical epochs are an indication of the believed relationship between epilepsy and the supernatural: the holy illness, morbus divinus (the divine), morbus deificus (created by God), morbus coelestis (the heavenly illness), morbus astralis (the stars' illness) and morbus lunaticus (the moon-induced illness). In Germany in the Middle Ages, a large number of colloquial expressions for epilepsy illustrate the influence of supernatural and divine forces and "the falling sickness": Zuchtrute Christi (rod of Christ), Gewalt Gottes (power of God), schedelnde (schüttelnde) Gottesstraf (shaking punishment from God). Even the term "Gichterle," used to describe epileptic fits suffered by small children, which is still a very common expression in Southern Germany, refers to the supposed supernatural (albeit demonic rather than divine) cause of the illness: "gichtige Krankheit" ("Gichterle" is a diminutive of this term) means something like "illness passed on through witchcraft and magic."[24] (p. 213)

However, if one approaches psychological pain and functional decline from within a spiritual or supernatural attitude, then supernatural causes are consistent and plausible. In the Bible the well-known story of the man possessed by "Legion," spokesman for a number of spirits who all possessed the man, could have been a description for Tourette's, intermittent explosive disorder, or paranoid schizophrenia, but in the Biblical texts it is described as having a spiritual etiology. It is not the only instance of such a perspective.

In the first chapter of the letter from St. Paul to the church in Rome, Paul describes the results of a person not acknowledging God, that is, not worshipping God as creator and instead worshipping the creation or aspects of the creation. Paul says that such a person, cut off from the life of God, develops a "depraved mind" and ends up doing things that are not proper and are self-destructive. These things include " . . . being filled with all unrighteousness, wickedness, greed, evil; full of envy, murder, strife, deceit, malice; they are gossips, slanderers, haters of God, insolent, untrustworthy, unloving, unmerciful"[i] (Romans 1:28-31, *New American Standard*). That could just as easily be seen as a description of axis two pathology—personality or character traits largely understood as interpersonal or relational dysfunctions. Certainly, people with that list of traits would experience ultimate brokenness and loss in terms of their relationships with other people. Here, however, instead of a direct attack from outside the person, caused by demons and the like, psychopathology finds its etiology in a lack of being appropriately related to God. In a correlated passage, St. Paul wrote to the church in Galatia, and he contrasted people who are guided by the Holy Spirit, who have the fruit of the Spirit, with those who do not and who function according to the base desires of the flesh:

> But I say, walk by the Spirit, and you will not carry out the desire of the flesh. For the flesh sets its desire against the Spirit, and the Spirit against the flesh; for these are in opposition to one another, so that you may not do the things that you please. But if you are led by the Spirit, you are not under the Law. Now the deeds of the flesh are evident, which are: immorality, impurity, sensuality, idolatry, sorcery, enmities, strife, jealousy, outbursts of anger, disputes, dissensions, factions, envying, drunkenness, carousing, and things like these, of which I forewarn you, just as I have forewarned you, that those who practice such things will not inherit the kingdom of God. But the fruit of the Spirit is love, joy, peace, patience, kindness, goodness, faithfulness, gentleness, self-control; against such things there is no law. Now those who belong to Christ Jesus have crucified the flesh with its passions and desires. (Galatians 5:16–24, *New American Standard*)

Both these descriptions feature intrapsychic and interpersonal dynamics that manifest in psychological pain and personal and interpersonal dysfunction. They are directly attributed to being out of sync with the supernatural power, guidance, or provision of God through the Holy Spirit. The dynamic involved is a natural consequence, a follow-up, to not being in relationship with God. The pain and dysfunction arise from within because of a lack of connection with an external spiritual entity; however, there are other examples, more predictable, of the pain and dysfunction resulting from the presence of, and contact with, external spiritual entities.

Perhaps the greatest example of a spiritual force tormenting a human being is the example of Job. Satan was granted permission from God to test Job, and so Satan attacked Job's family, wiped out all his assets, afflicted him physically, and harassed him emotionally through the critical advice of his wife and friends. He was alone with his faith and his sense of who he was in the world, and he cursed the day he was born. As the story unfolded, Job cried out to God but got no answer. He was distressed emotionally, and he had physical complications that exacerbated his psychological pain. He was left with the advice of his so-called friends until the end of the book, when finally God addressed Job, and Job received a fresh revelation of God. That is when he repented and his entire demeanor changed:

> Then Job answered the Lord and said,
> I know that You can do all things,
> And that no purpose of Yours can be thwarted.
> Who is this that hides counsel without knowledge?
> Therefore I have declared that which I did not understand,
> Things too wonderful for me, which I did not know.
> Hear, now, and I will speak;
> I will ask You, and You instruct me.
> I have heard of You by the hearing of the ear;
> But now my eye sees You;
> Therefore I retract,
> And I repent in dust and ashes.
> (Job 42:1–6, *New American Standard*)

A glimpse into the spiritual life and warfare supposedly going on around people is found in the story of Daniel, chapter 10. There Daniel saw a vision, and although the men with him did not see the vision, the presence of the spiritual entity Daniel saw, an angel, was enough to produce a sense of dread in these people, and they ran away. Daniel reported that when he saw the angel,

> . . . no strength was left in me, for my natural color turned to a deathly pallor, and I retained no strength. But I heard the sound of his words; and as soon as I heard the sound of his words, I fell into a deep sleep on my face, with my face to the ground. Then, behold, a hand touched me and set me trembling on my hands and knees. (Daniel 10: 8–10, *New American Standard*)

Daniel had an experience of the numinous, and it was utterly unsettling. The angel informed him that the angel had been in a battle with another angel and prevented from coming to Daniel's assistance until another angel came to help him. This is a picture of another dimension that people with a spiritual attitude readily accept. They speak of spiritual warfare, a struggle for the hearts and minds of human beings. This same kind of struggle is described in *The Screwtape Letters*, by C. S. Lewis,[25] an allegory describing the ways demons attempt to distract and dismay believers even while they sit in church.

CONCLUSION

The supernatural has been scaring people ever since people peered into the darkness, wondering what made a sound. Rather than providing an exhaustive list of things that qualify as supernatural, and then correlating them to various disorders, a general approach has been taken. The supernatural is part of a larger category known as non-naturalism or anti-naturalism, which is one end of a polarity—the other being naturalism.

Psychopathology has been categorized in the DSM into various clusters of symptoms, but for simplicity's sake, I have listed three main categories of psychopathology: thought disorders, mood disorders, and anxiety disorders. Thought disorders pertain to one's grip on reality, mood disorders pertain to one's dominant emotional tone, and anxiety disorders describe the way worry and fear play on a person.

An attitude is the lens that influences one's gaze of interest, such that one looks for what is colored by that lens and one does not look for what is not colored by that lens. In a naturalist or scientific attitude, one looks for that which can be measured empirically. In a non-naturalist or spiritual attitude, interest drives one to attend to spiritual matters, religious practices and concerns, and supernatural explanations for what naturalists and others explain using methodical naturalistic processes of evaluation. Thus, a psychologist or anthropologist is more apt to discard a spiritual explanation for phenomena than is a clergyman or a shaman. The opposite is also true.

That said, by using mainline examples from the Bible, links were provided between supernatural causes and physical, emotional, and relational pain and dysfunction.

REFERENCES

1. Brown, J. F., & Menninger, K. A. (1940). The historical development of psychopathology. In J. F. Brown & K. A. Menninger, *The psychodynamics of abnormal behavior*, pp. 23–47. New York, NY: McGraw-Hill, p. 23.

2. Horst, S. (2007). *Beyond reduction: Philosophy of mind and post-reductionist philosophy of science*. New York, NY: Oxford University Press.

3. Aho, K. A. (2012). Assessing the role of virtue ethics in psychology: A commentary on the work of Blaine Fowers, Frank Richardson, and Brent Slife. *Journal of Theoretical and Philosophical Psychology*, 32(1), 43–49.

4. Flanagan, O. (1997). Understanding consciousness: The case of sleep and dreams. In M. Ito, Y. Miyashita, & E. T. Rolls (Eds.), *Cognition, computation, and consciousness*, pp. 45–65. New York, NY: Oxford University Press.

5. Moran, D. (2000). *Introduction to phenomenology*. New York, NY: Routledge.

6. Slife, B. D., Mitchell, L. J., & Whoolery, M. (2004). A theistic approach to therapeutic community: Non-naturalism and the Alldredge Academy. In S. Richards & A. Bergin (Eds.), *Casebook for a spiritual strategy in counseling and psychotherapy*, pp. 35–54. Washington, DC: American Psychological Association.

7. Papineau, D. (2009, Spring). Naturalism. *The Stanford Encyclopedia of Philosophy*, E. N. Zalta (ed.), downloaded April 8, 2012, from http://plato.stanford.edu/entries/naturalism

8. Bishop, R. C. (2009). What is this naturalism stuff all about? *Journal of Theoretical and Philosophical Psychology, 29*(2), 108–113.

9. Gallaher, S., & Zahavi, D. (2008). *The phenomenological mind: An introduction to philosophy of mind and cognitive science*. New York, NY: Routledge.

10. Hood, R. (2008). Mysticism and the paranormal. In H. J. Ellens (ed.), *Miracles: God, science, and psychology in the paranormal*, vol. 3, *Parapsychological perspectives*, pp. 16–37. Westport, CT: Praeger.

11. Joubert, N. L., & Joubert, Z. E. (2011). Evil in film: Portrayal and biblical critique. In J. H. Ellens (Ed.), *Explaining evil*, vol. 1, *Definitions and development*, pp. 215–236. Santa Barbara, CA: Praeger/ABC-CLIO.

12. Otto, R. (1950/1923). *The idea of the holy*. Oxford, UK: Oxford University Press.

13. Lovecraft, H. P., & Bleiler, E. (1973). *Supernatural horror in literature*. Mineola, NY: Dover Publications.

14. Brownell, P. (2008). Faith: An existential, phenomenological, and biblical integration. In J. H. Ellens (ed.), *Miracles: God, science, and psychology in the paranormal*, vol. 2, *Medical and therapeutic events*, pp. 213–234. Westport, CT: Praeger.

15. Brownell, P. (2010). Intentional spirituality. In J. H. Ellens (Ed.), *The healing power of spirituality*, vol. 1, *Personal spirituality*, pp. 19–40. Santa Barbara, CA: Praeger/ABC-CLIO.

16. Baker, J., & Draper, S. (2010). Diverse supernatural portfolios: Certitude, exclusivity, and the curvilinear relationship between religiosity and paranormal beliefs. *Journal for the Scientific Study of Religion, 49*(3), 413–424.

17. Leavey, G. (2010). The appreciation of the spiritual in mental illness: A qualitative study of beliefs among clergy in the UK. *Transcultural Psychiatry, 47*(4), 571–590.

18. Ruggles, A. H. (1934). *Mental health: Past, present and future. The Colver lectures in Brown University 1932*. Baltimore, MD: Williams & Wilkins Co.

19. Sonesson, O., Tjus, T., & Arvidsson, H. (2010). Reliability of a functioning scale (GAF) among psychiatric ward staff. *Nordic Psychology, 62*(1), 53–64.

20. Aristotle (2008). *De anima*. New York, NY: Cosimo Classics.

21. Crocker, S. (1999). *A well-lived life: Essays in gestalt therapy*. Cambridge, MA: Gestalt Press.

22. Doyle, A. C. (1926/2011). *The history of spiritualism*. New York, NY: Cambridge University Press.

23. American Psychiatric Association (2000). *Diagnostic and statistical manual of mental disorders*, 4ᵗʰ edition, with text revision. Washington, DC: Author.

24. López-Ibor, J., Jr., & López-Ibor Alcocer, M. (2010). Religious experience and psychopathology. In Peter Verhagen, Herman van Praag, Juan López-Ibor Jr., John Cox & Driss Moussaoui (Eds.), *Religion and psychiatry: Beyond boundaries*, pp. 211–233. Hoboken, NJ: John Wiley & Sons.

25. Lewis, C. S. (2001) *The screwtape letters*. New York, NY: HarperCollins.

NOTE

[i] Scripture taken from the *New American Standard Bible*, copyright 1995 by the Lockman Foundation. Used by permission.

Chapter 10

Film Portrayal of Psychopathology and Its Treatment

Brooke J. Cannon

Since the first "photoplays" were introduced in the early 20th century, movies have been a mainstay of entertainment for all ages. The initial allure of the movie theater, or nickelodeon, raised some concerns among psychologists of the time. Several studies found effects of movies on children's social attitudes and prejudice. Peterson and Thurstone (as cited in Cressey[1]) assessed attitudes before and after viewing certain films, and their results indicated that "appropriate photoplays affect the social attitudes of youth toward such stereotyped groups as 'Negroes,' 'Chinese,' and 'Germans,' and upon controversial issues such as warfare, patriotism and the punishment of criminals"[1] (p. 516). Given such influence of movies on the audience, there is increasing concern regarding the cinematic portrayal of characters with mental illness and their treatment.

As the 20th century progressed, psychodynamic concepts became increasingly prominent in films. Screenwriters studied Jungian archetypes and Freudian theory.[2] Psychoanalytic motivations for characters became common. The tripartite model of personality—the Id, the Ego, and the Superego—became an effective formula. It is still well-utilized in today's movies, such as in the tripartite personality representation in the *Dark Knight* series: Joker, Batman, and Alfred, respectively. By the 1950s, movie analysts were routinely seeking psychoanalytic concepts in the films they reviewed, perhaps arising from the psychodynamic orientation of the first *Diagnostic and Statistical Manuals* (I, published in 1950, and II published in 1968). This tendency to ascribe psychoanalytic concepts to movies was not fully accepted, however. For example, Siegfried Kracauer's 1950 book review[3] of *Movies: A Psychological Study*, by Wolfenstein and Leites, concludes

> We increasingly come to *mythologize psychoanalytic concepts*, even in fields where we had better face the facts, however obvious or intricate, instead of eternally plumbing psychological depths underneath. . . . The rise of this mythology with its specious father and mother images also represents an attempt to elude real encounters with real things. It is a form of escapism.[3] (p. 580)

Beginning slowly at first, with movies such as *Now, Voyager* (1942) and *The Three Faces of Eve* (1957), main characters with identifiable, realistic psychopathology appeared. The notable exception is film portrayals of combat-related trauma, which have existed since World War I. By the latter quarter of the 20th century, movies more often explicitly focused on psychopathological disorders, such as gambling addiction (*The Gambler*, 1974), schizophrenia (*I Never Promised You a Rose Garden*, 1977), depression (*Ordinary People*, 1980), autism (*Rain Man*, 1988), bipolar disorder (*Mr. Jones*, 1993), obsessive-compulsive disorder (*As Good As It Gets*, 1997), and gender-identity disorder (*Boys Don't Cry*, 1999). *Lars and the Real Girl* (2007) is a wonderful portrayal of a family's and community's supportive, and curative, response to mental illness.

Portrayal of the treatment of mental illness has not followed the same evolutionary arc. Inpatient treatment facilities, "asylums," continue to be depicted as horrific places (e.g., *Gothika*, 2003; *Shutter Island*, 2010). Electroconvulsive therapy has virtually always been presented with significant drama and often as painful (with the notable exception of *Fear Strikes Out*, 1957). Current films continue this misrepresentation (e.g., *Dark Shadows*, 2012).

Cinema's mental health professionals perpetually are depicted in an unrealistic manner. There are some exceptions, but by and large, portrayals are distorted, either negatively or positively, and the characters are rarely shown maintaining professional practice standards and ethics. Romantic relationships between therapists and clients occur in movies throughout the 20th century. Typically, female therapists fall in love with their male clients; some are even shown to leave their professions to pursue the romance, such as in *Mr. Jones* (1991) and the recent *50/50* (2011). The hope of a more accurate portrayal triggered by the arrival of films such as *Prime* (2005), which appropriately addressed conflict of interest, confidentiality, and boundary issues, was dashed by films such as *Shrink* (2009), in which the psychiatrist violates all of these areas AND treats his own depression with marijuana.

Professional organizations are attempting to influence moviemakers to improve these portrayals (e.g., Division 42, Media Psychology, of the American Psychological Association). However, as long as such depictions of mental health professionals foster entertaining movies, it is unlikely that portrayals will change significantly.

Indeed, movies are filled with characters who display odd behaviors and act irrationally. Without such idiosyncrasies films would be dull, indeed. The collection of these behaviors may be consistent with a psychopathological disorder, intentionally or not, or may be solely a cinematic device. For filmographies and additional analyses of psychopathology in film, the reader is referred to several comprehensive texts.[4,5,6,7,8] This chapter will provide a general overview and examples of American movie portrayals across the 20th century, the settings and methods used to treat these characters, and the portrayal of mental health professionals.

PSYCHOPATHOLOGY

Psychotic Disorders

The dramatic symptoms of schizophrenia—hallucinations, delusions, thought disorder, and other bizarre behaviors—provide screenwriters with a wide range of portrayal options. For example, in *I Never Promised You a Rose Garden* (1977), Deborah, a 16-year-old girl with schizophrenia, is admitted to Ward D ("D" for disturbed"). She experiences command hallucinations from a primitive tribesman and uses neologisms (nonsensical words) as the tribe's language. The audience experiences the hallucinations through film cuts to jungle scenes and music.

Less severe schizophrenia is portrayed in the independent film *Clean, Shaven* (1993). This slice-of-life film follows Peter as he is discharged from a mental institution, returns to his mother's home, and searches for his daughter, who has been adopted. Peter experiences heightened auditory senses; for example, he hears the electricity running through the power lines. He has somatic delusions, believing that he has transmitters embedded in his body and that his body has been contaminated, requiring excessive scrubbing. Peter's mother appears to have many negative symptoms of schizophrenia. Her communication with Peter is dysfunctional: she offers to make him a sandwich; he politely states that he is not hungry; she proceeds to make the sandwich, anyway, and then chastises him for not eating it. Nonetheless, Peter is functioning fairly well and others in the film are the ones to experience a faulty reality.

The impact of schizophrenia on a supportive family is nicely portrayed in *Benny & Joon* (1993). Benny (Aidan Quinn) is the caretaker for his sister, Joon (Mary Stuart Masterson), who has chronic schizophrenia. Joon does well with a set routine, but when she meets the quirky Sam (Johnny Depp) and they fall in love, her life changes. Conflict over this relationship with her brother triggers a psychotic episode. The realities of Joon's needs and limitations are accurately illustrated, as well as the positive effects of supportive loved ones.

A dramatic portrayal of schizoaffective disorder (manic) is given in the Academy Award–winning movie *Shine* (1996). Based on the true story of master pianist David Helfgott, played by Jeremy Rush, bizarre behaviors and beliefs are well-exhibited. David enjoys "clanging," speaking in rhyming words. He also shows impulsive, childlike behavior and excessive energy. His thinking is concrete. Like many other films, the etiology of David's disorder is suggested to be faulty parenting, for he has an overbearing father, who exhibits symptoms of paranoid personality disorder.

Patients with delusional disorders often appear in movies with inpatient settings, typically as humorous background characters—for example, a patient who believes he is Napoleon. A prominent delusional character in *Arsenic and Old Lace* (1944) believes that he is Teddy Roosevelt, supervising the digging of the Panama Canal. Johnny Depp believes that he is the great lover Don Juan in *Don Juan DeMarco* (1994). The development of paranoid delusions is portrayed in *The Conversation* (1974), with Gene Hackman decompensating into dysfunction by the film's end. Mel Gibson's chronic paranoia in *Conspiracy Theory* (1997) serendipitously hits truth, as reflected in Roger Ebert's review, "Sometimes, like a stopped clock, he's on the money."[9]

Mood Disorders

Mood disorders, not surprisingly, are most likely to appear in heavy dramas. A notable exception is the generally accurate portrayal of bipolar disorder by Richard Gere in *Mr. Jones* (1993), which also unfortunately includes the stereotypical romance with his female treating psychiatrist (Lena Olin). Very strong portrayals of the different faces of depression are provided in the Academy Award–winning *Ordinary People* (1980). While trying to maintain their image as the "perfect" family, the Jarretts struggle, following the accidental death of the "favored" son. Conrad (Timothy Hutton) has been hospitalized for depression and sees Dr. Berger (Judd Hirsch) for outpatient therapy, uncovering the negative impact of his detached mother and his ineffective father. Ultimately, Conrad's survivor guilt is exposed, and he is able to begin to move on. In contrast, Conrad's mother (Mary Tyler Moore) cannot confront her emotions, choosing instead to maintain her suppression and leave the family. Conrad's father (Donald Sutherland) finally recognizes the need to deal with his grief and to support his remaining son; he, too, enters therapy.

An often overlooked film, *Don't Bother to Knock* (1952), stars a surprisingly good Marilyn Monroe. Nell is hired as a babysitter for a young girl in a hotel room. We learn that her fiancé was killed in a plane accident, and it becomes clearer as the film progresses that Nell has a psychotic depression. As she decompensates, there is the possibility that she may become homicidal, in addition to threatening another self-harm attempt. Unfortunately, the myth that patients with mental illness are dangerous is promoted by this storyline.

Anxiety Disorders

Movies depicting combat-related posttraumatic stress disorder (PTSD) usually appear in the post-war eras. The traumas of World War I are evident in the silent film *The Big Parade* (1925) and in *Behind the Lines* (1998). As in *Behind the Lines*, which portrayed aphonia (loss of voice) as a result of war trauma, several post–World War II films coupled PTSD and conversion disorder symptoms, such as amnesia in *Spellbound* (1945) and paralysis in *Home of the Brave* (1949) and *12 O'Clock High* (1949). *Shock Corridor* (1963) includes the aftermath of the Korean War, with a delusional veteran. Adjustment to returning home from service during the Vietnam War appears in numerous films, such as *The Deer Hunter* (1978), *Coming Home* (1978), *Birdy* (1984), and *Born on the Fourth of July* (1989).

PTSD also is depicted in the movies as a result of non-combat traumas. For example, different presentations after an airplane accident are masterfully portrayed in *Fearless* (1993) by Jeff Bridges and Rosie Perez. Bridges becomes numb and has a sense of invulnerability; Perez is devastated by the loss of her child and associated guilt. John Turturro attempts to be effective as the airline-hired psychologist. Both *Ordinary People* (1980) and *Analyze This* (1999) have characters with elements of PTSD arising from the death of a loved one.

Acrophobia, as paired with PTSD, figures prominently in Hitchcock's *Vertigo* (1958), being the cornerstone of the suspenseful plotline. Scottie (Jimmy Stewart) even makes an attempt at self-directed exposure treatment, using a stepladder. Scottie's fear of heights keeps him from preventing his love interest's falling from a bell tower; he is blamed by others for her death, which causes him to become virtually catatonic, diagnosed with "acute melancholia, together with a guilt complex." Perhaps in an effort to deny feelings of guilt, upon Scottie's release from the hospital, he begins to believe that the dead woman, Madeleine, is still alive. His desire for her becomes obsessive. Scottie ultimately faces his fear of heights when he climbs the bell tower while in an emotional state which conflicts with fear—anger.

Perhaps the best portrayal of obsessive-compulsive disorder is by Jack Nicholson as Melvin Udall in *As Good As It Gets* (1997). The obsessive thoughts are only alluded to by his behaviors. Melvin exhibits multiple compulsions—cleaning, checking, avoiding cracks, and fearing contamination from contact with others. He has an abrasive personality, perhaps developed as a defense mechanism. As occurs all too often in film, it is the love of a woman (Helen Hunt), not his therapist, which softens his heart and improves his symptoms.

Dissociative Disorders

The *Three Faces of Eve* (1957) was the first major motion picture to portray multiple personality disorder. Joanne Woodward won an Academy Award for her portrayal of Eve, a woman with three distinct personalities. Her individual therapy with Dr. Luther (Lee Cobb) and his use of hypnosis are presented in a professional manner. Both Luther and a male staff member appropriately rebuff the advances of Eve's promiscuous alter personality, Eve Black.

A TV movie of the 1970s about multiple personality disorder may have had the greatest impact on mental health practices of all time. *Sybil* (1976) launched a multiple personality disorder–diagnosing frenzy. Indeed, only a handful of patients were diagnosed with this disorder prior to the appearance of the book and the subsequent movie. The diagnosis flourished, creating significant controversy in the field, particularly as evidence contradicting the diagnosis came to light.[10]

The ability to accurately diagnose multiple personality disorder is at issue in *Primal Fear* (1996). A homeless altar boy (Edward Norton) is on trial for murdering the archbishop. He presents as a mild-mannered, stammering young man, hardly likely to commit murder. After his arrest, however, another personality appears, which is irreverent and highly aggressive, and that person confesses to the murder. The plot then revolves around the legal defense strategies, considering this discovery. The movie parallels the feigning of multiple personality disorder by Kenneth Bianchi, known as the "Hillside Strangler," after his arrest in 1979.

Substance Use Disorders

When not a primary movie focus, alcohol use is an innocuous, or even glamorous, activity. McIntosh, Smith, Bazzini, and Mills[11] examined 832 characters in 100 top-grossing films from 1940 to 1989. Drinkers were more physically attractive, wealthier, and more sexually active than nondrinkers. There was no difference across decades. Cape[12] examined 51 movies involving substance use, from 1900 to 1999. He found four predominant stereotypes: tragic hero, rebellious free spirit, demonized addict/homicidal maniac, and humorous/comedic user. Examples of the tragic hero would include the Academy Award–winning *The Lost Weekend* (1945) and *Leaving Las Vegas* (1995). Rebellious free spirits are apparent in *Harvey* (1950), a movie which suggests that hallucinations are caused by alcohol consumption, but interestingly, the main character is never actually shown drinking, and *Fear and Loathing in Las Vegas* (1997), portraying Hunter S. Thompson's significant drug use (this movie contains some fantastic drug-induced hallucinations). Substance use associated with demonized addicts or homicidal maniacs occurs in *Blue Velvet* (1986), in which Dennis Hopper inhales from a tank of amyl nitrate, and the classic propaganda film, *Reefer Madness* (1936). Many contemporary teen movies include humorous or comic use of drugs and alcohol. Films of the early 20th century were more likely to feature use of opioids, such as in *The Mystery of the Leaping Fish* (1916), in which Douglas Fairbanks Sr. uses cocaine extensively.[12]

Personality Disorders

Most movie villains display characteristics of antisocial personality disorder. The majority of these characters are male. However, the Academy Award–winning film *All About Eve* (1950) gives us a great female character, Eve (Anne Baxter), with antisocial personality disorder features. Eve smoothly manipulates those around her, feigning innocence. Although often used as an example of histrionic personality disorder, Scarlett O'Hara in *Gone with the Wind* (1939) also exhibits antisocial personality disorder traits. Scarlett marries for material benefits, not love. She blatantly uses sex appeal to manipulate others and seeks out excitement when she is understimulated.

Paranoid personality disorder is wonderfully portrayed by Humphrey Bogart in *The Caine Mutiny* (1954). It is apparent how the symptoms of the disorder can be functional in certain settings, such as hypervigilance by a wartime ship captain, but also how they can cause dysfunction, such as when the captain becomes obsessively paranoid over trivialities, in this case, missing frozen strawberries. Bogart's cross-examination during a court martial hearing demonstrates his attempt to maintain his composure, until asked about the strawberries ("Ah, but the strawberries, that's . . . that's where I had them . . .").

Fatal Attraction (1987) depicts Glenn Close as Michael Douglas's spurned lover. Her labile affect, black/white thinking, and fears of abandonment are typical symptoms of borderline personality disorder; boiling the family's pet rabbit is not! That she also becomes homicidal furthers the mental illness and aggression myth. Similar portrayals occur in *Play Misty for Me* (1971) and *Single White Female* (1992).

Other Disorders

There are movies which deal with less common disorders quite accurately. *What's Eating Gilbert Grape* (1993), *Forrest Gump* (1994), and *Sling Blade* (1996) have main characters with intellectual disabilities. *Rain Man* (1988) won Dustin Hoffman an Academy Award for his portrayal of autism. Julianne Moore suffers from "multiple chemical sensitivity syndrome" in *Safe* (1995), or could it be somatization disorder? Alzheimer's disease is presented in *On Golden Pond* (1981) and *Safe House* (1998), and dementia resulting from porphyria is illustrated by *The Madness of King George* (1994). Hilary Swank won an Academy Award for her portrayal of Brandon Teena, a biologically female young adult with gender identity disorder, in *Boys Don't Cry* (1999).

TREATMENT

Inpatient Facilities

The "insane asylum" has been a setting for movies across the 20th century. Early cinematic glimpses inside mental health facilities most often depicted the patients as eccentric yet harmless. By mid-century, mental hospitals were depicted more often as inhumane treatment facilities, housing both benign and dangerous patients. As we reached the end of the century, mental hospitals were either used as an explanation for the homicidal maniac's behavior (e.g., he escaped from an asylum), or were depicted more as custodial centers.

Although mental health treatment was a rare topic in the silent film era, *Dr. Dippy's Sanitarium* (1906) is perhaps the earliest portrayal of a mental institution and mental health professional. This 20-minute silent film portrays childlike patients who run amok, taking over the institution, causing playful chaos as they torment a new guard. They are easily brought back into order by Dr. Dippy, as he provides each of them with a pie. Much like the German existentialist film, *The Cabinet of Dr. Caligari* (1919), asylum patients in *Dr. Dippy's Sanitarium* are depicted primarily as eccentric and benign. As in most portrayals of inpatient settings, these early movies contain stereotypical patients: the catatonic patient standing silently in the corner, the somnambulist wandering around at night, the delusional patient dressed as a famous figure, and the patient who initially doesn't seem "crazy," but then demonstrates severe psychosis as time passes. This concept of "masked insanity" is depicted in *The Cabinet of Dr. Caligari*, as we learn that it is the asylum's director who is behind a series of murders. In parallel, 1919's *When the Clouds Roll By* includes an escaped asylum patient masquerading as a "mind doctor." This plot device persists today (e.g., *Mr. Brooks*, 2007).

The 1930s brought a more sophisticated portrayal of mental health treatment. *Private Worlds* (1935) focuses primarily on the relationships among the staff but also reflects a more medical, scientific approach to mental illness in a hospital setting. *Carefree* (1938) casts the classy Fred Astaire as a psychiatrist, complete with tuxedo and dance numbers. High-class mental health treatment continues in *Now, Voyager* (1942), with a beautiful pastoral setting for the treatment facility.

As the 1940s progressed, mental institutions took on a more sinister character. Three films, in particular, focus on horrific, inhumane settings but counter with the healing power of caring professionals. The first, *Stairway to Light* (1945), is an Academy Award–winning short film based on Philippe Pinel's reforms of a French asylum in the late 1700s. Through respect and kindness, Pinel systematically brought patients out of the dark dungeons in which they were chained for decades. His humane treatment, referred to as "moral therapy," allowed patients to be cured and discharged from the asylum. The French community feared the release of these "madmen," and Pinel was nearly killed on the street by an angry mob when, miraculously, he was saved by one of the very patients he had helped.

A similar message was sent the following year, when *Bedlam* (1946) was released. Starring the noted horror film actor Boris Karloff, *Bedlam* gives us a fuller view inside a British asylum during the late 1700s, prior to Pinel's work. Karloff serves as the head of the asylum. He views the "loonies" as animals, and charges admission to the public to view them, much as in visiting a zoo. Some are chained; some are in cages. They are in a dungeon with straw on the floor for beds. It becomes clear that some are admitted to the asylum for political reasons. A young woman and her Quaker friend work to expose Karloff and the inhumane treatment. The film is based on the history of London's Bethlehem Royal Hospital.

Combining both horrific conditions and treatment with one of the best portrayals of a mental health practitioner, *The Snake Pit* (1948) garnered several nominations for academy awards, including a win for sound. Starring Olivia de Havilland as Virginia, a young woman with amnesia and psychosis, the film is set in a state mental institution. Although some of the wards are more custodial, there also is "the pit," where the most severe patients are confined together. It is clear that the facility is overcrowded, the staff is stressed, and there is a focus on administrative requirements. In a scene foreshadowing today's managed care issues, Virginia's psychiatrist, Dr. Kik, argues with hospital administrators about length of stay issues. *The Snake Pit* also brings us one of the first sadistic head nurse portrayals. The rest of the nursing staff also exhibit dominance over the patients through verbal abuse and harsh punishments. This behavior is consistent with the results of Zimbardo's 1973 Stanford Prison Experiment, which demonstrated how power differentials and dehumanizing conditions can lead to abusive behavior.[13] We continue to see portrayals of malevolent staff in many films, most notably *One Flew Over the Cuckoo's Nest* (1975).

Mental health treatment during the next decade focused primarily on individual work, with few institutional film settings. *Fear Strikes Out* (1957), the story of professional baseball player Jimmy Piersall's family dynamics and mental breakdown, includes a period of psychiatric hospitalization. The setting is realistic, benign, and professional. Another of the decade's movies with an asylum is the comedy *Harvey* (1950), starring Jimmy Stewart. Again, the facility is presented as professional, although the treatment and conduct of the staff are far from professional.

Three films of the 1960s portray love found in a mental institution. *Splendor in the Grass* (1961) briefly mentions that Deanie met her soon-to-be husband, now a physician, during her time in a psychiatric hospital. Greater focus on such a relationship is found in *David and Lisa* (1962), both students at a school for mentally disturbed adolescents. The facility is portrayed professionally; the schoolmaster, a psychiatrist, demonstrates a caring, accepting attitude. As found in many movies, however, the suggestion is that it is the love between David and Lisa that is curative. The third film, *Lilith* (1964), reflects both love between patients and between a staff member and a patient. Love in this case, however, is destructive. Warren Beatty portrays Vincent, a returning war veteran learning to become an occupational therapist at a private psychiatric facility for the wealthy. He quickly discovers the beautiful and unpredictable Lilith, played by Jean Seberg, falling obsessively in love with her. Another patient, Stephen (Peter Fonda), also loves Lilith. As time passes, both Lilith's and Vincent's psychopathologies are revealed. Their involvement with one another results in catatonia for Lilith, hospitalization for Vincent, and the suicide of Stephen. *Lilith* is a rare film which counters the "love cures all" theme. Lilith's portrayal by Jean Seberg is all the more powerful when considering the actress's personal life. Seberg had multiple unsuccessful romantic relationships and annual suicide attempts on the anniversary of her infant daughter's death, leading ultimately to her death from drug overdose at the age of 40.[14]

Lilith (1964) also promotes another mental illness myth: that schizophrenia is contagious. During a staff training, a psychiatrist presents results of a "study" which compared web building by spiders injected with the blood from a schizophrenic patient with webs built by unaffected spiders. As you might predict, the "schizophrenic" spiders' webs were grossly distorted and disorganized. The plotline of *Lilith* suggests the possibility that Vincent was exposed to her blood before he began exhibiting signs of psychopathology.

Sam Fuller's *Shock Corridor* (1963) is perhaps the most sociopolitical 1960s film set in a mental hospital. According to Fuller, he "was dealing with insanity, racism, patriotism, nuclear warfare, and sexual perversion. . . . My madhouse was a metaphor for America"[15] (p. 403). The plot revolves around an overzealous newspaper reporter, Johnny, played by Peter Breck, who hopes to win the Pulitzer Prize by solving the murder of an institution's psychiatrist. In order to gain admission to the facility, Johnny feigns a mental illness, described as "erotic dementia" in the original movie ad campaign. He seeks out the three patients who were witnesses to the crime. These include a Southern bigot who collaborated with the communists during the Korean war and now believes that he is a Confederate general; a young black man who snapped from the stresses of being part of the first college desegregation and now believes that he is a racist KKK member; and a nuclear scientist who helped develop the A-bomb and now has the mind of a six-year-old. Adding to the diagnostic inaccuracies is the "nympho ward," which Johnny accidentally enters and then is attacked therein by the women. Although warned by those who helped him prepare for his façade, Johnny becomes truly mentally ill, perpetuating the "mental illness is infectious" myth. *Shock Corridor* was initially banned in Great Britain, due to the inaccuracies of mental illness and treatment facility portrayals. As time passed, however, the merit of the film was acknowledged; it is one of the official 200 films named by the Library of Congress as "American Classics."[15]

The 1970s brings us THE movie about mental hospitals— *One Flew Over the Cuckoo's Nest* (1975), as well as a few others with negative portrayals of treatment facilities. Continuing the legacy of evil head nurses (e.g., *The Snake Pit*, 1948, and Joan Crawford in *The Caretakers*, 1963), *One Flew Over the Cuckoo's Nest's* Nurse Ratched (Louise Fletcher) has become the template of such a character. The facility, into which psychologically sound McMurphy (Jack Nicholson) is admitted in order to dodge a jail term, reflects the institutional climate of the time. Nurses stay in "the cage," only emerging to administer pills or deal with a crisis. Patients are left to their own devices, while remaining within the locked ward, resulting in the suicide of one patient. The accuracy of such settings is reflected in Rosenhan's famous "pseudopatients," who were admitted to facilities after feigning illness; they reported similar behaviors from the staff and patients.[16]

Another film of the period, *I Never Promised You a Rose Garden* (1977), reflects 16-year-old Debra's experiences during her hospitalization on a female ward for schizophrenia. Although the treating psychiatrist is overly dedicated and benevolent, a male nurse, Hobbs, routinely physically and sexually abuses patients. One patient (portrayed by Martine Bartlett) refers to Hobbs as her "chief rapist" (ironically, Bartlett also played the schizophrenic mother in *Sybil*, 1976). When Debra reports his behavior to the psychiatrist, Dr. Fried indicates that she does not run the hospital and cannot do anything other than file a formal complaint. There are repeated instances of Debra's return of functioning through her work one-on-one with Dr. Fried, but then horrific experiences on the ward knock her back into psychosis, including Hobbs' particularly violent attack of another patient. This resulted in his being fired, but no clear criminal charges. Patients learn that Hobbs committed suicide, which launches increased psychotic behaviors fueled by guilt. Thus, inpatient films of this era portrayed inpatient settings not only as merely custodial but also as dangerous.

The plot device of the "escaped lunatic" was brought back with *Halloween* (1979) and its sequels, as homicidal former patient Michael Meyers is pursued by his psychiatrist. Asylums and their patients continue to be portrayed as scary and dangerous to this day.

Paralleling the "deinstitutionalization" movement of the 1980s, far fewer movies depicted inpatient treatment in the remainder of the century. *Frances* (1982) is one of the few, chronicling actress Frances Farmer's mental illness and its treatment during the 1940s. As in *I Never Promised You a Rose Garden*, she is physically and sexually abused by male staff. Other inpatient settings are generally benign, as in *Girl, Interrupted* (1999), or more positively portrayed, as in *Don Juan DeMarco* (1994) and *Awakenings* (1990). Both *Clean, Shaven* (1993) and *Sling Blade* (1996) begin with the main characters being released from an inpatient setting. Little is shown of Peter's release in *Clean, Shaven*, but Karl's discharge in *Sling Blade* is hurried and impersonal, with no preparation for return to community living.

Treatment Methods

The treatment method most often exploited for its dramatic effect is electroconvulsive therapy (ECT). The treatment is presented as horrific, often with equipment reminiscent of Frankenstein's laboratory. Patients are awake, usually thrashing about. It may be used as a punishment for bad behavior. Films such as *The Snake Pit* (1948), *Shock Corridor* (1963), and *One Flew Over the Cuckoo's Nest* (1975) present ECT in this fashion. More positive portrayal occurs in few films. For example, in *Fear Strikes Out* (1957), ECT occurs off camera and the patient walks calmly into the treatment room. In *The Caretakers* (1963) the caring psychiatrist administers the treatment, reassuring the patient and explaining the procedure to the observing nurse; however, subsequent post-treatment care by another nurse is unsupportive. Even the overdramatic portrayal of ECT in *The Snake Pit* (1948), complete with jarring music and camerawork, results in behavioral improvement.

Other less commonly used treatment methods have appeared in feature films. These include hydrotherapy (e.g., *The Snake Pit*, 1948; *Shock Corridor*, 1963; and *Girl, Interrupted*, 1999), cupping (e.g., *Dangerous Liaisons*, 1988), lobotomy (e.g., *One Flew Over the Cuckoo's Nest*, 1975), hypnosis (e.g., *Three Faces of Eve*, 1957), and sodium pentothal (e.g., *Captain Newman, M.D.*, 1963). The standard treatment of neurasthenia, going on an extended, relaxing vacation, appears in *Now, Voyager* (1942) and *Enchanted April* (1999).

Portrayal of "talk" therapy in feature films arose during the 1940s, typically presented with a psychoanalytic flavor. Often there is a "search and seizure" approach to treatment, with the therapist seeking some repressed trauma.

The climactic point of the film is the uncovering of the memory, resulting in a complete cure of the client. Hitchcock's *Spellbound* (1945) is clear in its focus on psychoanalysis. Hitchcock employed a psychiatric consultant and the movie begins with the text, "Our story deals with psychoanalysis, the method by which modern science treats the emotional problems of the sane . . ." In *Spellbound*, Dr. Constance Peterson (Ingrid Bergman) is the sole female psychiatrist at a mental asylum. She discovers that the man who showed up as the new head of the facility (Gregory Peck) actually has amnesia and does not know his true identity. Through various Freudian interpretations, particularly of symbols in a dream sequence designed by Salvador Dali, the repressed memory is uncovered. Peterson's elderly mentor does most of the work, as her mind is too clouded by love. He is the stereotypical psychoanalyst, complete with Austrian accent and goatee. Although blatant in his use of psychoanalytic concepts, Hitchcock's primary goal was to create suspense, with less consideration of the accuracy of treatment portrayal.

Similar therapeutic success is achieved in *The Snake Pit* (1948), as the psychiatrist works to uncover the source of the patient's disturbance. Both *Spellbound* (1945) and *The Snake Pit* have guilt as the primary source of amnesia. A particularly competent psychiatrist in *Three Faces of Eve* (1957) traces the source of his patient's multiple personalities to a childhood trauma. Hitchcock's *Psycho* (1960) provides the most blatant demonstration of bad parenting causing psychopathology, more benignly presented in *Fear Strikes Out* (1957). In *Pressure Point* (1962), Sidney Poitier, a prison psychiatrist, treats a sociopathic Neo-Nazi. The prisoner chronicles multiple instances of horrific behavior, which seemingly stemmed from his experiences with an abusive father. Guilt over a past event, childhood traumatic events, and toxic parents are frequent etiologies for cinematic psychopathology.

All three of these sources of conflict are used in Hitchcock's *Marnie* (1964), with continued focus on psychoanalytic content. Starring Sean Connery as rich, handsome, successful Mark, and Tippi Hedron as the beautiful, mysterious Marnie, the plot line of repressed memories causing dysfunction continues. Mark loves a challenge, and Marnie provides it for him. She is not interested in romance and instead engages in kleptomania. Mark uses his discovery of her illegal activities to coerce her into marrying him. On their wedding night, she refuses his sexual advances and becomes unresponsive. In a controversial scene, Mark sexually assaults her. Marnie responds by making a suicide attempt the next morning. This sets Mark off to find an answer to the puzzle. He reads "Sexual Aberrations of the Criminal Female" and employs various psychoanalytic techniques, such as word association and dream analysis. (There was to have been a psychiatrist character, but Hitchcock chose to give this content to Mark, instead.[17]) As would be predicted, the uncovering of the childhood trauma results in a freeing of Marnie from her inner turmoil, ostensibly to then allow her to love Mark freely.

Paralleling advances in psychotherapy, 1963's *The Caretakers* focuses on the "new" approach to inpatient treatment—group psychotherapy. Considered to be a radical deviation from standard care, Dr. MacLeod (Robert Stack) confronts resistance from the head nurse, Lucretia Terry (Joan Crawford). While MacLeod is treating patients with compassion and freedom, Terry is teaching her nurses judo. MacLeod achieves his goal of creating a day hospital for the "experimental" group therapy patients.

Another portrayal of a dedicated, perhaps overly so, mental health professional occurs in *Sybil* (1976). Dr. Cornelia Wilbur (Joanne Woodward, who ironically portrayed the title character in *Three Faces of Eve*, 1957) treats Sybil and her various personalities in an intensive, one-on-one approach. Again, the psychiatrist searches for the source of Sybil's dysfunction. She finds it in Sybil's experiences with an abusive, schizophrenic mother. The therapeutic approaches portrayed in *Sybil* go beyond typical professional boundaries, unlike the treatment in *Three Faces of Eve* (1957). Wilbur is shown finding Sybil's childhood doctor and searching her childhood home.

I Never Promised You a Rose Garden (1977) reflects another strong female psychiatrist–female patient connection. The boundaries are more rigid in this film, and, as noted above, the psychiatrist does not extend herself (e.g., does not help deal with an abusive staff member).

Woody Allen's films routinely include reference to, or portrayal of, psychoanalysis. Allen is consistently neurotic through his films. *Annie Hall* (1977) utilizes scenes of psychoanalysis to demonstrate the differences in perceptions between Annie and Alvy and the state of their relationship. Psychoanalysis is presented in a matter-of-fact, almost expected way, further normalizing mental health interventions for the movie audience. Therapists are generally faceless in these scenes.

Perhaps the most accurate portrayal of psychotherapy occurs in *An Unmarried Woman* (1978). Erica (Jill Clayburgh) is dealing with the aftermath of her husband's affair and the end of their marriage. Although there are only a few therapy sessions in the movie, they are quite accurate depictions of psychotherapy. This is not surprising, as the therapist is portrayed by real-life psychologist, Dr. Penelope Russianoff, who was able to alter her lines to have more realistic dialogue.[18]

Although Russianoff brought realism to psychotherapy in *An Unmarried Woman* (1978), it is Judd Hirsh's portrayal of a psychiatrist, Dr. Berger, in *Ordinary People* (1980) that is often cited as a positive portrayal of a mental health professional. No longer the detached, psychoanalyst, Dr. Berger is a flawed human being who cares deeply about his patient. Even his raising his voice at the client is accepted and not considered abusive. The therapeutic approach reflects guided discovery, rather than omniscient interpretation by the expert.

Hereafter, movies with significant portrayal of individual therapy tend to present therapists as multidimensional human beings. We see this in Robin Williams' role as the reluctant, emotionally wounded psychologist in *Good Will Hunting* (1997). As in *Ordinary People* (1980), Williams lashes out at the client, this time physically in response to the client's personal insult. Risky treatment methods without proper authorization occur in *Awakenings* (1990), as Williams portrays Oliver Sacks in his treatment of patients with encephalitis lethargica. Yet a survey of the best portrayals of treatment/treating professionals finds these three movies of the 20th century to be the most favored.[19] Unfortunately, this multidimensional portrayal of mental health professionals has also led to less than positive characterizations.

MENTAL HEALTH PROFESSIONALS

Although there are several different professions which provide mental health services, movies rarely make this distinction. In a review of popular movies from 1990 to 1999, the professional identity was only clear in 29 percent of the movies (10 percent psychologists, 19 percent psychiatrists), with either "doctor" or "therapist" used in the remaining films.[20] This confusion is best exemplified in *The Dark Mirror* (1946), in which the mental health professional's credentials read, "Dr. Scott Elliott, M.D., Ph.D., M.S., Psychologist."[5]

As mental health professionals became increasingly popular characters in motion pictures, various categories of stereotypes have been offered. Gabbard and Gabbard, in their comprehensive review of approximately 450 films featuring mental health professionals, found portrayals in the first half of the 20th century fall into three categories: the Alienist (e.g., *The Front Page*, 1931), the Quack (e.g., *Carefree*, 1938), and the Oracle (e.g., *Blind Alley*, 1939).[5] Addressing more recent films, Schneider termed movie portrayals as Dr. Dippy (e.g., *What's New, Pussycat?*, 1965), Dr. Evil (e.g., *Dressed to Kill*, 1980), or Dr. Wonderful (e.g., *Ordinary People*, 1980).[21] Two more types were added by Schultz: Dr. Rigid (e.g., *Miracle on 34th Street*, 1947) and Dr. Line-Crosser (e.g., *Color of Night*, 1994).[22] Wedding and Niemiec offered eight primary themes of mental health professional portrayal: Arrogant and Ineffectual (e.g., *What About Bob?*, 1991); Cold-Hearted and Authoritarian (e.g., *One Flew Over the Cuckoo's Nest*, 1975); Dangerous and Omniscient (e.g., *Silence of the Lambs*, 1991); Learned and Authoritative (e.g., *Three Faces of Eve*, 1957); Motivating and Well-Intentioned (e.g., *Good Will Hunting*, 1997); Passive and Apathetic (e.g., *There's Something About Mary*, 1998); Seductive and Unethical (e.g., *Mr. Jones*, 1993); and Shrewd and Manipulative (e.g., *Basic Instinct*, 1992).[23]

Dine Young et al. attempted to empirically assess the motivations of mental health practitioners in popular movies. They reviewed the most popular films from 1990 to 1999 (200 movies) and determined that 34 featured at least one mental health professional. Through a rigorous analysis of the movies, they determined that most appeared in dramas, just fewer than half played a significant character, most were male (69 percent), and virtually all were white (95 percent). Regarding motivation, "concern for others" was determined to be the most frequent, although these characters typically also were portrayed as having personal flaws and weaknesses (e.g., *The Sixth Sense*, 1999; *Awakenings*, 1990; *Good Will Hunting*, 1997).[20]

Portrayal of mental health professionals is not equal when it comes to sex of the therapist. Dine Young et al. found that female therapists in the movies were more likely to be motivated by love than male therapists, particularly if they were young.[20] Male mental health professionals are more likely to be portrayed as incompetent, and female mental health professionals are more likely to fall in love with their male clients.[24] Gabbard and Gabbard found 29 movies across the 20th century in which female therapists had a romantic relationship with their male clients, ranging from *The Flame Within* (1935) to *Deconstructing Harry* (1997). In contrast, during this same period, they found only 17 movies depicting a male therapist falling in love with a female client, from *Carefree* (1938) to *Sphere* (1998). Even more disturbing is the difference in frequency with which therapists successfully treat their clients. During the 20th century, only 2 films portrayed a female therapist successfully treating a male client without romantic involvement, contrasted with 32 films featuring a successful male therapist with a female client.[5]

Female therapists also are often portrayed as single, without satisfying personal lives, emotionally restricted, and sexually repressed. The classic example of this template is Dr. Constance Peterson (Ingrid Bergman) in *Spellbound* (1945). At the start of the film, she spurns the advances of a male colleague. Others comment on her professional dedication. She resides at the institution, her bedroom adjacent to her office space. Only with the arrival of the handsome amnesiac (Gregory Peck) does she, literally, let her hair down. As her love blossoms, her elderly Freudian mentor comments, "Women make the best psychiatrists until they fall in love. After that they make the best patients."

In addition to romantic involvements with clients, other ethical violations occur frequently among cinema's mental health professionals. Confidentiality is violated for various reasons. In *Nightmare Alley* (1947), a psychologist works with a con man, giving him information about her clients in order to run a psychic scheme. Unintentional violation of confidentiality occurs in *Another Woman* (1987), when therapy sessions are overheard in a neighboring apartment. Among many other ethical infractions, Billy Crystal's character in

Analyze This (1999) tells his girlfriend and the authorities (without just cause) about his client, and his teenage son reports routinely listening to therapy sessions through the heating vent.

Criminal conduct by mental health practitioners ranges from falsifying records (*Angel Heart*, 1987), boundary crossing and participating in con games with a client (*House of Games*, 1987), and sex therapy (*Bliss*, 1997) to numerous examples of murder by mental health professionals, including: *Spellbound* (1945), *Dressed to Kill* (1980), *Bad Timing* (1980), *Manhunter* (1986), *Silence of the Lambs* (1991), and *Raising Cain* (1992).

Clearly, accurate portrayal of mental health professionals is not a primary goal of movie makers. Take, for example, *Mumford* (1999). This film portrays a psychologist routinely violating confidentiality, crossing boundaries, treating patients rudely, and a myriad of other professional practice violations. Even his clients note the unconventional conduct. However, his approaches work; his clients get better. By the end of the movie, when it is revealed that he, indeed, has no training in psychology, the message is clear—both training and ethical conduct are not required for successful treatment! This does little for public perception of the field, particularly when paired with the many movies sending the message that the patients are more "sane" than the mental health professionals (e.g., *What About Bob?*, 1991; *One Flew Over the Cuckoo's Nest*, 1975).

CONCLUSION

Psychological concepts appear in movies across the 20th century. Some are more explicit than others in identification of psychopathology. When considering portrayal of mental illness and its treatment, the latter part of the 20th century brought increased focus on specific disorders.

Films with a psychological focus have long been nominated for academy awards, and actors portraying a lead character with a mental disorder often win an Oscar (e.g., Ray Milland in *The Lost Weekend*, 1945; Cliff Robertson in *Charly*, 1968; Henry Fonda in *On Golden Pond*, 1982; Dustin Hoffman in *Rain Man*, 1988; Anthony Hopkins in *Silence of the Lambs*, 1992; Tom Hanks in *Forrest Gump*, 1994; Nicolas Cage in *Leaving Las Vegas*, 1996; Geoffrey Rush in *Shine*, 1997; and Jack Nicholson in *As Good As It Gets*, 1998).

During this same period, there were far fewer best actress Oscars awarded to women in such roles, and often the psychopathology was not explicit, typically only suggesting personality disorders (e.g., Bette Davis in *Dangerous*, 1936, and *Jezebel*, 1938; and Vivien Leigh in *Gone With the Wind*, 1939, and *A Streetcar Named Desire*, 1952). A few movies of this period won Oscars for their lead actresses, who did clearly portray characters with psychological disorders (e.g.,

Joanne Woodward in *The Three Faces of Eve*, 1958; Ingrid Bergman in *Anasta-sia*, 1952; Jane Fonda in *Klute*, 1971; Jodie Foster in *The Accused*, 1988; Holly Hunter in *The Piano*, 1994; and Hilary Swank in *Boys Don't Cry*, 1999). Fortu-nately, this award-winning trend for a female lead with a psychological disorder has continued, with films such as *The Hours* (2002), *Monster* (2003), and *The Black Swan* (2010).

Although the acting may be superb, as discussed above, not all character por-trayals are accurate. A survey of psychology students, psychologists, and mem-bers of the National Alliance on Mental Illness[19] reported the "best" and "worst" portrayals of mental illness and its treatment. *A Beautiful Mind* (2001), *Ordinary People* (1980), *Girl, Interrupted* (1999), and *As Good As It Gets* (1991) were the top-rated film portrayals of mental illness. *Good Will Hunting* (1997), *Ordinary People* (1980), *A Beautiful Mind* (2001), and *Awakenings* (1991) were deemed the best portrayals of treatment.

The overwhelming choice for the "worst" portrayals of mental illness was Jim Carey in *Me, Myself, and Irene* (2000), garnering more than half of the top votes.[19] Carey's portrayal of multiple-personality disorder, in which the main personality is passive and the alternate personality is "an advanced delusionary schizophrenic with involuntary narcissistic rage," was wrought with many ste-reotypes and stigmatizing behaviors. The only near-accuracy in the film is the disappearance of the alternate personality once the primary personality gained the ability to be assertive.

Perhaps reacting to the multiple ethical violations portrayed, survey respon-dents found 1991 to be a particularly bad year for cinematic mental health practitioners, reflecting the "worst" portrayal of the treatment of mental illness. This was the release year of the top three films in this category: *The Prince of Tides*, *What About Bob?*, and *Analyze This*.[19]

Moving beyond mere entertainment, more recently movies have been "prescribed" as treatment tools, often termed "cinematherapy." In their survey of psychologists' use of motion pictures in their clinical practice, Lampropoulos, Kazantzis, and Deane report that *Ordinary People* (1980), *Philadelphia* (1993), *The Great Santini* (1979), and *On Golden Pond* (1981) are the top four most frequently recommended.[25] Given the potential for inaccuracies of both mental illness and mental health practitioner portrayal, Lampropoulos et al. provide guidance in movie selection for the practitioner.[25]

From the first simplistic photoplays to today's computer-generated imag-ery, the film industry has evolved dramatically. Movies continue to provide entertainment to millions of viewers. Although most of the audience is seek-ing entertainment, movies have the power to affect attitudes. Unfortunately, in many cases, portrayal of disorders and particularly of mental health practitio-ners is not accurate. With proper selection, however, movies serve not only as entertainment but also as education about accurate, and inaccurate, portrayals of mental illness, and as tools useful in the treatment of psychopathology.

REFERENCES

1. Cressey, P. G. (1938). The motion picture experience as modified by social background and personality. *American Sociological Review, 3*, 516–525.

2. Blumenfeld, R. (2006). *Tools and Techniques for Character Interpretation: A Handbook of Psychology for Actors, Writers, and Directors*. Pompton Plains, NJ: Limelight Editions.

3. Kracauer, S. (1950). Review of *Movies: A Psychological Study* by Martha Wolfenstein and Nathan Leites. *The Public Opinion Quarterly, 14*, 577–580.

4. Fleming, M., & Manvell, R. (1985). *Images of Madness: The Portrayal of Insanity in the Feature Film*. Cranbury, NJ: Associated University Presses.

5. Gabbard, G. O., & Gabbard, K. (1999). *Psychiatry and the Cinema* (2nd ed.). Washington, D.C.: American Psychiatric Press.

6. Robinson, D. J. (2003). *Reel Psychiatry: Movie Portrayals of Psychiatric Conditions*. Port Huron, MI: Rapid Psychler Press.

7. Wedding, D., Boyd, M., & Niemiec, R. M. (2009). *Movies and Mental Illness: Using Films to Understand Psychopathology* (3rd ed.). Cambridge, MA: Hogrefe.

8. Zimmerman, J. N. (2003). *People Like Ourselves: Portrayals of Mental Illness in the Movies*. Lanham, MD: Scarecrow Press.

9. Ebert, R. (August 8, 1997). Conspiracy theory. *Chicago Sun Times*. Retrieved from http://www.rogerebert.suntimes.com

10. Nathan, D. (2011). *Sybil Exposed*. New York, NY: Free Press.

11. McIntosh, W. D., Smith, S. M., Bazzini, D. G., & Mills, P. S. (1999). Alcohol in the movies: Characteristics of drinkers and nondrinkers in films from 1940 to 1989. *Journal of Applied Social Psychology, 29*, 1191–1199.

12. Cape, G. S. (2003). Addiction, stigma and movies. *Acta Scandinavia, 107*, 163–169.

13. Haney, C., Banks, W. C., & Zimbardo, P. G. (1973). Study of prisoners and guards in a simulated prison. *Naval Research Reviews, 9*, 1–17.

14. Turner Classic Movies (2012). Jean Seberg: Biography. *Turner Classic Movies*. Retrieved on September 1, 2012 from http://www.tcm/com

15. Fuller, S. (2002). *A Third Face: My Tale of Writing, Fighting, and Filmmaking*. New York, NY: Knopf.

16. Rosenhan, D. L. (1973). On being sane in insane places. *Science, 179*, 250–258.

17. Spoto, D. (1992). *The Art of Alfred Hitchcock: Fifty Years of Motion Pictures*. New York, NY: Anchor Books.

18. Saxon, W. (2000, September 5). Penelope Russianoff, psychologist, dies at 82. *The New York Times*. Retrieved September 1, 2012 from http://.www.newyorktimes.com

19. Cannon, B. J. (August, 2009). *Best and worst movie portrayals of mental illness and its treatment*. Paper presented at the 117th annual meeting of the American Psychological Association, Toronto, Ontario, Canada.

20. Dine Young, S., Boester, A., Whitt, M. T., & Stevens, M. (2008). Character motivations in the representation of mental health professionals in popular film. *Mass Communication & Society, 11,* 82–99.

21. Schneider, I. (1987). The theory and practice of movie psychiatry. *American Journal of Psychiatry, 144,* 996–1002.

22. Schultz, H. T. (2005). Hollywood's portrayal of psychologists and psychiatrists: Gender and professional training differences. In E. Cole & J. H. Daniel (Eds.), *Featuring Females: Feminist Analyses of Media* (pp. 101–112). Washington, DC: APA Books.

23. Wedding, D., & Niemiec, R. M. (2003). The clinical use of films in psychotherapy. *JCLP/In Session: Psychotherapy in Practice, 59,* 207–215.

24. Bischoff, R. J., & Reiter, A. D. (1999). The role of gender in the presentation of mental health clinicians in the movies: Implications for clinical practice. *Psychotherapy, 36,* 180–189.

25. Lampropoulos, G. K., Kazantzis, N., & Deane, F. P. (2004). Psychologists' use of motion pictures in clinical practice. *Professional Psychology: Research and Practice, 35,* 535–541.

Chapter 11

Historical Perspectives on the Nature versus Nurture Debate and Where We Stand Today

Andrea Knestel, Amy Pitchforth, and Aaron J. Jeffrey

The study of abnormal behavior dates back thousands of years. Two ancient manuscripts (Edwin Smith ca. 1600 B.C., Ebers ca. 1500 B.C.) are believed to be among the first to outline early attempts to understand both medical and mental functions.[1] Demonology (possession by evil spirits) was an early explanation of abnormal behavior that often involved the casting out of evil spirits (exorcism) in an attempt to liberate individuals and restore them to normal functioning. Hippocrates (460–377 B.C.), a Greek physician and the father of modern medicine, who rejected the notion of demonology, believed that mental disorders were the result of brain pathology rather than the result of punishment by God. He advocated for mental illness to be viewed and treated in ways similar to other physical health conditions.[2] Hippocrates believed in the concept of somatogenesis (the idea that difficulties with thought and action stem from physical/bodily complications) and viewed heredity as playing an important role in understanding mental disorders. He classified mental disorders into three categories: 1) mania, 2) melancholia (depression), and 3) phrenitis (brain fever) and prescribed, for example, sobriety, celibacy, a vegetable diet, exercise, and bleeding for the treatment of melancholia. Hippocrates' notion of abnormal behavior further rested upon his view of balance among the four humors (bodily fluids)—blood, black bile, yellow bile, and phlegm—believing that an imbalance of the humors could result in a number of mental health problems, such as irritability, sluggishness, and changeable temperament. Although Hippocrates' views eventually gave way to modern scientific inquiry/methods, his emphasis on the importance of physical balance was most certainly a precursor for contemporary thought on what constitutes mental health/illness.

Hippocrates' views of mental illness were followed by Plato (429–347 B.C.), who saw psychological problems as growing out of the whole organism as well as sociocultural factors. Aristotle (384–322 B.C.), however, subsequently viewed mental illness, as did Hippocrates before him, as the result of improper bile functioning. Galen (A.D. 130–200) categorized psychological disorders as having physical (e.g., injuries to the head, menstrual changes) and mental (e.g., fear, shock, economic challenges) causes. In the Middle Ages (ca. A.D. 500–1500), incidences of abnormal behavior were quite prevalent, and historical records suggest that Europe experienced occurrences of mass madness (hysterical group behavior) and lycanthropy (belief in the possession by wolves and wolf-like behaviors). The observation of mass madness was particularly prevalent during times of extreme famine, social oppression, and epidemic diseases (e.g., Black Death). Demonology and witchcraft were also seen as causes of mental illness during that time. Robert Burton[3] differentiated between physical and spiritual possession by demons. According to Burton's views, those who were possessed physically were classified as mad, whereas those who were possessed spiritually were classified as witches.

More consistent with today's views, additional thoughts about the causes of mental illness were introduced during the latter part of the Middle Ages and Renaissance. For example, Paracelsus (1490–1541) believed that mental disorders were a form of disease (in the case of mania) or had psychic causes. Teresa of Avila (1515–1582) suggested that there could be an illness of the mind. Similarly, Johann Weyer (1515–1588), a physician who specialized in mental disorders and denounced witchcraft, believed that those who appeared to be possessed were in fact dealing with illnesses of the mind and/or body. Reginald Scot (1538–1599) also rejected the notion of demonology and suggested that sicknesses can have powerful effects on the brain and impair one's ability to make sound judgments.[4]

Early classification systems of mental disorders espoused somatogenic views. Wilhelm Griesinger (1817–1868), a German psychiatrist, believed that mental health diagnoses could be explained in terms of biological causes, specifically brain pathology. Griesinger's student, Emil Kraepelin (1856–1926), developed a classification system that focused on biological explanations of mental illness. Kraepelin viewed each mental illness as distinct from all others and regarded the grouping of specific symptom patterns (syndromes) as having an underlying biological cause. Kraepelin's classification system became the basis of today's diagnostic system, the DSM-IV-TR.[5]

As can be seen from this brief history, biological explanations of mental illness prevailed well into the 20th century. Interestingly, these medical explanations extended into "psychosocial theorizing by adopting a symptom/underlying-cause point of view"[1] (p. 51), where it was assumed that even psychological problems were caused by an underlying illness or pathology that was not necessarily biological in nature. These medical views were interspersed with theological thought that sin, possession by evil spirits, and witchcraft were potential causes of mental disorders. As described above, some views took social and environmental factors into consideration when explaining abnormal behavior. Additionally, psychological factors received more credibility during the so-called Nancy School/Charcot debate, wherein it was agreed upon that hysteria, as well as other behavioral disorders, may be the result of underlying psychological causes. Current views on mental illness are multifaceted and extend the nature versus nurture debate to the present day. In the next section we will review more contemporary paradigms of abnormal behavior with a specific focus on the emphasis given to explanations of nature and nurture.

BIOLOGICAL PERSPECTIVES

The biological perspective, or medical model, is an outgrowth of somatogenesis, espousing the notion that mental disorders have, at their root, abnormal biological functions.[1,2] A variety of biological factors have become implicated in the pathophysiology of mental illness. For example, neurotransmitter imbalances often play a role in schizophrenia, depression, anxiety, and suicide. Hormonal imbalances are most frequently noted in gender-related behaviors such as aggression. Genetic components of mental illness have been found in depression, alcoholism, and schizophrenia; chromosomal abnormalities can be seen in disorders such as Down syndrome. Further, differences in temperament are seen as stemming from prenatal and postnatal environmental factors and can be observed as differences in emotional and arousal responses and are often implicated in behaviors such as neuroticism. Physical handicaps may result from embryonic abnormalities or environmental factors, such as alcohol use by the mother during pregnancy. Mental disorders often associated with physical handicaps include learning disabilities and emotional and behavioral disturbances. Brain dysfunction can be seen in disorders such as dementia of the Alzheimer's type, and the deprivation of basic physiological needs such as food or sleep can lead to feelings of depersonalization or depression.

PSYCHOSOCIAL PERSPECTIVES

Explanations of mental illness that favor more of a nurture approach include the psychoanalytic, cognitive-behavioral, and behavioral perspectives.[1] According to the psychoanalytic model, mental illness results from unconscious conflicts, the repression of which may lead to abnormal behaviors. Cognitive-behavior theory's view of mental illness posits that maladaptive cognitive processes may lead to abnormal behavior. The behavioral perspective views learning as central to the development of human behavior, both normal and abnormal. It is believed that nature does not play a role in the acquisition of abnormal behavior and that changing environmental conditions can modify or eliminate undesirable behaviors.

Perspectives for explaining abnormal behavior abound and there does not seem to be a paradigm that is superior at explaining abnormal behavior. The model that will be explained below takes this into account and views abnormal behavior as the result of the interplay of multiple causes.

DIATHESIS-STRESS MODEL

According to the diathesis-stress model, or biopsychosocial model, mental illness results from the combination of nature and nurture, where nature refers to a person's biological vulnerability (diathesis) and nurture refers to a person's life experiences (e.g., stress).[2] Predispositions for mental illness can arise from a range of biological, psychological, and cultural factors, such as genetics, oxygen deprivation at birth, feelings of hopelessness, abuse, or cultural ideals. For example, a biological diathesis has been found to be a key player in the development of schizophrenia, and a cognitive diathesis appears to have a strong influence in the development of anxiety and depression. However, having a diathesis for a particular disorder does not mean that the disorder will develop; it only suggests that a person is more likely to develop it. This is where the second part of the model comes into play. Stress refers to some sort of life event that is experienced as stressful (e.g., divorce, death, or unemployment). The diathesis-stress model suggests that it is the interplay between diathesis and stress that brings about the development of a particular mental disorder.[1] In other words, the experience of stress may be needed to activate a disorder. The model further posits that a number of factors are likely at play in the development of mental illness and that the contribution of each is important in understanding abnormal behavior.

CONTEMPORARY METHODS OF ASSESSING AND EXPLAINING NATURE AND NURTURE

A variety of contemporary methods have been used to assess the genetic and environmental influences on mental health disorders. Twin and adoption studies, molecular analysis, and genetic and environmental interaction studies have introduced new understandings of the role of nature and nurture in the development and persistence of mental disorders. These methods also present a picture of questions that remain unanswered.

Twin and adoption studies involve examining how traits are presented similarly and differently for individuals based on common genes, common environments, or a combination of both.[6] By assessing the genetic trait expression of monozygotic twins, where siblings share the same genetic makeup, and dizygotic twins, where siblings share approximately half of their genetic makeup, researchers have been able to identify mental disorders that have a clear genetic component. These include disorders such as schizophrenia, bipolar disorder, attention-deficit/hyperactivity disorder (ADHD), and autistic disorder. Adoption studies, in which an individual resides in a genetically dissimilar environment to that of his birth family, have provided some evidence for a genetic component to schizophrenia.

Although the study of genetics dates back more than a century, modern molecular genetic analysis continues to provide answers in identifying specific genes involved in traits that are shared by the members of a family. Linkage analysis, the study of gene location on a given chromosome and their nonadherence to Mendel's law of independent assortment, and allelic association, the study of the locations and connections between certain alleles and concomitant gene expression, are promising methods of ascertaining the genetic root of some mental disorders. These types of analyses have been successful in identifying specific gene forms of disorders such as early-onset dementia of the Alzheimer's type and other early onset dementias.[6]

Gene × Environmental (G × E) interaction studies rely on the assumption that "complex mental disorders require an understanding of the interplay between genetic and environmental factors"[7] (p. 200). G × E interplay researchers seek to understand how certain environmental factors lead to mental health disorders in the presence of certain genetic makeups. Conversely, they also work to ascertain how individuals with specific genetic makeups only develop disorders when combined with specific environmental factors. G × E research has been conducted, and sometimes replicated, on mental health disorders such as depression, ADHD, schizophrenia, and substance use.

Although much progress has been made in the examination of nature/ nurture influences, there is still much that is unknown. The next steps and challenges in this area of study, articulated over a decade ago by Rutter,[8] are the same that continue to face contemporary mental health researchers. Those areas include: 1) identifying susceptibility genes, 2) explaining environmentally mediated causal risk processes, 3) examining nature-nurture interplay, 4) deciphering the effects of psychosocial adversity on the organism, 5) outlining the causal processes in rates of disorders for differing groups, and 6) understanding changes due to age in psychopathological characteristics.

Having reviewed both historical and contemporary views on the influence of nature and nurture on mental illness, we now present specific examples of mental disorders and the confluence of factors that contribute to them.

MOOD DISORDERS

According to the DSM-IV-TR,[5] mood disorders can be categorized as follows: 1) depressive disorders (unipolar depression), 2) bipolar disorders, and 3) disorders based on etiology (mood disorder due to a general medical condition and substance-induced mood disorder). There has been a longstanding debate in psychiatry on the respective contributions of nature and nurture to psychopathology in mood disorders, which has been reconciled by the assumption that both serve as contributing factors.[9]

Depressive Disorders

Depressive disorders is a broad diagnostic category which includes major depressive disorder (MDD; single episode or recurrent), dysthymic disorder, and depressive disorder not otherwise specified.[5] Research suggests that the lifetime risk for developing MDD is between 1 percent and 25 percent for women and 5 percent and 12 percent for men. The prevalence rates of dysthymic disorder are approximately 6 percent for both men and women. The prevalence rates for MDD and dysthymic disorder appear to be unrelated to ethnicity, education, income, or marital status.

These findings have led to speculations in the DSM-IV-TR[5] about the role of familial patterns in the development of MDD and dysthymic disorder. Specifically, it has been found that MDD is 1.5–3 times more common among first-degree biological relatives of individuals with this disorder when compared to incidences of MDD in the general population. Similarly, dysthymic disorder is more common among first-degree biological relatives than in the general population.

Nature. Changes in the brain (decreased levels of brain activity or lesions in the left anterior or prefrontal cortex) have been found in individuals with depression.[1,10] It has been shown that activation of the inflammatory response system (IRS) in depression is related to incidences of hypothalamic-pituitary-adrenal-axis (HPA) hyperactivity, suggesting that HPA-hyperactivity in depression is induced by pro-inflammatory cytokine. The hypothalamic-pituitary-thyroid axis has also been shown to be involved in depression.[1] Individuals with hypothyroidism, for example, show higher rates of depression. The neurotransmitters norepinephrine, dopamine, and serotonin have been implicated in depression, with no conclusive evidence to their precise involvement in the etiology of depression.[1] Similarly, disturbances in biological rhythms have gained some research support; however, more research is needed to fully understand the involvement of these biological factors in depression.[1]

Nurture. Parental mental health, the treatment of the child during childhood, and the long-term outcome of an individual's risk of depression stand in an inverse relationship. It has been found that children who are maltreated (physical abuse, psychological abuse, neglect) have a four-times greater risk of having a depressive episode turn into a chronic disorder.[11] In addition to the factors that impact the onset and course of depression, the question of what leads to "a cure" remains. For example, neuroimaging studies have shown that psychotherapy impacts brain physiology (i.e., chemicals). These findings have led researchers to question the validity of genetics/biology in explaining the cause of depression.[12] Furthermore, research suggests that an individual's body mass index, lean body mass, and level of activity have a direct impact on diagnosis, severity, and duration of depression.[13] Precipitating environmental circumstances in depression include situations that lower self-esteem (failing, being fired), the thwarting of an important goal or facing of insoluble dilemmas, the development of a physical disease or disability, a single overwhelming stressor or several stressors happening in a series, and insidious stressors that are unrecognized by the individual they are impacting.[14]

Nature × Nurture Interaction. The key to understanding the nature × nurture interaction for depressive disorders is the discovery of the mechanism whereby nature (genes) influences risk of a depressive disorder as a function of nurture (environmental stimuli). However, research in this area has confirmed the complexity of the nature × nurture interaction, making it difficult to provide clear or simple explanations about their influence on psychopathology. This has led to many studies examining each factor individually, limiting our understanding of an individual's vulnerability to mood disorders and associated development of treatment modalities. Thus, the diathesis-stress/dual-risk hypothesis has become the framework for research in depression. For example, it has been found that some individuals have a disproportionately high risk of being adversely affected by environmental stressors because of a genetic vulnerability.[15] The authors of another study found that chemical imbalance or change may be inherited and later mediated by environmental factors that lead to depression.[10]

Bipolar Disorders

The diagnostic criteria of bipolar disorders include episodes of depression, mania, and hypomania. Bipolar I Disorder is characterized by one or more episodes of mania followed by at least one depressive or mixed episode. Bipolar II

Disorder is characterized by at least one episode of depression followed by an episode of hypomania, with cyclothymic disorder being characterized by a rapid (short duration between episodes) cycle of depressive and hypomanic episodes.

The prevalence rates of bipolar disorders range from 0.4 percent to 5 percent in community-based samples. Additionally, the familial patterns of bipolar disorders suggest that first-degree biological relatives of individuals with a diagnosis of bipolar disorder or cyclothymic disorder have elevated rates of Bipolar I Disorder (4 percent–24 percent), Bipolar II Disorder (1 percent–5 percent), and MDD (4 percent–24 percent). Additionally, individuals who have first-degree relatives with mood disorders are more likely to experience an earlier onset of bipolar disorder.[5]

Nature. With the support of twin, family, and adoption studies, there is strong evidence of a genetic influence for bipolar disorders. Although there is an abundance of evidence for gene involvement, there is no overwhelming evidence for only one single gene being the main contributor to bipolar disorder. There is evidence, however, that the interaction of multiple genes and environmental factors contributes to the development of bipolar disorder.[16] The genetic nature of bipolar disorder is further supported by pharmacotherapy trials that point to the effectiveness of lithium and anticonvulsive drugs in the treatment of bipolar disorders. Imbalances of the neurotransmitters norepinephrine, serotonin, and dopamine are also believed to be involved in bipolar disorder.[1] As in depression, research points to the involvement of the HPA-axis in bipolar disorder and disturbances in biological rhythms have been reported.[1]

Nurture. Research has examined two types of environmental factors that may play a role in bipolar disorder: recent life events and social support. It has been found that individuals with bipolar disorder experience an increase in stressful life events before the initial onset and recurrence of mood episodes. Additionally, most research suggests that negative life events precede the manic/hypomanic and depressive episodes in bipolar disorder. The social support research has found reasonable evidence to suggest that social support from significant others leads to a more positive course of bipolar disorder, whereas negative support from significant others predicts a worse course.[17]

ANXIETY DISORDERS

The category of anxiety disorders in the DSM-IV-TR[5] includes the following diagnoses: 1) panic disorder with/without agoraphobia, 2) agoraphobia without history of panic disorder, 3) specific phobia, 4) social phobia, 5) obsessive-compulsive disorder (OCD), 6) posttraumatic stress disorder, 7) acute stress disorder, 8) generalized anxiety disorder (GAD), 9) anxiety disorder due to a general medical condition, 10) substance-induced anxiety disorder, and 11) anxiety disorder not otherwise specified. Prevalence rates of anxiety disorders vary considerably and can be as low as 1 percent and as high as 23 percent, depending on the specific disorder.

Familial patterns for anxiety disorders vary significantly between disorders but there is some agreement that individuals who have a first-degree biological relative with an anxiety disorder are up to eight times more likely to develop an anxiety disorder themselves as compared to individuals who do not have a first-degree relative with an anxiety disorder. The variation in the familial patterns suggests that anxiety is not a homogeneous diagnostic category, despite efforts to categorize these disorders. Research is inconclusive about the degree to which serotonin, autonomic activity, and physiological reactivity are involved in the cause and course of the disorder; however, it is clear that they are important contributing factors either alone or in conjunction with other biological and/or environmental factors.[5]

Nature. Across anxiety disorders, there is considerable variation in the biological and genetic factors associated with each disorder. In phobias, both genetic and temperamental/personality factors have been found to affect the speed and strength of the conditioning response, with an estimated 30 percent of the variation being due to genetic factors. While the literature on the genetic contributions to the development of GAD is mixed, OCD has received the strongest research support in this area.[18] It is further assumed that most anxiety disorders have a heritability component. A specific gene affecting the brain's ability to use the neurotransmitter serotonin has been identified in anxiety and neuroticism.[1]

Nurture. The experience of anxiety is generally an adaptive response to protect the individual from harm. However, for an individual with an anxiety disorder, the experience of anxiety is immediately preceded by distress or a highly stressful life event. Carson, Butcher, and Mineka[1] report that 80–90 percent of individuals across studies were found to experience their first symptoms of an anxiety disorder immediately following the occurrence of a stressful life event.

NEUROLOGICAL/DEVELOPMENTAL DISORDERS

We have defined neurological/developmental disorders as those that occur either early in life or have a slow onset in later adulthood, marked by multiple cognitive and/or social deficits. The disorders included in this review are dementia of the Alzheimer's type, dementia, and autistic disorder. The prevalence rates for dementia of the Alzheimer's type are 1.4 percent–1.6 percent for adults ages 65–69 and 16 percent–25 percent for adults over the age of 85. The prevalence rates for dementia are 3 percent, and the DSM-IV-TR[5] reports 2–20 cases per 10,000 individuals for autistic disorder.

Research suggests that being a first-degree biological relative of an individual with dementia or dementia of the Alzheimer's type increases one's risk of being diagnosed with the disorder. There is also an increased risk of autistic disorder within families among siblings of individuals with the disorder, with approximately 5 percent of siblings also exhibiting the condition.[5]

Nature. Dementia of the Alzheimer's type is inherited as an autosomal dominant trait with linkage to several chromosomes, including chromosomes 2, 14, and 21. However, the cases linked to specific inherited abnormalities are not known. Research has shown that individuals carrying one or both allele codings for apolipoprotein E-4 on chromosome 19 have an elevated risk for later-onset dementia of the Alzheimer's type, although the gene itself does not appear to be a cause of the disease.[19] While autistic disorder does not have a known cause, there is some evidence for genetic contribution from studies implicating copy number variation and single nucleotide polymorphisms associated with the disorder. In addition to twin and family studies which indicate considerably higher concordance rates among monozygotic than dizygotic twins, siblings of individuals with autistic disorder have a more than 20-fold risk of developing the disorder themselves. Additionally, there is evidence of subtle differences in social interaction, communication, and flexibility among family members of individuals with autistic disorder, which have been hypothesized to reflect genetic liability.[1] There may further be a link between autistic disorder and brain damage.[2] Research has shown that changes in central nervous system functioning may be brought on by meningitis, encephalitis, or tuberous sclerosis and may mimic autistic disorder.

Nurture. The non-biological factors believed to be associated with dementia and dementia of the alzheimer's type have fluctuated over time. For example, research shows that individuals who are exposed to lead in even small doses experience a decline in cognitive function that persists into adulthood and that manifests itself as a persistently lower IQ and alteration in behavior (both seen in later adulthood).[20] This is of particular importance because it has been found that work-related exposure to lead in adulthood is associated with poorer neurobehavioral test scores and with deficits in manual dexterity, executive ability, verbal intelligence, and verbal memory. There are no current trends in the research literature suggesting that environmental factors play a role in the causation or determined severity of autistic disorder.

BEHAVIORAL/ADDICTIVE DISORDERS

The disorders that will be covered in this section include eating disorders (bulimia nervosa, and anorexia nervosa) and substance-related disorders, such as disorders related to drug use or abuse, including alcohol, prescription medications, and toxins. The prevalence rates for eating disorders range from 0.5 percent among women to less than 0.01 percent for men. Researchers believe that these numbers reflect an underreporting of these disorders by both men and women. There are no clear prevalence rates of substance-related disorders; however, it is estimated that approximately 5 percent of the population have a substance-related disorder.

The familial patterns for eating disorders show that individuals are at higher risk of developing an eating disorder if they have a first-degree biological relative with the disorder. The familial patterns of substance-related disorders are striking, with an estimated 40–60 percent of the variance of risk being explained by genetic influences. The risk of dependency is three to four times higher in close relatives of individuals with substance dependency. Additionally, this higher risk is associated with a greater number of affected relatives, closer genetic relationships, and severity of the individual's dependence on the substance.[5]

Nature. When considering the risk and contributing factors of eating disorders from a biological perspective, the most potent factor is the female gender. Twin and family studies suggest that anorexia nervosa and bulimia nervosa are complex genetic diseases and that, for each disorder, the proportion of heritability ranges between 50 percent and 83 percent. It has also been found that about a third of the genetic risk for eating disorders, depressive disorders, anxiety disorders, and substance use disorders is shared.[21] Additionally, biochemical research suggests that endogenous opioids (e.g., beta-endorphin) and serotonin levels may play a role in eating disorders.[2]

Research into the susceptibility to substance-related disorders shows that biology plays an important role. It has been found that a key factor is a person's biological makeup or constitution. However, it has not been determined to what extent or how this influences an individual's susceptibility of developing an addiction. It has further been found that genetics are directly tied to cravings and the learning aspects of addiction.[1]

Nurture. Environmental factors involved in the development of eating disorders are believed to start prenatally. For example, mothers of individuals who later develop an eating disorder are more likely to be exposed to stress during pregnancy. Within the context of social values and social ideas of thinness, negative comparisons between an individual's body shape and that of the ideal may contribute to poor self-esteem and behavioral patterns.[21]

Individuals with parents who are addicted to a substance are significantly more vulnerable to developing a substance-related disorder. Additionally, children who are exposed to negative role models early in life and who have limited adult guidance often struggle with addiction to substances.[1] Research further suggests that many potential alcoholics tend to be emotionally immature, have high expectations of the world, need constant praise and admiration, and respond to failure with extreme hurt and feelings of inferiority.

SCHIZOPHRENIA/PSYCHOTIC DISORDERS

The disorders that will be examined in this section include schizophrenia, schizophreniform disorder, and schizoaffective disorder. The definition of schizophrenia has shifted from a historical definition based on the severity of functional impairment to a present-day definition based on presence and severity of symptoms.[5] The prevalence rates for schizophrenia range from 0.5 to 1.5 percent, while the prevalence rates for schizophreniform disorder are low (possibly five times fewer than the rates of schizophrenia). The prevalence rates for schizoaffective disorder are not known, but it appears that they are less common than the rates for schizophrenia.

The familial patterns for schizophrenia suggest that individuals with first-degree biological relatives who suffer from schizophrenia have a 10-times greater risk of developing schizophrenia themselves. Individuals with a first-degree biological relative with schizophreniform disorder or schizoaffective disorder have an undetermined greater risk of developing a psychotic disorder, and they are more likely to develop a mood disorder in the case of schizoaffective disorder.[5]

Nature. Research has shown that concordance rates for schizophrenia are higher in monozygotic twins than in dizygotic twins. Adoption studies suggest that biological relatives of individuals with schizophrenia have a substantially greater risk for developing schizophrenia, whereas adoptive relatives do not have the same increased risk.[5] Research into the biochemistry of schizophrenia further suggests that dopamine, serotonin, and glutamate may also play a role in the development and course of schizophrenia.[2] Neurophysiological factors, such as imbalances in neurophysiologic processes, have also received attention in the research literature. However, research in this area is still trying to make sense of and piece together the vast array of available theories and findings.

Nurture. It is important to note that there is ample discussion about the interaction between biological and psychosocial factors in schizophrenia. However, there is little research that supports these discussions. It has been found that family dynamics (including the mental health of a parent) are correlated with a diagnosis of schizophrenia. One such example is the high incidence of emotional disturbance and conflict in families from which individuals with schizophrenia emerge. Independent life events (getting fired, ending a relationship, experiencing a traumatic event) have also been found to precede the onset of a schizophrenic episode.[22] Relationships between social class and schizophrenia have been reported, with the social-selection theory (that those with schizophrenia experience a downward drift in social class) having received stronger support than the sociogenic hypothesis (that being in a lower social class contributes to the development of schizophrenia).[2]

CONCLUSION

Throughout history humankind has devised many explanations in an effort to understand the genesis and perpetuation of mental illness. In this search for understanding, biological, psychological, and environmental factors have been regarded as contributing elements. Over the course of time in the mental health field, we have scrapped, built on, and revised past theories to hone our conceptualization of mental disorders. We have moved from a predominantly biological explanation of mental illness into a debate on the influences of broader factors and now find ourselves embracing a more complex and integrative perspective. Modern technology and research now allow us to look at the microscopic building blocks of life, as well as the social environment, to delineate a more detailed picture than what was known historically. Although our more advanced methods are able to shed new light, they also present different challenges to the field in terms of replication studies and present new questions about the power of what we are able to explain.

Mental health professionals know more today about the roots and influences of mental disorders than ever before in history, and our knowledge base continues to expand. Our understanding, however, is bound to our culture and time. Just as the explanations of Hippocrates, Plato, or Galen could seem rudimentary compared to current perspectives, so may ours compared to the increasingly complex understandings of the future. In our current zeitgeist, mental health professionals and researchers can continue to study and present accurate information about nature, nurture, and the intricate interactions between them.

REFERENCES

1. Carson, R. C., Butcher, J. N., & Mineka, S. (2000). *Abnormal psychology and modern life* (11th ed.). Boston, MA: Allyn and Bacon.
2. Davison, G. C., & Neale, J. M. (2001). *Abnormal psychology* (8th ed.). New York, NY: Wiley & Sons.
3. Burton, R. (1624). *Anatomy of Melancholia*. Oxford, England: Oxford.
4. Castiglioni, A. (1946). *Adventures of the mind*. New York, NY: Knopf.
5. American Psychiatric Association (2000). *Diagnostic and statistical manual of mental disorders* (4th ed., text rev.). Washington, DC: Author.
6. Tandon, K., & McGuffin, P. (2002). The genetic basis for psychiatric illness in man. *European Journal of Neuroscience, 16*, 403–407. doi:10.1046/j.1460-9568.2002.02095.x

7. Wermter, A.-K., Laucht, M., Schimmelmann, B. G., Banaschweski, T., Sonuga-Barke, E. J. S., Rietschel, M., & Becker, K. (2010). From nature versus nurture, via nature and nurture, to gene × environment interaction in mental disorders. *European Child & Adolescent Psychiatry, 19*, 199–210. doi:10.1007/s00787-009-0082-z

8. Rutter, M. (2002). The interplay of nature, nurture, and developmental influences: The challenge ahead for mental health. *Archives of Genetic Psychiatry, 59*, 996–1000. doi:10.1001/archpsyc.59.11.996

9. Homberg, J.R. (2011). The stress-coping (mis)match hypothesis for nature x nurture interactions. *Brain Research, 1432*, 114–121. doi:10.1016/j.brainres.2011.11.037

10. Maes, M. (2011). Depression is an inflammatory disease, but cell-mediated immune activation is the key component of depression. *Progress in Neuro-Psychopharmacology & Biological Psychiatry, 35*, 664–675. doi:10.1016/j.pnpbp.2010.06.014

11. Brown, G. W. (2012). The promoter of the serotonin transporter genotype, environment and depression: A hypothesis supported? *Journal of Affective Disorders, 137*, 1–3. doi:10.1016/j.jad.2011.09.015

12. Bailey, C. (2002). Is it really our chemicals that need balancing? *Journal of American College Health Association, 51*, 42–47. doi:10.1080/07448480209596328

13. Chi Choy, W., López-León, S., Aulchenko, Y. S., Mackenbach, J. P., Oostra, B. A., van Duijn, C. M., & Janssens, A. C. J. W. (2009). Role of shared genetic and environmental factors in symptoms of depression and body composition. *Psychiatric Genetics, 19*, 32–38. doi:10.1097/YPG.0b013e328320804e

14. Kessler, R. C. (1997). The effects of stressful life events on depression. *Annual Review of Psychology, 48*, 191–214. doi:10.1146/annurev.psych.48.1.191

15. Nettle, D. (2004). Evolutionary origins of depression: a review and reformulation. *Journal of Affective Disorders, 81*, 91–102. doi:10.1016/j.jad.2003.08.009

16. Meltzer, H. Y. (2000). Genetics and etiology of schizophrenia and bipolar disorder. *Biological Psychiatry, 47*, 171–173. doi:10.1016/S0006-3223(99)00303-0

17. Alloy, L. B., Abramson, L. Y., Urosevic, S., Walshaw, P. D., Nusslock, R., & Neeren, A. M. (2005). The psychological context of bipolar disorder: Environmental, cognitive, and developmental risk factors. *Clinical Psychology Review, 25*, 1043–1075. doi:10.1016/j.cpr.2005.06.006

18. Baer, L. (2002). *The imp of the mind*. New York, NY: The Penguin Group.

19. Pitman, R. K. (2010). Posttraumatic stress disorder and dementia: What is the origin of the association? *The Journal of the American Medical Association, 303*, 2287–2288. doi:10.1001/jama.2010.767

20. Landrigan, P. J., Sonawane, B., Butler, R. N., Trasande, L., Callan, R., & Droller, D. (2005). Early environmental origins of neurodegenerative diseases in later life. *Environmental Health Perspectives, 113*, 1230–1233. doi:10.1289/ehp.7571

21. Treasure, J., Claudino, A. M., & Zucker, N. (2010). Eating disorders. *Lancet, 375*, 583–593. doi:10.1016/S0140-6736(09)61748-7

22. Lukoff, D., Snyder, K., Ventura, J., & Nuechterlein, K. H. (1984). Life events, familial stress, and coping in the developmental course of schizophrenia. *Schizophrenia Bulletin, 10*, 258–292. doi:10.1093/schbul/10.2.258

Chapter 12

Biological Views

James W. Sturges

As early as the Stone Age, there were biological approaches to mental illness. Some prehistoric skulls have holes drilled in them, with subsequent bone growth to indicate the individuals were alive and survived. This "trepanning" procedure happened around the world, and in some cases it was probably done to allow illness-related agents to escape.[1] Whether those agents were considered biological or spiritual, it was an early mechanistic approach to illness and probably mental illness.

About 475 B.C., the Greek philosopher-scientist Alcmaeon of Croton noticed that human senses of sight, sound, smell, and taste are located in the head and was the first to identify the brain as the location of intelligence. Plato and others came to accept Alcmaeon's view.[2] (Aristotle believed that information from the senses was perceived by the heart.) The well-known historical figure Galen (131–201 AD), who spent four years as a physician to gladiators, recognized that brain injuries meant changes in perceptual abilities, personality, and behavior.

In 400 BC, Hippocrates looked to natural causes in medicine and applied the ancient concept of humorism to human temperament. He believed that the imbalance of bodily fluids led to distinct emotions and behavior. Galen labeled these temperaments sanguine, choleric, melancholic, and phlegmatic. Arabic and European writers perpetuated the humoral theory, and though disputed in the Renaissance period, it persisted into the 19th century.[3]

Increasingly careful anatomical studies of the brain were conducted in the 1300–1500s, and in the 1600s, the microscope was developed. There was more to life than met the eye! Cells and tiny organisms were discovered. Germ theory emerged. Inoculation was discovered in Turkey and found to prevent severe cases of smallpox.[4] Sanitary conditions were undertaken for surgeries. Thomas Willis published an illustrated book on brain anatomy in 1664 and later invented the term "neurology."[4] There was a rise in mechanistic thinking, such as that of René Descartes (1596–1650), who envisioned the body controlled in a way similar to the hydraulic moving statues in the Royal Gardens in St. Germain, France. (Galen had been similarly inspired by the Roman aqueducts in his thinking of the role of bodily fluids.) There was a greater understanding of the developing of reflexive responses to stimulation, controlled by nerves.

Psychiatric conditions became recognized to be a product of disease, in part because the connection between syphilis infection and general paresis (or general paralysis of the insane) was well-recognized by the late 1800s. General paresis and other mental illnesses were lumped together under the label "dementia."

In 1872, Darwin published *The Expression of Emotions in Man and Animals*, which examined the evolutionary origins of facial expressions and other behavior. There was increasing recognition of the role of heredity (and natural selection) in behavioral characteristics. The French physician Benedict Morel (1809–1873) understood that in addition to "degeneration" caused by factors such as infection and alcohol or drug use, heredity played a role in mental illness. "Dementia praecox," as Morel called it (precocious dementia), was increasingly becoming recognized as a disease of the brain (e.g., by Emil Kraepelin, in 1893). Eugen Bleuler labeled it "schizophrenia" in 1908, recognized that patients with schizophrenia sometimes improved, and saw that it was not the same as dementias associated with aging.

Like humoralism, some speculation regarding brain-behavior relations seemed plausible but was simply wrong. Franz Joseph Gall (1758–1828) believed that regions of the brain were associated with personality traits and that stronger traits had larger brain areas that could be detected by differences in skull shapes. This launched the popular practice of phrenology in Britain and the United States, which lasted from about 1810 until about 1840.[5]

Jean Pierre Flourens (1794–1867) removed or destroyed the cerebral hemispheres, cerebellum, or brainstem in living animals, demonstrating that those structures were necessary for cognitive functions, movement, and autonomic functions, respectively. Later, Karl Spencer Lashley (1890–1958) would notice that the more rat cortex that was destroyed, the more impairment there was in learning mazes (the concept of mass action). He believed that this was because association cortex has "equipotentiality"—equal potential for carrying out complex activities—as seen in recovery of function after injury.

Charles Bell (1774–1842) and François Magendie (1783–1855) studied spinal nerves in animals, finding separate and unidirectional anterior spinal sensory and posterior spinal motor nerves (the Bell-Magendie law; though the existence of motor and sensory nerves had been noted by Galen). Johannes Müller (1801–1858) recognized that the information conveyed by nerves differed across the senses (the doctrine of specific nerve energies).

At times, human brain injuries supplied localization information, such as in 1848, when an explosion drove a railroad spike through Phineas Gage's left frontal lobe and he underwent a personality change. Frontal lobe functions include planning ability and social behavior, and Gage was reported to have deficits in both areas after his injury. In 1861 Pierre-Paul Broca treated a patient with almost no verbal expression and discovered at autopsy a left-frontal lobe tumor. In 1874, Carl Wernicke found speech comprehension deficits associated with upper left temporal lobe damage. These are the now familiar "Broca's area" and "Wernicke's area," respectively.

Camillo Golgi (1843–1926) developed a cell-staining method that allowed visualization of individual neurons, and soon scientists began studying synaptic junctions between neurons, including nerve conduction speed across synapses, and the resulting chemical changes around the cells. This allowed an understanding of neurotransmission. Resting neurons are polarized, but when stimulated, gates open and positive ions flow in. When a threshold is reached, the cell fires, releasing neurotransmitters into the synapse. Cell membrane permeability and specialized pumps return the neuron to equilibrium. There has been an explosion of pharmacology research on neurotransmitter agonists and antagonists over the last few decades, in large part to better understand and treat psychological disorders. Serotonin, the catecholamines, and other neurotransmitters are integral in psychological functioning and physical functioning in general. Neurotransmission facilitates rapid messaging; the endocrine system is its slower-acting and slower-resolving counterpart.

PHYSIOLOGICAL ORIGINS OF PSYCHOLOGY

In 1874, Wilhelm Wundt published the first textbook in psychology: *Principles of Physiological Psychology*.[6] He viewed it as only logical that psychology would make use of physiology and experimental methods to analyze mental processes. Often drawing on studies done with other species, Wundt began with illustrated descriptions of nerve cells and experiments on nerve conduction. He discussed reflexes and voluntary movements. He went on to lay out brain development, anatomy, and nerve connections. He often commented on differences across species, with a clear eye to evolutionary changes. He provided very detailed descriptions of human brain structures, surfaces, vascularization, myelination, cavities, and connections. He outlined olfaction, vision, and motor pathways. Using work by Wernicke and others, and the knowledge obtained by aphasias from various brain lesions, he described what he called speech centers. He created theories and schematics of associative thought and the formulation of verbal ideas. By the publication of the fifth edition in 1902, there were three volumes, including theories of mental elements and ideas and sections on emotion and the interconnections among mental processes.

Wundt's work was fundamental in establishing that psychology would include the biological perspective at its core. The empirical and at times materialistic approach of William James's *The Principles of Psychology* (1890) and the James-Lange theory of emotion (i.e., we feel sorrow because we cry, etc.) were also early endorsements of the inherent somatic nature of the study of psychology. Lange postulated that the formation of neural connections was a component of conditioned responses.[7] (Lange, James, and others believed vasomotor changes preceded emotional states.) James was often on the fence between philosophy and physiology. He tried, for example, to reconcile determinism with free will.

DETERMINISM VERSUS FREE WILL

Psychology studies determinants of behavior, such as heritable contributions to personality and psychological disorders, learning histories, situational factors, and internal physiological events. In these ways we explain the variance in behavior and mental processes. A retrospective perspective makes the concept of determinism more understandable; that is, if we look back at what led to behavior, cause and effect is more evident.

Some of our behaviors are well learned and fairly automatic, compulsive or impulsive, or symptomatic of Tourette's syndrome or other disorders. Others involve thoughtful decisions. The microstructure of the brain contains the genesis of both the automatic and the considered, however. Interestingly, there is evidence of measurable events indicating readiness potentials in the brain even prior to our own awareness that we are about to act. This was initially shown with electroencephalography (EEG) by Libet[8] but has been replicated with other technologies. It seems that, at least in some cases, we act first and then rationalize our "decision," reminiscent of the James-Lange theory of emotions. Regardless of whether that is always the case, we are certainly making our decisions because of underlying causes, many of which are not clear to us. The brain as a whole functions as a decision-making organ. Neural circuits have been shaped by both genes and what they have been exposed to. These circuits are stimulated by hormonal messages and neurotransmission, often triggered by events in the environment, as we perceive them.

It is often obvious to an individual that his or her own behavior is due to outside factors, while not obvious to observers, who primarily focus on the individual's acts rather than on the situation—the so-called "fundamental attribution error." Even acts and choices without visible external factors have causes, though, of course. And although we hold people accountable for their actions, even the criminal justice system looks at mitigating factors when determining sentencing and recognizes its own deterministic role in deterrence of future crimes.

James Cantor, psychologist at University of Toronto, discussed issues of legal accountability in the face of biological determinism with regard to the Jerry Sandusky case. Sandusky, a well-known college football coach, was convicted of sexually abusing 45 boys over a 15-year period. Cantor believed that whereas pedophilia is an uncontrollable condition, predatory sexual behavior is not. Stanford neuroscientist Robert Sapolsky took the analysis one step further, however, stating that we have to consider how biology applies to all aspects of behavior and that there is no part of us that is separate from our biological existence. By way of examples, he pointed out that brain damage leads to impulse-control problems, genes are associated with risk-taking, and that there are deleterious effects of stress on cognitive functioning.[9]

MATERIALISM

Francis Crick's "astonishing hypothesis" in 1995 was that consciousness is entirely due to the activity of neurons.[10] How that happens is still largely a mystery. One possible theory that might be helpful in our understanding of this mechanism was formulated in 1949 by Lashley's former student, Donald Hebb,[11] in his postulate of synaptic modification. Cells fire together, change, and become more efficient at doing so; neural circuits used repeatedly become easily kindled and triggered. Similarly, purposive activity develops when reward strengthens neural activity patterns, probably even in the high-level functions of the prefrontal cortex.[12]

The postulate of synaptic modification is the neuroanatomical parallel to experimentally derived laws of conditioning, learning, and memory. What is perhaps more surprising, though, is how plastic the brain is and how rapidly its connections change. Of interest along these lines, in the treatment of psychological disorders, is how changes in the way we use our brains can create desirable changes in circuitry.[13] For example, meditation creates changes in the white matter (mostly glial/support cells and message-sending myelinated axons) in the anterior cingulate cortex, which is the front part of a sort of collar-shaped formation around the corpus callosum (the bundle of nerves that connects the brain's left and right hemispheres). Among other functions, this part of the brain is associated with self-regulation, which is involved in many clinical problems, such as attention deficit hyperactivity disorder, substance use problems, and borderline personality disorder.[14]

Periodically, forward-looking artificial intelligence researchers will predict that by creating silicon versions of the brain, we will be able to replicate consciousness. Sometimes this is described as a way of instantiating the unique characteristics of an individual and thereby allowing some form of immortality. Unfortunately, although this might benefit others, it would not allow the individual to experience immortality. The individual would still die and cease to experience consciousness and have no awareness of the ongoing similar mental processes embodied in the re-creation. What is more useful, for the purpose of life extension, are the increasingly available artificial replacements for diseased or injured body parts. In one exciting application of this, rats and owl monkeys have been able to control robotic arms wired to the motor cortex.[15,16] Even neural prostheses are coming, beginning with the sensory system, using neural-silicon interfaces.[17]

NATURE vs. NURTURE

Our inherited characteristics and life experiences act together as the components of the well-known nature-nurture discussion. Psychology leaned a little too heavily on nurture's explanatory value from the 1930s through the 1970s. Some of this was due to the influence of behaviorism, exemplified by John Watson's 1930 assertion that given a dozen healthy infants, he could take any one and create a doctor, thief, and so on, through behavioral principles. Behaviorism had, in turn, been influenced by the British empiricists, such as John Locke (1632–1704), who believed we were born *tabula rasa*, a blank slate.

The approach of Johns Hopkins psychologist John Money in the 1960s and 1970s was a striking example of an overemphasis on environment as responsible for the characteristics of the individual. Believing that gender roles and identities were learned, he encouraged the use of sexual reassignment surgery for infants with ambiguous or damaged genitalia. This proved problematic, and it is now more widely recognized that genetically driven factors such as prenatal androgenization of the brain by testosterone from the developing testes play a stronger role in gender identity.

Careful twin and adoption studies have helped explicate the role of heredity and environment in the case of psychological disorders and personality traits. In terms of psychological disorders, it is clear, for example, that bipolar disorder and schizophrenia have a large heritable contribution while other disorders, such as major depressive disorder, have less of one. In terms of the so-called Big Five personality characteristics, heritability averages around 50 percent. Perhaps a more important point, however, is that environment and heredity act in a reciprocal fashion. For example, a child with an easy-going temperament elicits a different set of responses from the environment than does a child with a difficult temperament. The elicited environmental characteristics then further influence the child's behavior, and so on.

THE ADVENT OF PSYCHOTROPICS

Antihistamines developed in the 1930s and 40s had sedative properties, but there were already sedating drugs available (such as chloral hydrate). One derivative had euphoric and calming effects (promethazine), however, which led to the development of the first antipsychotic (chlorpromazine), trade-named Thorazine, in 1954, eventually prescribed to millions of patients for psychiatric conditions.[18] The antipsychotics did not represent a fundamental shift in the treatment of mental illness because somatic therapies were often used in the early 1900s, such as insulin shock, electroconvulsive shock therapy (ECT), and lobotomies (severing nerves to the frontal lobes). Lobotomies were done on tens of thousands of people in modern times, into the 1980s. A modified version of ECT is still in use, especially for chronic suicidality unresponsive to medication.

Because antipsychotic medication became widely and easily applicable, it propelled biological approaches and eclipsed other treatment approaches, especially for serious mental illnesses. Psychoanalysis, already being superseded by behavior therapy and humanistic counseling, now had added competition. The practice of psychiatry became primarily oriented toward prescribing medication. There were other societal ramifications of the new medications as well, such as contributing to the trend toward deinstitutionalization of patients, such as those whose positive symptoms of schizophrenia remitted with medication. This had both beneficial and negative effects for patients; it facilitated less restrictive treatment but coincided with serious problems of limited resources for outpatient treatment and housing and resulted in increased homelessness among the mentally ill.

Other medications followed the antipsychotics, of course, including antidepressants, mood stabilizers, and new anxiolytics. An interesting aspect of psychotropics is that they are used to target specific psychiatric conditions. This buttressed the general understanding of various psychopathologies as tied to particular neuropsychiatric conditions and reified disorders. For example, the identification of attention deficit hyperactivity disorder has increased since the 1980s, as medications became widely used in its treatment. Similarly, marketing of serotonin reuptake inhibitors in the 2000s influenced public perceptions regarding depression.

Primarily because of a shortage of psychiatrists, and after a successful long-term Department of Defense pilot program, New Mexico (in 2002) and Louisiana (in 2004) adopted laws allowing psychologists with extensive training in clinical pharmacology to prescribe psychiatric medications. There have also been prescribing psychologists operating with the Indian Health Service. Such legislation is opposed by physician groups and has been defeated in a number of other states.

RISE OF NEUROPSYCHIATRY

Fewer than 40 years ago, there was a question of whether schizophrenia was a brain disorder. General paresis was once treated with moral therapy (essentially morale building). Today, whereas the role of the brain is now clearly accepted, the link between genetic anomalies and brain anomalies is still under scrutiny.[19] Whereas the portions of genes being implicated in current research in psychopathology are often quite specific, there is the more longstanding general approach, through twin and adoption studies, of simply trying to quantify the degree to which particular disorders are heritable and the degree to which various personality traits are heritable.

Genotypes manifest in brain phenotypes, such as when male sexual differentiation occurs in utero because the sex chromosomes led to the development of the testes and thus testosterone. Phenotypes interact with environments, eliciting and affecting environmental responses, which in turn further shape the organism. Because even highly heritable disorders such as schizophrenia are not entirely predictable on a genetic basis (only 40 percent of monozygotic twins of those with schizophrenia have it themselves), it is clear that there are environmental triggers involved. The diathesis-stress phenomenon—a pre-existing vulnerability interacting with the environment—is ubiquitous in health, not just mental health.

THE IMPACT OF IMAGING TECHNOLOGIES

The research and clinical uses of positron emission tomography (PET scans) and functional magnetic resonance imaging (fMRIs) have been phenomenal. In PET technology, mildly radioactive glucose is injected into the cerebrospinal fluid, and the radiation in the glucose can be detected and visualized as it is metabolized throughout the brain. Magnetic resonance imaging, on the other hand, uses magnets to align the nuclei of atoms and then radio waves to alter the alignment. This results in nuclei rotating at different speeds in various locations and allows contrast to be seen across types of tissue. Very useful images are generated. Functional MRIs map changes in blood flow as the blood is used by cells. Both PET scans and fMRIs can therefore allow visualization and identification of the brain regions that are active during a variety of mental activities. fMRI has come to be used more than PET in the last 20 years, having the advantage of not requiring the radiated glucose injections.

Imaging has greatly supplemented the information gathered by neuropsychological testing and electroencephalography. Brain abnormalities have been identified in the risk for posttraumatic stress disorder (PTSD), autism, and other disorders. Activity in specific brain regions has been identified with mood disorders. Anxiety and depression involve complex interactions of genetics, biology, and the environment, and technology is allowing a revolution in this research. Even personality disorders are likely to involve poor cortical regulation of affect, and personality research now makes use of molecular neuroimaging and neuroendocrine findings.

Clinically, fMRI has allowed better identification of problem areas prior to surgery, shown whether medications have crossed the blood-brain barrier, and dramatically demonstrated the effectiveness of cognitive behavior therapy. It is now being used to predict which patients will benefit from psychotherapy and other interventions and to evaluate the results of various treatments for anxiety disorders and depression. Some have even called MRI the tool of choice in this regard.

PSYCHOPHYSIOLOGICAL ASSESSMENT

Biofeedback as a way of conditioning autonomic responses emerged in the 1960s. Reducing muscle tension as a part of relaxation became the focus of a great deal of research. Changes in heart rate and bronchodilation, body temperature, and electrical brain waves have also been measured in clinical interventions, and arguably underused. We know that anxiety problems involve not only cognitive and emotional difficulties but many somatic complaints as well. People with panic sometimes believe they are having heart attacks or will not be able to continue breathing, children with school refusal often have stomach aches, folks with generalized anxiety and PTSD experience chronic sympathetic nervous system arousal. PTSD is one area in which psychophysiological assessment has clear utility in treatment. Therapy involves carefully exposing those with PTSD to cues associated with distress, with the goal of extinguishing the distress reactions. A voluntary exposure trial is continued until the person's distress has diminished (e.g., by 50 percent). This can be better governed by monitoring the individual's physiologic responses, in addition to collecting subjective ratings of distress. There may also be diagnostic value in measuring changes in heart rate, blood pressure, galvanic skin response, pupillary response, EEG and electromyographic changes, or even brain activity as measured by fMRI.

MEDICAL VS. BIOPSYCHOSOCIAL MODELS

The wide acceptance of biological explanations for psychological disorders and medical conditions in general has had its pros and cons. The medical model has been remarkably resistant to change even as the biopsychosocial model has been widely touted in training and textbooks. The treatment of pain conditions and psychosomatic illness underutilizes the biopsychosocial model, for example. Effective pain management and treatment of other conditions involving psychological factors clearly requires an interdisciplinary approach yet is often treated without the benefit of appropriate behavioral medicine interventions.

In the case of the treatment of chronic pain, it is accepted that pain treatments should be addressed via somatic interventions (medication, physical therapy, nerve stimulators, and surgery) in combination with behavioral, psychological, and environmental change. The standard of care is an interdisciplinary approach that helps patients to identify behavioral and psychological approaches that serve to reduce their distress and increase their adaptive functioning. A variety of self-report measures help identify qualitative, quantitative, and temporal aspects of pain as well as its antecedent conditions. Treatment may include environmental and behavioral changes, relaxation training, stress management, and family therapy that takes into account operant factors maintaining pain behavior or low activity levels.

Physicians and patients alike ask inappropriate questions, such as whether the pain has (solely) a medical cause or (solely) a psychological one. To make matters worse, patients often feel stigmatized by psychological treatment for their pain conditions. Because pain patients are often referred to mental health providers as a last resort, they may sense an implication that the pain is imagined. Therefore, it is wise to start with validation of patient distress, which is composed of pain and anxiety. Their pain is what they are reporting; it is real and true. This can be followed with setting reasonable expectations for treatment: its goal is to reduce pain and increase functioning. In conjunction with addressing patient expectations, individualized examples can help illustrate the role of behavior medicine. Patients can often think of situational factors in their own lives that relate to changes in their pain experiences. Being engrossed in an activity may be associated with different perceptions of pain than is being unoccupied. Similarly, they may be able to see that the intolerability of pain depends somewhat on the significance of it: pain during exercise versus that associated with chronic conditions results in different levels of distress because of how it is interpreted.

Even beyond the well-known placebo effect, psychological factors play a role in effectiveness of medication administration. Scheduled or self-administered medications elicit fewer pain behaviors than occur with as-needed ("prn"), nurse-administered schedules, in which patients essentially need to demonstrate their pain. The more predictability and control that people have, the better they cope, and the better their subsequent health. This has been true across a range of conditions and populations.

Psychosomatic (psychophysiologic or somatic conditions) with psychological, behavioral, and environmental factors involve medical conditions influenced by lifestyle factors such as health-related behaviors and stress management. Not to be confused with somatoform disorders (e.g., hypochondriasis), these somatic problems include cardiovascular disease, ulcers, migraines, and many other conditions. Being more depressed, for example, makes recurrences of heart problems four times as likely.[20] Mechanisms for this include both direct physiological pathways (e.g., the hypothalamic-pituitary-adrenal [HPA] axis) and effects on mediating health-related behaviors. A common misperception is that lifestyle factors, as well as psychological and behavioral interventions, are irrelevant, and that causes of disease are almost exclusively genetic.

PSYCHONEUROIMMUNOLOGY

In 1915 Walter Cannon had shown the actions of the sympathetic and parasympathetic nervous systems on digestion—the so-called fight or flight response. By the 1950s Hans Selye's evidence of the physically damaging effects of stress on animals was well-established. But it was not until the 1980s that it became well accepted that the nervous system and the immune system work together to fight pathogens and suppress illness. It had been shown that emotional conditions reduced antibody responses in human patients, and that (originally drug-induced) immunosuppression could be conditioned to occur in rats in response to a saccharin taste. More of the neural connections to the immune system have since been discovered, and much more is now known about the relevant neurotransmitters and endocrine functions. The HPA axis is frequently identified in this regard, in which the limbic system triggers the pituitary gland to release adrenocorticotropin hormone, which causes the release of the stress hormone cortisol by the adrenal gland (which in turn causes feedback to the limbic system to curtail the process). Extended periods of elevated cortisol levels are damaging to the body.

PUTTING IT ALL TOGETHER

The human experience involves the body as a whole: nervous, endocrine, immune, cardiovascular, respiratory, digestive, reproductive systems. Understanding the physiology of these systems—how they carry out their functions—is implicit to psychology. Physiological psychology has experienced the convergence of work in biology, neuroscience, engineering, and other fields. It has, in turn, been at the foundation of psychology as a discipline, reflecting the fundamental material nature of the human organism. There is a clear trend over time toward an increasing understanding of the biological nature of mental processes. Psychological disorder after disorder has become, in some sense, the province of biology as more is understood about them. On the other hand, psychology is more essential than ever in the biopsychosocial era. There is an increasing and appropriate recognition that not only are brain functions biological in nature, but that our biology is shaped by experience, habit, environment, and psychological interventions.

In the future, we will see a better understanding of the microstructure of the brain and its originating genetic codes. The applications of this knowledge will be far-reaching. An ongoing challenge in biological psychology will be developing a more complete understanding of how information is encoded in the brain. Neuronal connections continually change, and neurons store information over time via molecules in the cell.[21] The distinction between brain as hardware and thought processes as software is obsolete. It is an integrated system.

Even as we come to better understand how cells store information, the sheer complexity of the number of pieces of information is overwhelming. It is inconceivable to imagine guessing the content of thought by looking at the brain. Or is it? Imaging can detect the type of mental activity that is occurring, whether it is of an emotional nature, whether it relates to new information or old, and whether it is challenging or automatic. Facial expressions reveal emotions and can point to deception. Psychophysiological assessment shows agitated versus relaxed bodily states in a variety of dimensions. Neuropsychological assessment quantifies myriad aspects of cognitive functioning. All of this supplements or is integral to one historically unique role of psychology, which is that of psychological assessment.

Some understanding of the biological aspects of psychology is crucial for all mental health practitioners but especially those in cognitive rehabilitation (e.g., for brain injuries and stroke), dementia, pain-related disorders, obesity, learning disorders, attention-deficit hyperactivity disorder, substance use disorders, obsessive compulsive disorder, the autism spectrum, anxiety, and depression, to name a few. Psychology and behavioral medicine are increasingly a part of all aspects of health care. Suzanne Bennett Johnson, president of the American Psychological Association, put her thoughts about the future this way:

> The mental health expert must be able to address a host of other behavioral issues important to health and well-being—medical regimen compliance, pain management, coping with disability or a life-threatening diagnosis, lifestyle behavior change. . . . This will require adapting to a culture of evidence-based practice and treatment guidelines, as well as communication and collaboration with a wide range of health providers from varying backgrounds.[22]

It is an exciting time in the field. We have come back to our physiological roots. What began as a graft of the study of the mind onto the study of the body has formed one strong tree with many branches.

REFERENCES

1. Glass, N. (1998). Brain surgery was done in the Stone Age. *Lancet, 351,* 1865.
2. Huffman, C. (2008). Alcmaeon. *Stanford encyclopedia of philosophy.* Retrieved from plato.stanford.edu/entries/alcmaeon/
3. Harvard University Library Open Collections Program (2012). Humoral theory. *Contagion: Historical views of diseases and epidemics.* Cambridge, MA: Harvard Library. Retrieved from http://ocp.hul.harvard.edu/contagion/humoraltheory.html
4. Boeree, C. G. (2006). The *history of psychology: Part three: The 1800s.* Retrieved from http://webspace.ship.edu/cgboer/historyofpsych.html
5. Sokal, M. M. (2001). Practical phrenology as psychological counseling in the 19th-century United States. In C. D. Green, M. Shore, & T. Teo (Eds.), *The transformation of psychology: Influences of 19th-century philosophy, technology, and natural science* (pp. 21–44). Washington, D.C.: American Psychological Association.
6. Wundt, W. M. (1904). *Principles of physiological psychology* (5th ed.). (E. B. Tichener, Trans.). New York: Macmillan. (Original work published in 1902).
7. Wassmann, C. (2010). Reflections on the "body loop": Carl Georg Lange's theory of emotion. *Cognition and Emotion, 24,* 974–990.
8. Libet, B., Gleason, C. A., Wright, E. W., and Pearl, D. K. (1983). Time of conscious intention to act in relation to onset of cerebral activity (readiness-potential). The unconscious initiation of a freely voluntary act. *Brain, 106,* 623–642.
9. Sapolsky, R. M. (2012, July 15). Head case puzzle. *Los Angeles Times.*
10. Crick, F. (1995). *Astonishing hypothesis: The scientific search for the soul.* New York: Touchstone.
11. Hebb, D. O. (1949). *The organization of behavior.* New York: Wiley & Sons.
12. Miller, E. K., & Cohen, J. D. (2001). An integrative theory of prefrontal cortex function. *Annual Review of Neuroscience, 24,* 167–202.
13. Slagter, H. A., Davidson, R. J., & Lutz, A. (2011). Mental training as a tool in the neuroscientific study of brain and cognitive plasticity. *Frontiers in Human Neuroscience, 5*(17). Retrieved from http://www.frontiersin.org/Human_Neuroscience/10.3389/fnhum.2011.00017/full
14. Tang, Y.-Y., Lu, Q., Fan, M., Yang, Y., & Posner, M. I. (2012, June). *Proceedings of the National Academy of Sciences.* Retrieved from http://www.pnas.org/
15. Mussa-Ivaldi, S. (2000). Real brains for real robots. *Nature, 408,* 305–306.
16. Nicolelis, M. A. (2001). Actions from thoughts. *Nature, 409,* 403–407.
17. Berger, T. W., & Glanzman, D. L. (Eds.) (2005). Toward replacement parts for the brain: Implantable biomimetic electronics as neural prostheses. Cambridge, MA: MIT Press.

18. JRank Science & Philosophy Science Encyclopedia (2012). *Psychology and psychiatry–therapeutics: From behavioral control to biological disease.* Retrieved from http://science.jrank.org/pages/10912/Psychology-Psychiatry-Therapeutics-From-Behavioral-Control-Biological-Disease.html

19. Frith, C. (2008). Editorial: In praise of cognitive neuropsychiatry. *Cognitive Neuropsychiatry, 13,* 2.

20. Frasure-Smith, N., & Lesperance, F. (2005). Depression and coronary heart disease: Complex synergism of mind, body, and environment. *Current Directions in Psychological Science, 14,* 39–43.

21. Black, I. B. (1994). *Information in the brain: A molecular perspective.* Cambridge, MA: MIT Press.

22. Johnson, S. B. (2012, June). Psychology's paradigm shift: From a mental health to a health profession? *Monitor on Psychology, 43*(6), 5.

Chapter 13

Psychosurgery through the Ages: From Lobotomy to Deep Brain Stimulation

Santiago Valenzuela Sosa and Genomary Krigbaum

Human beings have always been interested in understanding the human mind and in ways to influence behavior. Gottlieg Burckhardt, a Swiss psychiatrist, performed the first experimental topectomy (selective remotion of brain portions) on December 29, 1888. Soon afterward he reported his results on cortical excisions on psychiatric patients.[1] He is considered the father of psychosurgery. Also, in 1935, Fulton and Jacobsen published the results of their research on the effect of frontal cortical resection in primates.[2] This work inspired Egas Moniz, a Portuguese neurologist, and with the help of Almeida Lima, a Brazilian neurosurgeon, he performed the first frontal leucotomies on psychiatric patients. This process entailed a burr 1 cm hole made bilaterally in the frontal bone, where a metallic cutting instrument, called a leucotome, was introduced several times and moved randomly to cut the white matter tracts in the frontal lobe. The results were published in 1936, and it promoted the progression of frequently replicating the practice of this closed, blind, dangerous surgical intervention in psychiatric patients throughout the western world.[3]

Walter Freeman (neurologist) and James Watts (neurosurgeon) promoted frontal leucotomies in the United States. Frontal leucotomies were prescribed for schizophrenia, depression, anxiety, and obsessive-compulsive disorder (OCD). Initially, Freeman and Watts worked as a team; together they performed a total of 625 frontal leucotomies. Afterwards, Freeman developed the metallic orbitoclast, an instrument that allowed him to enter the frontal lobe through the orbit. With this new tool he didn't need a neurosurgeon. The procedure, named transorbitary lobotomy, was conducted under local anesthesia, sterilized, simpler, very quick, and reproducible. For instance, in one 12-day period, Freeman lobotomized 225 patients. Thus, between 1939 and 1951 more than 18,000 lobotomies were performed in the United States alone, and Freeman conducted 2,400 of them.[4]

In the 1950s, with the manufacturing of Thorazine (Chlorpromazine), the ethical objections to these surgeries based on the unacceptable morbidity and mortality rate, and the potential use as tools to control undesirable behaviors and profound damage to personality as well as emotional life, led to a progressive and sustained decrease of the use of surgery as a tool to treat psychiatric disorders. Therefore, due to the documented historical background, modern surgical interventions to treat medically refractory, treatment-resistant, and disabling psychiatric disorders are subject to close ethical scrutiny as well as regulations. This chapter will focus on the neurosurgical options to treat psychiatric disorder.

NEUROPHYSIOLOGICAL BASIS OF PSYCHOSURGERY

In recent decades much progress has been made in the understanding of the delicate intricacy of the encephalic circuitry. With modern advances in science, the way in which we understand the brain and its structures (including motor and emotional, as well as centers controlling the senses) is clearer now compared to decades ago. The cerebral cortex, corpus callosum, cerebellum, basal ganglia, reticular formation, brain stem, and spinal cord, are all integrated into a synergistic, interdependent, cohesive system.

With the advances in the neurosciences, the emerging insights gained from animal models, clinical surgical data, and (functional) Magnetic Resonance Imaging (fMRI, MRI) regarding the anatomical and functional basis of *behavioral and cognitive networks*, are amazing and impactful due to the high incidence of psychiatric disorders. It is interesting that out of 10 worldwide disabilities, four are of psychiatric origin: depression, obsessive-compulsive disorder (OCD), schizophrenia, and bipolar disorder. Depression, the number one cause of disability in the world, affects more than 120 million people worldwide, and in the United States it affects more than 18 million patients and is the cause of 30,000 suicides a year. Depression kills more Americans than breast cancer.[5] Thus, the high incidence of psychiatric disorders, its impact on the life of millions of patients and their families worldwide, skyrocketing costs of healthcare, and the financial burden impacting countries everywhere are primary motivators in the increased interest for evidence-based data that can add to our understanding of the disorders, as well as the implications in treatment.

The medical and psychological treatment of psychiatric disorders in the U.S. alone has an annual cost of over 20 billion dollars, which in a struggling economy, as well as in health care services, has a negative impact and long-term implications for treatment. For instance, 100,000 electroconvulsive therapy (ECT) procedures are conducted in the United States every year for severely clinically depressed patients, in order to induce some level of relief and stability. Nonetheless, it is a frustrating reality that even with all therapeutic efforts, 10 percent of patients do not respond to treatment, and in that group there is a 15 percent suicide rate.[5]

It is this environment of uncertainty and lack of multiple treatment alternatives that have made psychosurgery emerge from the shadows of the 1950s to become a promising and exciting therapeutic tool to help individuals with severe and treatment-resistant psychiatric disorders. The rationale for more aggressive therapeutic strategies depends on the severity of the disorder, which is determined by evaluating the level of the following:

Impairment. Limited functionality (personal, professional, and socially significant impairment).

Treatment resistance. Failed trials of several psychotropic medications and the lack of effective treatment choices.

Aside from psychotropic medications, ECT, transcranial magnetic stimulation (TMS) psychotherapy, and neurosurgical options, there are not many other options offered within modern medicine. An ethical principle that must be respected in all cases is to obtain an informed consent from the individual who will undergo a psychosurgery, because in the absence of a psychosis, individuals retain their faculties (insight and reasoning).

BEHAVIORAL AND COGNITIVE NETWORKS

Chronicity. Years of struggling with an uncontrollable disease.

Behavioral and cognitive networks have been localized in the cortical and subcortical structures of the frontal lobe. Current data indicates that *behavioral and cognitive networks* control motivation and drive, anxiety, reward and punishment, behavioral self-awareness and regulation, decision-making, mood regulation, and emotion. They also play a key role in memory and intellectual processes.

Psychiatric disorders are closely related to the frontal lobe circuitry dysfunction and can have different clinical presentations in an array of individuals.[6] Thus, it is important to understand the neuroanatomy of the brain; such concepts are outlined as follows:

The prefrontal cortex. It is the front part of the brain. Its dorsal and ventral compartments have intricate connections with the basal ganglia, thalamus, hypothalamus, and brain stem centers, closely integrating motor and limbic system functions.

The prefrontal cortex entails two functional compartments, which are as follows:

The dorsal compartment. Includes the dorsolateral prefrontal cortex (DLPFC) and the lateral orbital prefrontal cortex (LOPFC) and perigenual cingulate. Its functions include cognition and planning.

The ventral compartment. Includes the middle orbito frontal cortex and the subgenual cingulate. Its related functions are drive, motivation, reward, and punishment.

The dorsal ventral compartment (in relationship to the frontal lobe). It regulates the mediation of behavior and cognition. For example, depression can be present due to an overactivation of the ventral compartment over the dorsal compartment. More so, an overactivation in both compartments would be present in OCD.

The limbic circuitry. It regulates emotion, motivation, and reward. It has two components:

Cortical structures. It resides in the ventromedial prefrontal cortex, particularly in the orbitofrontal cortex and the subgenual cingulate. Recently, the agranular insular cortex has been included as a cortical part.

Subcortical structures. It entails the ventral striatum (nucleus accumbens, ventromedial caudate, ventral pallidum). All the subcortical structures are related directly with the amygdala and the hypothalamus. The anterior internal capsule is responsible for the whole connectivity.

Cognitive associative circuitry. It regulates the limbic pathway to facilitate conduct, plan behaviors, and act accordingly. Acts as a limbic system modulator, suppressing negative feelings and painful (things) stimulus for the top-down control of limbic responses to sensory stimuli and motor activity. Its cortical structures are located in the dorsolateral prefrontal cortex, the lateral orbitofrontal cortex, the parietal cortex, and the dorsal anterior cingulate. Also, the anterior internal capsule plays a key role in the connectivity process.

Function of the anterior internal capsule. It is key for the cognitive associative circuitry to run smoothly. The anterior internal capsule is a dense collection of white matter tracts, placed in the center of the basal ganglia system (caudate nucleus, lenticular nucleus and thalamus), and it mediates ample connections between the cingulate cortex, orbital and medial prefrontal cortex, and the vast extension of the prefrontal cortex (dorsolateral prefrontal cortex, dorsomedial prefrontal cortex). The function of the anterior internal capsule of enabling a smooth process in the cognitive associative circuitry makes it a great candidate for deep brain stimulation (DBS) procedures, which targets planned behaviors and the emotional regulation that happens in the limbic system.

The ventral striatum. It entails the nucleus accumbens and the olfactory bulb, and the ventromedial parts of the caudate nucleus and putamen. This area of the striatum mediates most of the emotional and motivational aspects of behavior. The ventral striatum connected/related structures have the function of their source and are as follows:

Amygala. Emotional aspect.

Hippocampus. Contextual information.

Midline thalamus. State of arousal, awareness.

Prefrontal cortex. Executive/cognitive information.

The structural and functional disturbances in the ventral striatum have shown a close relation to psychopathologies such as OCD, schizophrenia and addictive behaviors.

BEHAVIORAL NETWORK ORGANIZATION, FRONTOSTRIATAL PROJECTIONS

Health disturbances affecting the dopamine system can induce emotional, cognitive, and motor dysfunction. The parallel organization of specific corticostriatal pathways is well-documented, but mechanisms by which dopamine might integrate information across different cortical/basal ganglia circuits are less well understood. Haber, Fudge, and McFarland[7] analyzed a collection of retrograde (tracing from the end point) and anterograde studies (tracing from the beginning source) to understand how the striatonigrostriatal (SNS) sub-circuit directs information flow between ventromedial (limbic), central (associative), and dorsolateral (motor) striatal regions.

Haber et al.[7] indicated that there exists a sequential flow of information, which supports an anatomical basis for the limbic/cognitive/motor interface via the ventral midbrain. The ventromedial striatum projects to a wide range of the dopamine cells, and it receives a relatively small dopamine input. In contrast, the dorsolateral striatum (DLS) receives input from a lot of dopamine cells and has a limited input to the substantia nigra (SN). Nonetheless, the central striatum (CS) receives input from and projects to a relatively wide range of the SN. Three SN components have been identified: 1) a dorsal group of nigrostriatal projecting cells; 2) a central region containing both nigrostriatal projecting cells and its reciprocal striatonigral terminal fields; and 3) a ventral region that receives a specific striatonigral projection, and not a reciprocal nigrostriatal projection.

Thus, between different striatal regions via the midbrain, there exists an interface in which dopamine cells form an ascending interconnected spiral between brain regions.[7] With all this knowledge available, the medical and surgical neuropsychiatry community has been able to address psychiatric problems in a variety of ways that range from non-surgical to surgical approaches (i.e., psychotherapeutic interventions, psychotropic medications, and psychosurgeries).

SURGICAL OPTIONS TO TREAT PSYCHIATRIC DISORDERS

Lesioning. Surgically intervening in a key brain structure, causing a purposeful lesion through a well-directed lesioning tool. Two distinct key techniques emerge in the literature:

The stereotactic radiosurgery with gamma knife. Using the Leksell stereotactic frame, attached with four pins to the head, the patient's targeted intervention (to a selected brain structure) is located with 1.5 or 3 Tesla in the MRI. The outcome is a well-conformed oval lesion of variable volume, done using the strength of 201 rays of Cobalt 60 collimated to 4 mm diameter, coinciding in a precise point located exactly on the selected target.[8]

The stereotactic radiofrequency surgery. Using insulated electrodes with a 1 cm exposed tip placed into a stereotactically determined target (a selected brain structure), radiofrequency current is applied to the electrode at a temperature of approximately 90°C (194°F) for 90 seconds, making one or several lesions.[9] In some countries the microsurgical resection of 3 cms of the dorsal cingulum is still practiced in refractory (resistant) cases of OCD or patients with schizophrenia who have a trajectory of aggressive/criminal behavior. This is also called the Cairns-Paillas Cingulectomy.[10]

Stimulators, based on the DBS technique. It is the most advocated technique because of its good tolerance, reproducibility, and lack of harm to the encephalic tissue.[11] It started in the 1980's, initially stimulating deep brain regions to help manage and treat movement disorders. It was noted that the patients would improve in depressive or even hypomanic states, opening an opportunity for DBS to be considered in resistant psychiatric disorders (i.e., chronic depression and OCD, to name a couple). It usually consists in a stereotactic brain surgery, where electrodes (of approximately four poles) are implanted. The electrodes emit high-frequency electrical impulses (in a continuum), thus modulating neuronal communication. After the surgery, different electrical frequencies and stimulation can be operated in the patient in a remote-control manner.[12]

WHICH SURGICAL TARGETS ARE SELECTED?

The specific cortical and subcortical areas of the brain that are related to the regulation of mood, obsession/compulsion, anxiety, impulsivity, behavioral self-regulation and decision-making, aggression, reward and motivation, and apathy are typical surgical targets. The most frequently used targets are the subthalamic nucleus, subgenual cingulate, ventral capsule/striatum, dorsolateral prefrontal cortex, dorsomedial thalamus, inferior thalamic peduncle, posteromedial hypothalamus, and the amygdala. In practical terms, the surgical targets in relationship with the disease are focused on OCD: ventral capsule/ventral striatum, and the subthalamic nucleus; and depression: subgenual cingulate cortex, ventral capsule/ventral striatum, and the dorsolateral prefrontal cortex.[12]

THE MAIN DECISIVE FACTORS IN PSYCHOSURGERY: THE PATIENT AND THE TREATING TEAM

The patient selection is the most critical thing to do. It must be the result of a thorough case review and exhausting of all the therapeutic options available. In order to be selected, the patient must have met the following criteria:

+ Must have a proven disability that affects the individual personally, professionally, and in the overall quality of life. Also, the patient must have a proven track record of more than five years of chronicity and severity.
+ Must have a set diagnosis, taking into account multiple informants, a differential diagnosis (including a clinical interview, psychometric tests), and an analysis of co-morbid variables.
+ Must have exhausted all therapeutic options available, such as psychotropic medications, psychotherapy, TMS, and ECT (without positive results).
+ Be under the care of a multidisciplinary treatment team that includes a neurosurgeon, a psychiatrist, a psychologist, a social worker, and any other related health professional who has similar dedication and expertise.
+ Must consent to the psychosurgery. The patient must have exhausted all available treatment options and be informed of and understand the pros and cons associated with the surgery.

DBS FOR PSYCHIATRIC DISORDERS

The use of DBS for psychiatric disorders is supported by several years of evidence based on data with promising long-term results, suggesting that it is an effective strategy for the treatment of movement disorders such as Parkinson's disease, and now for resistant psychiatric disorders such as OCD and chronic depression.[12]

More than 200 patients with DBS implants in the following brain-targeted structures have been published: ventral capsule/ventral striatum: for OCD and depression; subgenual cingulate (BA25): for depression; subthalamic nucleus: for OCD. These procedures have a documented high level of safety and a reported 50 percent success rate consistently through a decade.

The transcendent work of Professor Alim Louis Benabid from Grenoble, France, in 1987, introduces the concept that high frequency stimulation (between 100 and 2000 Hertz) (DBS) induces a functional inhibition and excites the neural fibers in all cellular targets experimented on, thus inducing a positive therapeutic effect in different neurological disorders with secondary psychiatry symptoms. Benabid's work sets the stage for expanding DBS beyond neurological disorders.[13]

The First DBS procedure was designed to treat Tourette's syndrome, published in 1999.[14] It was followed (the same year) by the revolutionary work of Nuttin, Gabriels, Cosyns, Meyerson, Andreewitch, Sunaert, Maes, Dupont, Gybels, Gielen, and Demeulemeester, treating OCD by electrical stimulation in the anterior limb of the internal capsule.[15]

The DBS technique is based on stereotactic principles. The targeted brain structure/region is identified with fMRI/MRI. An anatomical map of the patient's basal ganglia is utilized to orient the neurosurgeon, but the exact location where the electrode will be implanted is decided on a case-by-case basis, depending on the patient's unique brain structure. To enter the brain and introduce the electrodes, a trepanation (burr hole) is made for each hemisphere. The use of microelectrodes to perform neurophysiological recordings or stimulation of the selected brain target gives the neurosurgeon a security about its exact location. Once the target location has been determined, a macroelectrode with four poles is implanted. In a remote-control manner, the electrodes are connected to a neurostimulator or pulse generator located in an area around the clavicle. After the DBS surgery, a follow-up visit is made at a psychiatric outpatient facility. The treating team that evaluated the patient before surgery makes the necessary adjustments regarding DBS programming, as well as follow-up decisions regarding the continuation of care (such as the management of psychotropic medication and psychotherapy).

DEPRESSION AND DBS

DBS performed in the subgenual cingulated gyrus and other frontocortical areas, such as the ventral caudate/ventral striatum and the nucleus accumbens, is associated with antidepressant effects in individuals who fail to respond to available treatments for major depressive disorder (MDD). The DBS exact mechanism of action is unknown. A viable theory is that DBS facilitates the connectivity and regulation of dysfunctional network activity, as well as modulates executive functioning (frontal lobe), mood/anxiety (limbic system), and reward networks.

Kopell, Halverson, Butson, Dickinson, Bobholz, Harsch, Rainey, Kondziolka, Howland, Eskandar, Evans, and Dougherty[16] implanted an electrode over

Brodman areas 9 and 46 (dorsolateral prefrontal cortex) in the left hemisphere of 12 patients suffering from MDD, who were resistant to available treatment. This was performed in a controlled study, randomized, single-blinded, and with 104 weeks outpatient follow-up (after the DBS surgery). The Hamilton Depression Rating Scale-28 (HDRS-28), Montgomery-Asberg Depression Rating Scale (MADRS), Global Assessment of Function (GAF), and Quality of Life Enjoyment and Satisfaction (QLES) questionnaire were administered as outcome measures. The results of the study showed a positive trend toward efficacy. Six patients had 40 percent or greater improvement, five patients had 50 percent or greater improvement, and four patients achieved remission during the study.[16]

Another target in the DBS treatment of chronic depression is the Subcallosal Cingulate Gyrus Brodman Area 25 (SCG BA25). In a recently published, 12-month, three-center prospective, open-label trial of DBS on the SCG BA25, in patients with treatment-resistant depression, the authors examined the reduction in depressive symptoms as defined by the Hamilton Rating Scale for Depression (HRSD-17) score in comparison to the scores before the DBS. The response rate, after 12 months of DBS, was 62 percent.[17]

Mayberg, Lozano, Vons, McNeely, Seminowicz, Hamani, Schwab, and Kennedy observed that the SCG BA25 is metabolically overactive in treatment-resistant depression.[18] They also indicated that antidepressant effects were associated with a marked reduction in local cerebral blood flow, as well as changes in downstream limbic and cortical sites, which were measured using positron emission tomography. Mayberg et al. implanted DBS electrodes to modulate the overactive SCG BA25 in six patients presenting with treatment-resistant depression. Deep stimulation of white matter tracts adjacent to the subgenual cingulated gyrus was associated with a sustained remission of depression in four of six patients. It was concluded that disrupting the focal dysfunctional activity in the limbic-cortical circuits, using electrical stimulation in the subgenual cingulated white matter, could effectively reverse symptoms in otherwise treatment-resistant depression.[19]

Also, the use of DBS in the ventral capsule and ventral striatum (VC/VS) could also be beneficial for patients suffering from chronic treatment-resistant depression. An open label study of 15 patients, using as outcome measures the Hamilton Depression Rating Scale-24 item (HDRS-24), the Montgomery-Asberg Depression Rating Scale (MADRS), and the GAF, showed a 53.3 percent reduction of main symptoms with 40 percent remission sustained for more than three years. The authors stated that DBS was well tolerated in all patients.[20]

Another DBS technique, with positive results, to treat chronic treatment-resistant depression, is the bilateral epidural prefrontal cortical stimulation. Nahas, Anderson, Borckardt, Arana, George, Reeves, and Takacs located the electrodes (in both sides of the brain) over the anterior frontal and midlateral prefrontal cortex in five adults who failed available treatments. All of them were followed (post–DBS surgery) for seven months and were administered the Hamilton Rating Scale for Depression and the Inventory of Depressive Symptoms Self-Report. Three participants reached remission. Thus, DBS (bilateral) in the epidural prefrontal cortical brain region poses a promising new technology for the treatment of resistant depression.[21]

OCD AND DBS

OCD is classified as an anxiety disorder and is characterized by recurrent, unwanted, distressing thoughts (obsessions) of harm avoidance, order, cleanliness, and so forth. It is also mixed with repetitive irresistible behaviors (compulsions), such as checking, counting, and washing rituals. The patient acknowledged these (obsessions/compulsions) as senseless or excessive habits, at some point during the course of the disorder. The compulsions are usually helpful in reducing the experienced anxiety, yet they are not necessarily pleasurable. This disorder may be profoundly disabling. Two to three percent of the U.S. population is affected by this disorder, and 10 percent of the individuals affected are resistant to the available treatment.[22]

Many theories attempt to explain the physiological etiology of this disorder. Considered one of the most accepted physiological explanations, a new neuro-physiological theory involving basal ganglia/orbitofrontal cortex circuitry dysfunction is promising. It stipulates that OCD symptoms appear when striato-pallido-thalamic activity is abnormally decreased or orbitofronto-thalamic activity is abnormally increased. In this process, the interaction of the neurotransmitters gaba (inhibitory, decreases), glutamate (excitatory, increases), and aspartate (as a glutamate associated neurotransmitter) plays a key role.[22]

Many lines of evidence point to dysfunction of orbitofrontal-subcortical circuitry in patients with OCD. fMRI studies have shown that hyperactivity in the orbitofrontal-subcortical circuitry in OCD could be explained as the result of an abnormal neuroanatomical development, or as the failure in the pruning of neuronal connections between them during childhood development. Saxena and Rauch stated, first, that a phenotypic heterogeneity could account for many of the inconsistencies among previous neuroimaging studies of OCD; and second, that although an abundance of indirect evidence suggests serotonergic abnormalities in patients with OCD, no direct evidence demonstrates what those abnormalities are or whether they are primary or secondary phenomena in patients with OCD.[22]

For many health professionals this disease seemed to be hopeless and treatment-resistant. Psychotherapy (focusing on the exposure to the trigger and response prevention) can be more useful than psychotropic medication (such as selective serotonin reuptake inhibitors [SSRIs] like fluoxetine, sertraline, paroxetine) as a long-term continuation of care. In individuals with comorbid tic disorders, adding atypical antipsychotics (such as Quetapine, Risperidone) to their medication management has shown a 50 percent response rate. Also, non-pharmacological biological treatments like ECT, TMS, and repetitive transcranial magnetic stimulation (rTMS) have been used with mitigated results. Nonetheless, just as with psychotropic medication, they have not produced the clinical results for remittance and/or remission from the disorder.[23]

Lesional neurosurgery with the techniques of stereotactic thermocoagulation and gamma knife capsulotomy has been conducted with some success. The stereotactic thermocoagulation entails three types of procedures outlined as follows:

Cingulotomy. It includes the lesioning of the cingulum.

Limbic Leucotomy. It entails performing an anterior cingulotomy and a subcaudate tractotomy.

Anterior Capsulotomy. It involves the lesioning of the anterior limb of the internal capsule.[9]

The gamma knife capsulotomy entails creating a bilateral 8 mm oval-shaped lesion in the anterior limb of the internal capsule, at the putaminal midpoint, with stereotactic Cobalt 60–based radiosurgery. It has been reported that this can objectively ameliorate the symptoms of OCD in all the patients treated.[8]

Specific DBS Treatment for OCD

Milad and Rauch highlighted that new neuroimaging evidence indicates the critical involvement of the lateral and medial orbitofrontal cortices, the dorsal anterior cingulated cortex and amygdalo-cortical circuitry, and the cortico-striatal circuitry, in the pathophysiology of OCD.[23]

Nuttin, Cosyns, Demeulemeester, Gybels, and Meyerson decided to implant DBS quadripolar electrodes in both anterior limbs of the internal capsules in six patients with treatment-resistant OCD. They decided to perform this technique instead of lesioning because of the inherent risk of complications due to bilateral anterior capsulotomy.[9] A team of psychiatrists and psychologists performed a double-blind clinical assessment. A blinded random crossover design was used to assess four of those patients who underwent continuous stimulation for at least 21 months after surgery. As defined by the Clinical Global Improvement assessment, the scores were unchanged in one patient and highly improved in three other patients during stimulation. It was concluded that the bilateral stimulation led to increased signal on fMRI follow-up studies, especially in the pons (brain region). Fluorine-18-deoxyglucose (FDG) positron emission tomographic (PET) scans obtained after 3 months of DBS showed decreased frontal metabolism during stimulation. The researchers indicated that after 21 months of post–DBS surgery follow-up, the capsular stimulation mitigates the primary symptoms in patients with long-standing, chronic, treatment-resistant OCD.[24]

Patients who underwent DBS surgery for treatment-resistant OCD showed an improvement of 60 percent (as defined) in psychometric scales widely used in OCD testing protocols, such as the Hamilton Rating Scale for Depression (HAM-D) and the Yale-Brown Obsessive Compulsive Scale (YBOCS). The Food and Drug Administration (FDA) approved the DBS procedure for OCD under the US-Humanitarian Device Exemption (HDE) program on February 19, 2009.[25]

Greenberg, Malone, Friehs, Rezai, Kubu, Malloy, Salloway, Okun, Goodman, and Rasmussen published a three-year follow-up of eight patients who were affected by treatment-resistant OCD and underwent DBS surgery. Four of those patients experienced a strong improvement in their symptoms, defined by YBOCS and the GAF (including a decrease in depressive and anxiety symptoms and an increase in self-care and functioning in all areas—work/academic, personal, and social). During the course of the three-year follow-up, when the DBS was interrupted by stimulator battery depletion, the symptoms of the disorder immediately reappeared. Even with the promising prospect of DBS surgical treatment for treatment-resistant OCD, it is important to take into account that some adverse side effects may include a single seizure, asymptomatic hemorrhage, and a small (acute) infection.[26]

In the last 10 years, a multicenter collaboration has facilitated a very impressive improvement in the selection criteria of patients, the technical details of the surgery (the choice of a more posterior target at the junction of the anterior capsule, anterior commissure, and posterior ventral striatum), and the quality of post-operatory follow-up. This has produced long-term clinical benefits in two-thirds of the DBS-implanted patients. DBS is currently accepted as a robust tool to deal with the severely affected OCD patients.[27]

OTHER BEHAVIORAL AND PSYCHIATRIC DISORDERS CONSIDERED FOR DBS TREATMENT

The low morbidity, reversibility, and adaptability of DBS make it suitable to treat a wide array of clinical psychopathologies like addiction, aggressiveness, anorexia, obesity, minimally conscious states, mild cognitive impairment, or the memory deficits reported in Alzheimer's disease.[11]

As research and the DBS treatment exploration continue, some brain regions or targets have been identified for the treatment of the following conditions:

Addiction (Heroin, Alcoholism, and Opium). The nucleus accumbens
Aggressiveness. The posterior hypothalamus

Anorexia Nervosa. The ventral capsule/ventral striatum
Minimally conscious states. The thalamus intralaminar nuclei
Obesity. The ventromedial nucleus of the hypothalamus

Close attention has been given to the neurobehavioral circuits' dysfunction in addiction (particularly cocaine). This condition is associated with neuro-adaptative changes in the frontostriatal brain system. Ersche, Barnes, Jones, Morein-Zamir, Robbins, and Bullmore analyzed behavioral and structural MRI data of 60 cocaine-dependent individuals and compared it with a similar number of healthy participants. They investigated the relationship between gray matter–volume variations, duration of cocaine use, and measures of impulsivity and compulsivity in the cocaine-dependent group. After careful analysis of the data, they found that 1) Cocaine dependence was associated with an extensive system of abnormally decreased volume of gray matter in the orbitofrontal, cingulated, insular, temporoparietal, and cerebellar cortex, with a localized increase in gray matter–volume in the basal ganglia; 2) Greater duration of cocaine dependence was correlated with greater reduction in gray matter–volume in the orbitofrontal, cingulated, and insular cortex; 3) Greater impairment of attentional control was associated with reduced volume in the insular cortex and increased volume in the caudate nucleus; and 4) Greater compulsivity of drug use was associated with reduced volume in the orbitofrontal cortex. Based on these findings, the researchers concluded that the cocaine-dependent participants showed structural abnormality in the corticostriatal brain systems and variability in the extent of anatomical changes in orbitofrontal, insular, and striatal structures, which was highly correlated to individual differences in the intensity, frequency, and duration of the dependence, inattention, and compulsivity in the consumption of cocaine.[28] Although this research indicates that a structural abnormality was found, it is not possible to assert that the abnormality was always there, since drugs such as cocaine have been shown to produce anomaly in the brain structural circuitry.

Interestingly, in our quest for evidence-based treatment approaches, traditional chinese medicine (TCM), such as acupuncture, has been shown to also be an alternative type of brain stimulation treatment (in controlled clinical trials), conducted by skillful and expert TCM practitioners. For instance, it is endorsed by the World Health Organization (WHO) in the treatment of psychiatric (and related neurological) disorders that include, but are not limited to, depression/neurotic depression, stroke, stroke/depression, Tourette's syndrome, drug addictions, and pain disorders. It is reported that a collaborative study between Hong Kong and London yielded results of raised endorphin concentrations, stimulated by acupuncture in heroin-dependent individuals, which resulted in the effective suppression of the withdrawal symptoms. Due to the amount of evidence and research outcome, acupuncture is currently used as an adjunct treatment in substance-abuse recovery programs. Conversely, acupuncture has been found to positively affect depression with close to no side effects in comparison to psychotropic medication (such as Amitriptyline).[29] Although this is an at least 2,000-years-old treatment approach (for many of the known medical ailments), we are just in the beginning stages to understand its mode of efficacy and process. However, there is no doubt that, as psychosurgery, it is a viable and available treatment for chronic, treatment-resistant psychiatric disorders (as per standard of care protocols).

Nonetheless, psychosurgery has greatly developed since its beginnings, and it has claimed its place among the biomedical treatments as a feasible option for treatment-resistant psychiatric disorders. The expertise of the neurosurgeon and the skillful execution of lesional approaches through stereotactic techniques, coupled with advanced imaging and the high index of safety/efficacy of DBS, make of the modern psychosurgery a promising therapeutic approach to treat severely ill psychiatric patients.

REFERENCES

1. Burckhardt, G. (1891). Über Rindenexcisionen, als Beitrag zur operativen Therapie der Psychosen. *Allegemeine Z Psychiatry, 47,* 463–548.

2. Fulton, J. F., & Jacobsen, D. F. (1935). The functions of the frontal lobes: A comparative study in monkeys, chimpanzees, and man. *Advances in Modern Biology (Moscow), 4,* 113–125.

3. Moniz, E. (1936). Essai d'un traitement chirurgical de certaines psychoses. *Bulletin de l'Académie Nationale de Médecine, 115,* 385–392.

4. Freeman, W., & Watts, J. (Eds.) (1950). *Psychosurgery: In the treatment of mental disorders and intractable pain.* Springfield, IL: C. Thomas.

5. National Institute of Mental Health (n.d.). *Statistics.* Retrieved on June 19, 2012 from http://www.nimh.nih.gov/statistics/index.shtml

6. Bressler, S. L., & Menon, V. (2010). Large-scale brain networks in cognition: Emerging methods and principles. *Trends in Cognitive Sciences, 14,* 277–290. doi: 10.1016/j.tics.2010.04.004

7. Haber, S. N, Fudge, J. L., & McFarland, N. R. (2000). Striatonigrostriatal pathways in primates form an ascending spiral from the shell to the dorsolateral striatum. *Journal of Neuroscience, 20* (6), 2369–2382.

8. Kondziolka, D., Flickinger, J. C., & Hudak, R. (2011). Results following gamma knife radiosurgical anterior capsulotomies for obsessive compulsive disorder. *Neurosurgery, 68* (1), 28–32.

9. Montoya, A., Weiss, A. P., Price, H. P., Cassem, E. H., Dougherty, D. D., Nierenberg, A., Cosgrove, G. R. (2002). Magnetic resonance imaging-guided stereotactic limbic leukotomy for treatment of intractable psychiatric disease. *Neurosurgery, 50* (5), 1043–1052.

10. Valenzuela-Sosa, S. (2010). Cingulectomy type Cairns-Paillas: An effective, accessible and safe psychosurgery technique. *Proceedings from the VII Congress of the Latin-American Colleges of Neuropsychopharmacology*. The Dominican Republic: Bayahibe, La Romana.

11. Benabid, A. L., & Torres, N. (2012). New targets for DBS. *Parkinsonism Related Disorders, 18* (1), 21–23.

12. Kuhn, J., Gründler, T. O. J., Lenartz, D., Sturm, V., Klosterkötter, J., & Huff, W. (2010). Deep brain stimulation for psychiatric disorders. *Deutsches Ärzteblatt International, 107* (7), 105–113. doi: 10.3238/arztebl.2010.0105

13. Benabid, A. L., Pollak, P., Louveau, A., Henry, S., & De Rougemont, J. (1987). Combined (thalamotomy and stimulation) stereotactic surgery of the VIM thalamic nucleus for bilateral Parkinson disease. *Applied Neurophysiology, 50*, 344–346.

14. Vandewalle, V., Van der Linden, C., Groenewegen, H. J., & Caemaert, J. (1999). Stereotactic treatment of Gilles de la Tourette syndrome by high frequency stimulation of thalamus. *Lancet, 353,* 724.

15. Nuttin, B. J., Gabriels, L. A., Cosyns, P. R., Meyerson, B. A., Andreewitch, S., Sunaert, S. G., . . . Demeulemeester, H. G. (2008). Long-term electrical capsular stimulation in patients with obsessive-compulsive disorder. *Neurosurgery, 62* (6), 966–977.

16. Kopell, B. H., Halverson, J., Butson, C. R., Dickinson, M., Bobholz, J., Harsch, H., . . . Dougherty, D. (2011). Epidural cortical stimulation of the left dorsolateral prefrontal cortex for refractory major depressive disorder. *Neurosurgery, 69* (5), 1015–1029.

17. Lozano, A. M., Giacobbe, P., Hamani, C., Rizvi, S. J., Kennedy, S. H., Kolivakis, T., . . . Mayberg, H. S. (2012). A multicenter pilot study of subcallosal cingulated area deep brain stimulation for treatment-resistant depression. *Journal of Neurosurgery, 116* (2), 315–322.

18. Mayberg, H. S., Lozano, A. M., Vons, V., McNeely, H. E., Seminowicz, D., Hamani, C., . . . Kennedy, S. H. (2005). Deep brain stimulation for treatment-resistant depression. *Neuron, 45* (5), 651–660.

19. Giacobbe, P., Mayberg, H. S., & Lozano, A. M. (2009). Treatment resistant depression as a failure of brain homeostatic mechanisms: Implications for deep brain stimulation. *Experimental Neurology, 219* (1), 44–52.

20. Malone, D. A., Dougherty, D., Rezai, A. R., Carpenter, L., Friehs, G. M., Eskandar, E. N., . . . Greenberg, B. D. (2009). Deep brain stimulation of the ventral capsule/ventral striatum for treatment-resistant depression. *Biological Psychiatry, 65* (4), 267–275.

21. Nahas, Z., Anderson, B. S., Borckardt, J., Arana, A. B., George, M. S., Reeves, S. T., & Takacs, I. (2010). Bilateral epidural prefrontal cortical stimulation for treatment-resistant depression. *Biological Psychiatry, 67* (2), 101–109.

22. Saxena, S., & Rauch, S. L. (2000). Functional neuroimaging and the neuroanatomy of obsessive-compulsive disorder. *The Psychiatric Clinics of North America, 23* (3), 563–586.

23. Milad, M. R., & Rauch, S. L. (2012). Obsessive-compulsive disorder: Beyond segregated cortico-striatal pathways. *Trends in Cognitive Sciences, 16* (1), 43–51.

24. Nuttin B., Cosyns, P., Demeulemeester, H., Gybels, J., & Meyerson, B. (1999). Electrical stimulation in anterior limbs of internal capsules in patients with obsessive-compulsive disorder. *Lancet, 354* (9189), 1526.

25. US Food and Drug Administration (2009). *Medical devices.* Retrieved on June 19, 2012 from http://www.fda.gov/MedicalDevices/ProductsandMedicalProcedures/DeviceApprovalsandClearances/Recently-ApprovedDevices/ucm125520.htm

26. Greenberg, B. D., Malone, D. A., Friehs, G. M., Rezai, A. R., Kubu, C. S., Malloy, P. F., Salloway, S. P., Okun, M. S., Goodman, W. K., Rasmussen, S. A. (2006). Three-Year Outcomes in deep brain stimulation for highly resistant obsessive-compulsive disorder. *Neuropsychopharmacology, 31* (11), 2384–2393.

27. Greenberg, B. D., Gabriels, L. A., Malone, D. A., Rezai, A. R., Friehs, G. M., Okun, M. S., . . . Nuttin, B. J. (2010). Deep brain stimulation of the ventral internal capsule/ventral striatum for obsessive-compulsive disorder: worldwide experience. *Molecular Psychiatry, 1*, 64–79.

28. Ersche, K. D., Barnes, A., Jones, P. S., Morein-Zamir, S., Robbins, T. W., Bullmore, E. T. (2011). Abnormal structure of frontostriatal brain systems is associated with aspects of impulsivity and compulsivity in cocaine dependence. *Brain, 134* (7), 2013–2024.

29. World Health Organization (1996). *Acupuncture: Review and analysis of reports on controlled clinical trials.* Retrieved on June 19, 2012 from http://whqlibdoc.who.int/publications/2002/9241545437.pdf

Chapter 14

Through a Cultural Lens: Psychopathology within and across Borders

Alberto M. Bursztyn, Sarah Gathright Afonso, and Kimberly Black

This chapter addresses the role of culture in understanding and defining psychopathology (the terms psychopathology and abnormal psychology are used interchangeably throughout). We begin with the premise that notions of normalcy and abnormality are embedded in every culture. That is, different societies identify, frame, and treat similar disorders in different ways, and individual cultures may present singular manifestations of psychological disorders. Societies also attribute causes of psychological distress to culturally consistent etiologies, and in many cases these explanations are alien to mainstream psychiatric frameworks. Moreover, there are indications that a culture's characteristics or traditions may heighten the likelihood of mental distress among its most vulnerable individuals. As such, cultural variability challenges contemporary Western psychiatry's attempts to define psychopathology in universal terms. We propose that these unresolved tensions are evident not only in the description of "cultural syndromes" in the *Diagnostic and Statistical Manual of Mental Disorders* (DSM) but also in more subtle intersections between patients' culturally inflected symptoms and the Western-centric assumptions of practicing psychiatrists and other mental health workers.

THE DSM AND CULTURAL VARIABILITY

The fourth edition of the *Diagnostic and Statistical Manual of Mental Disorders—Text Revised* sets the professional standard for differentiating between normal and abnormal psychological functioning.[1] The implications of its definition of mental disorder, shown below, are far-reaching, for this definition provides a framework and justification for medical intervention. The DSM-IV-TR describes a mental disorder as

> A clinically significant behavioral or psychological syndrome or pattern that occurs in an individual and that is associated with present distress or disability, or with a significantly increased risk of suffering death, pain, disability, or an important loss of freedom. *In addition, this syndrome or pattern must not be merely an expectable and culturally sanctioned response to a particular event.* Whatever its original cause, it must currently be considered a manifestation of a behavioral, psychological, or biological dysfunction in the individual. *Neither deviant behavior nor conflicts that are primarily between the individual and society are mental disorders unless the deviance or conflict is a symptom of a dysfunction in the individual, as described above.*[1] (p. xxxi) (bold emphasis added)

In this definition, the authors implicitly recognize the interplay between mental disorders and society/culture but fail to address the larger question of cultural variability. Moreover, even within a culturally homogenous setting, the description of psychopathology in the DSM-IV-TR states that no one definition can adequately conceptualize and operationalize the characteristics of mental disorder across all situations.[1] Additionally, the DSM-IV-TR acknowledges that while a number of terms, such as distress and dysfunction, have been utilized as indictors of mental disorder, none "is equivalent to the concept"[1] (p. xxxi).

By excluding as psychopathology any "culturally expectable response to an event," the DSM-IV-TR describes abnormal functioning as a significant departure from cultural norms.[1] This conceptualization of psychopathology implies that the only valid frame of reference for "expectable" is the culture that gave origin to psychiatry. Additionally, while the DSM-IV-TR recognizes that individuals may be in conflict with society without meriting a psychiatric diagnosis, psychopathology is determined to be present only when the conflict or deviant behavior is a manifestation of a mental illness—therefore, mental illness represents a dysfunction "in the individual."[1] This view betrays a particularly ethnocentric understanding of mental illness that privileges culturally derived views of appropriate and inappropriate behaviors and locates psychopathology within individuals, as would be the case for medical conditions. Furthermore, the DSM-IV-TR definition of mental disorder retains a notable vagueness about potential causes of psychopathology.[1]

At the root of the difficulties concerning the role of culture in psychopathology is the unresolved, and perhaps irresolvable, tension between a school of thought that defines psychopathology as strictly a dysfunction of biophysiological systems, and the perspective that abnormal mental health is either entirely, or at least partially, a function of social processes that may be traced to environmental conditions and shaped within specific cultural contexts. While the first approach embraces a traditional medical formulation of disorder, the second embodies a multidisciplinary understanding of human experience and suffering. In recent decades, the biological perspective has gained prominence in Western societies with the advent of psychopharmacology as the treatment of choice and psychiatry's rejection of psychoanalysis.[2] This narrowed understanding of mental illness has been challenged within the field of psychiatry, as well as by researchers in allied disciplines. At issue is whether Western conceptions of psychopathology are objective and universal manifestations of the human condition or, instead, are manifestations of dysfunction in the cultures wherein psychiatry originated. Additional formulations suggest that psychopathology is present within all cultures, although its nature and symptomatology are intricately associated with the traditions and characteristics of the cultures wherein they are observed.

In the absence of a consensus definition of mental disorder, Lewis-Fernandez and Kleinman eloquently state that "the construct [of mental disorder] is itself a culture-bound belief that reflects the local biases of Western society, and that the science of psychopathology could be valid only in the sense that it is an accepted belief system of a particular culture"[3] (p. 381). Fundamentally, the act of diagnosing a mental disorder implies that optimal psychological functioning is both desirable and achievable. However, differing individuals and groups within a particular society may not necessarily agree as to what constitutes healthy and optimal functioning.[4] As such, identifying the markers of normal behavior and emotional functioning, and achieving consensus regarding what may be considered acceptable and typical functioning across cultures, is a great challenge.

Although the psychiatric and psychological literatures of over a century contain numerous examples of research on the effects of culture and ethnicity on human thought and behavior,[5,6,7] psychopathological conditions remain cross-culturally ambiguous. Therefore, it is critical to continue to examine cultural differences and their role in defining, conceptualizing, and treating dysfunction and psychopathology.

Psychopathology, as manifested by individuals' compromised psychological and mental health functioning, is a major global health concern. The World Health Organization reports that mental health conditions affect and debilitate millions of individuals around the world each year.[8] For example, in a report focusing on people with mental health issues as a vulnerable group, the WHO estimates that 151 million individuals around the world suffer from depression while 26 million suffer from schizophrenia.[8] To demonstrate the extent to which mental illness affects worldwide populations, the WHO notes that in low-income countries, depression affects nearly as many people as does malaria.[8] That is, depression is estimated to account for 3.2 percent of the total disease burden in these countries, while malaria comprises an only slightly higher 4 percent.

Despite increasing worldwide awareness of mental health conditions and their toll on individuals and communities, the purported causes and societal meanings of psychiatric symptoms vary widely. As described by Fabrega, "psychiatric illnesses are behavioral anomalies and breakdowns that are culturally shaped, explained, and dealt with in terms of established conventions and meanings"[9] (p. 3). For instance, "cultural idioms" may serve to explain the origins of individuals' behavior, such as attributing their actions to witchcraft, the evil eye, or a disturbance in one's hot-cold balance[10] (p. 406). Such phrases as "heat in the head" or "heart squeezed," although not present in the Western psychiatric lexicon, may reflect a range of personal or social experiences, and do not necessarily suggest psychopathology[10] (p. 406). In contrast, Western approaches to psychiatric diagnosis often assess culturally sanctioned expressions of distress, such as trance or possession states, fainting and seizure-like episodes, or hallucinations, as pathologic; moreover, medically trained clinicians frequently fail to acknowledge these conditions as possible manifestations of culture-specific, traditional practices, values, and beliefs.

Research evidence confirms that what is considered a disorder in one culture may fail to meet the same standard in another.[6] As expectations for behavior and emotional response vary widely, we argue here that holding different cultures to a Western standard of mental health classification and treatment (e.g., DSM-IV-TR) may in fact over-pathologize cultural behaviors typical of non-Western cultural expression and, at the same time, fail to recognize some manifestations of emotional distress unfamiliar to Western psychiatry. Abundant cross-cultural research supports this notion. For example, in a study conducted by Giosian, Glovsky, and Haslam, Brazilian, Romanian, and U.S. college students were presented with descriptions of mental disorders from the DSM-IV-TR.[11] The Romanian and U.S. students "correctly" identified most of the descriptions as mental disorders, while only a third of the Brazilian students agreed with these determinations. The researchers noted that the Brazilian sample's judgments showed no correspondence with DSM diagnostic criteria and regarded this result as evidence that varied perceptions of mental disorders exist within different cultures. Similar conclusions were drawn by researchers examining the perceptions of Attention Deficit Hyperactivity Disorder (ADHD) among U.S. and Chinese study participants. While the U.S. participants showed familiarity and alignment with the diagnostic characteristics of ADHD, as described in the DSM, the Chinese participants provided responses less consistent with the DSM criteria. Chinese participants were more likely to attribute ADHD symptoms to children's lack of effort and/or to their poor upbringing, suggesting that causal attributions of deviant behaviors are likely rooted in the social and cultural frameworks that establish standards for normal functioning and behavior.[12]

A HISTORICAL PERSPECTIVE

Fabrega reports that phenomena similar to Western psychiatric illnesses have been identified in Indian, Chinese, Islamic, Greek, and Roman medical literatures.[9] These psychiatric illnesses, as described in antiquity, were likely characterized by marked decline in individuals' physical, social, and emotional functioning, as well as in their overall well-being. During medieval times, mental illnesses that involved delusions or other evidence of insanity resulted in social stigmatization, with the most common interventions to address observed madness conducted by Christian churches in the form of exorcisms. Despite the lack of effective treatment, both classical and medieval conceptualizations of psychiatric illness ultimately allowed for demystification of their origins. It should be noted, however, that somatization of symptoms in such conditions as hysteria and mood disorders presented a different kind of problem and implied uncertainty regarding origin.

The somatization of psychiatric symptoms continues as a controversial area in today's Western medical system. Research that investigates biological processes as the sole origins of pathology often fails to integrate the cultural and social contexts within which these symptoms occur in the diagnostic and classification process.[9] Jahoda explained that utilizing a relatively homogenous population in conceptualizing the nature of psychopathology across cultures is not only limited, but also misguided.[13] Although current research efforts are often characterized by the inclusion of individuals of diverse backgrounds as research participants, Jahoda's statements remain relevant today. That is, Western medical perspectives on mental health and on the classifications of mental illness continue to dominate current research, diagnostic practices, treatments, and scholarship.

Emil Kraepelin, a founding figure in psychiatry, formulated the earliest diagnostic criteria for dementia precox and manic depressive disorder in late-19th-century Europe and linked those conditions to biological processes, thus affirming a medical conceptualization of the disorders. However, the emergence of the field of clinical psychology, also in the late 19th century, allowed for differentiation to begin between medical and psychological disorders. The role of culture in early diagnostic formulations was not entirely absent, with Kraepelin himself noting that the applicability of his classification system may have limited utility with non-Western groups.[2] Yet considerations about cultural variability and mental health did not come into focus until the 1960s and 1970s when scholars and researchers in psychology and psychiatry began to recognize and formalize cross-cultural perspectives, theory, and research.[5] While both academic and societal understandings of the range and variation of psychological functioning continue to emerge and garner serious consideration, cross-cultural psychiatry remains a relatively marginalized field and represents a niche concern among practitioners.

The introduction of the DSM formalized mental illness categories and began to transform the mental health field by unifying multiple currents into a single compendium of diagnostic categories. Perhaps the most influential was the third edition. Given the need for codification worldwide, the widely referenced DSM-III, published in 1980, became the "de facto classification of mental disorders in practically all countries," following its translation into more than 30 languages[14] (p. 132). Previous editions of the DSM were dominated by psychoanalytic language and psychobiological concepts that were less accessible to, and less accepted by, the international psychiatric community. While the DSM-III and its categorical approach to classification proved to be easily understood and less controversial,[14] the third edition lacked consideration for cultural variability and social context in psychiatric diagnoses. Despite this major failure, the DSM-III and its revised edition, the DSM-III-R, attained and maintained their status as the premier diagnostic assessment tools in international psychiatry; this sudden global prominence of the DSM allowed a distinctive American language and sensibility to pervade the description of psychopathology worldwide.

CONTEMPORARY CONTEXT

In describing the historical background of the classification of mental disorders, the DSM-IV-TR identifies the "need to collect statistical information" regarding the patient populations of mental hospitals in the United States as the impetus for developing a system of classification[1] (p. xxv). However, statistical classification was later subsumed by classification systems with increased clinical utility in diagnosing and treating patients with psychiatric and neurological disorders. That is, the DSM-IV-TR makes use of categorical classifications that include "criteria sets with defining features" to divide mental disorders into types[1] (p. xxxi). The manual makes provisions for its use in clinical work with culturally diverse populations and purports to address ethnic and cultural considerations through provision of three types of information. These include: 1) in-text discussions of cultural variations in the clinical presentation of mental disorders, 2) an appended chapter that describes twenty-five culture-bound syndromes, and 3) presentation of a framework for culturally sensitive case-formulation. Despite this attempt to address cultural-specific mental health phenomena, by isolating descriptions in a separate section—an appendix—culture remains an afterthought in the DSM-IV's mainstream approach to psychiatric diagnosis and classification. Flaskerud perceptively suggests that because culture-bound symptoms are presented in an appended format, it reinforces clinicians' views of them as "exotic" and allows for their very existence and validity to remain in question[10] (p. 406).

A history of coordination between the American Psychiatric Association and the World Health Organization has facilitated consistency between the development of the DSM and the *International Classification of Diseases* (ICD), respectively. The ICD-9-CM (Clinical Modification) and ICD-10 are compatible with the codes and terms utilized by the DSM-IV; the development of each was coordinated with the National Institute of Mental Health (NIMH), the National Institute on Drug Abuse (NIDA), and the National Institute on Alcohol Abuse and Alcoholism (NIAAA). Because the ICD was developed and endorsed by the World Health Organization, it may be expected to address culture in psychiatric diagnosis more effectively than the DSM. However, the ICD's discussion of culturally responsible diagnostic practices remains ambiguous and lacks focus.[14]

With a fifth edition of the DSM expected in 2013 and the ICD-11 slated for finalization in 2015, it is anticipated that "significant changes in structure, diagnostic modalities, clinical evaluation approaches, definition and scope of disorders, and measurements of severity and level of functioning" will occur[14] (p. 131). However, while the integration of cultural concerns is making inroads in these publications, it is still likely to follow established patterns of marginalization and continue to relegate cultural context to sidebar status.

The search for a universal psychiatry has been compared to other discourses, notably in the social sciences, wherein a single hegemonic narrative is challenged by diverse standpoint perspectives. These competing explanatory models often adopt the etic-emic lexicon, which originated in linguistics, but has been subsequently adopted by anthropology and other disciplines. The etic orientation may be loosely described as trans-cultural, focusing on phenomena that are inherent to the human condition. Emic perspectives, consistent with indigenous knowledge, are grounded on specific traditions and cultural contexts and may not have applicability or shared meaning beyond the setting observed.[15] While mainstream psychiatry remains focused on establishing a universal science of psychopathology, emic knowledge and practices qualify and question that agenda. In fact, taking a radical emic approach, one may argue that Western psychiatric knowledge, including its classification systems and treatment modalities, reflect a specific culture's response to human suffering.

PSYCHOPATHOLOGY ACROSS CULTURES AND CULTURAL DETERMINANTS OF PSYCHOPATHOLOGY

Draguns and Tanaka-Matsumi, among others, have sought to clarify the nature of psychopathology across cultures, as well as the role of culture in psychopathology.[6,7] In their comprehensive review of literature on the first theme, covering the last several decades, they evaluated the universality of major diagnostic conditions, such as depression, somatization, schizophrenia, anxiety disorders, and dissociative phenomena. They noted that applying scales and diagnostic criteria across cultures cannot escape the difficulty of standardizing procedures and minimizing observer bias. One of their inferences is that the impact of culture on psychopathology generates distinctive manifestations of mental illness. Nevertheless, they note that some researchers have observed a pattern whereby cultural variability of symptoms decreases as the condition becomes more severe[16,17] Epidemiological studies confirm that severe conditions such as schizophrenia and depression are evident cross-culturally and share core diagnostic elements. Specific manifestations of symptoms, however, are quite variable and often coherent with the cultural understanding of those conditions. Less severe conditions show even greater symptom variation and therefore may give rise to culture-specific syndromes. These emerging understandings regarding the role of culture on the expression of psychopathology are beginning to gain recognition with mental health professions. The reciprocal question (i.e., to what extent culture is implicated in the causation of psychopathology) has attracted relatively little research attention.[18]

Studies by the WHO specifically investigating schizophrenia in nine countries (1973, 1980) cross-culturally validated the core symptoms of the condition: lack of insight, flat affect, delusions, hallucinations, and experiences of control. A follow-up study yielded a rather surprising result: individuals affected with schizophrenia had a better prognosis in the developing countries surveyed than in the industrialized ones. Although some of the findings have been contested, Jablensky and Sartorios reviewed the extant data and asserted that schizophrenia is found at similar rates of incidence in all cultures and geographic regions, and although the course and prognosis vary greatly, the outcomes are significantly better in developing countries.[19] Multiple explanations have been proposed to account for these results, but all share a cultural dimension. For example, in the sampled countries, individuals with schizophrenia were more likely to be married and living in extended families and were less stigmatized by their conditions than those in the developed nations. Moreover, hallucinations in various rural communities may be interpreted as manifestations of communication with the spiritual world rather than as a sign of sickness. In other words, culture creates the context for interpreting behaviors as supernatural or psychopathological.[20] In societies in which intimate and intense interactions with the spiritual realm are part of everyday life, the reactions to mental distress and prescribed treatments reflect those worldviews. Within traditional collectivistic societies, mental suffering is often linked to a larger and coherent sense of the universe. If mental illness is seen as an intrusion of the spirit world on the individual or family, the burden of social stigma is reduced. In contrast, individualistic Western societies are more likely to place the onus of responsibility for mental distress on the sufferer, while inducing guilt and offering scant social support. These differences may affect the course of recovery because the individual suffering with mental illness is more likely to be embraced in one setting and marginalized in the other.

Recognition that cultural context should be addressed in psychopathology is gaining greater acceptance, even as contemporary diagnostic compendia continue to reflect a strong etic perspective. The notion that characteristics of cultures contribute to specific psychopathologies is an emerging and elusive area of research. Although patterns of behavior may be accepted or even valued and encouraged in particular societies or cultures, they do not necessarily indicate "optimal psychological functioning"[4] (p. 382). Instances of ritualistic behavior are common in religious practice, and some observers have posited that cultures condoning and enforcing rituals may predispose individuals to obsessive-compulsive symptoms, masking the condition when present.[21] That is, the congruence between various cultural practices and beliefs, and the presentation of some psychiatric symptoms, may inadvertently limit "insight into the irrationality of the symptoms."[21] As such, Kirmayer et al. emphasize the need for further research into the "tension between cultural styles and health consequences"[21] (p. 382). Cultural styles have been associated with personality development, but their links to specific psychopathological conditions, beyond "cultural syndromes," are less well established.[22,23,24]

Draguns and Tanaka-Matsumi propose that using Hoftede's cultural dimensions framework may serve to clarify the extent and nature of psychopathology in different societies.[7] Hoftede's typology identifies four dimensions of culture that describe the widely observed diversity of communication patterns, beliefs, and behaviors across the globe. His framework has been widely applied in international consulting and other fields, including cross-cultural psychology. Hoftede identified critical differences in the ways that people in various societies understand their lived-worlds (in effect, the patterns of thinking and feeling that guide individuals' choices and actions in culturally coherent ways).[25] Draguns and Tanaka-Matsumi, suggest that Hoftede's individualism-collectivism dimension may predict that mental distress in individualistic societies is associated with guilt, alienation, and loneliness.[7] In collectivist societies mental anguish may be linked to failed relations, social rejection, and shame. Since cultures play a central role in defining the boundaries of identity, the nature of human relations, and social role expectations, it stands to reason that these dimensions of culture contribute to the character and expression of psychopathology. Accordingly, mental health and psychopathology may vary across cultures in ways that are coherent with the supports and demands of each culture.[25]

TOWARD A CULTURALLY INFORMED
UNDERSTANDING OF PSYCHOPATHOLOGY

The field of psychiatry has taken a primarily descriptive and categorical approach to diagnosis in the past. Lacking clear neuro-biological indicators, the approach is likely to continue. However, an increasing number of researchers have argued that culturally informed research requires that investigators refrain from imposing diagnostic categories developed in one culture on conditions observed in another.[14,26,27] Also, although mental health research over the past three decades has yielded reliable assessment instruments for various psychopathologies, reliability does not constitute cultural validity.[27] Consequently, future research should focus on adapting current assessment instruments for use across various cultures. Additionally, limiting research to identifying practices and beliefs that differ across cultures has proven inadequate in efforts to gain cultural competence. Future research must also address the extent to which various cultural practices, values, beliefs, and worldviews are present and perhaps implicated in the development of psychopathology.[4] Perhaps the best diagnostic practices will emerge from a more nuanced and specific understanding that integrates the interaction between individuals and emic cultural expectations.

Current thinking is likely to be replaced in the near future as both cognitive neuroscience and social sciences continue to inform the field. For example, in our evolving understanding of disorders such as schizophrenia and depression, we view earlier formulations as inappropriate or misguided. Earlier errors in diagnosis could be seen retrospectively as a result of confounding disorders that we now understand differently. While this may be an acceptable explanation, a social constructivist perspective may propose that, in the past, "the social and cultural circumstances of individuals [identified as suffering from mental illness] and the way these individuals responded to stress were different. [Additionally,] these disorders were constructed by physicians in a different form and with a different content"[9] (p. 9).

Postmodern theorists and social constructivists propose a culturally relativistic view by asserting that absolute truths do not exist and that our understandings of reality are constituted by differing interpretations formed in language.[28] Postmodern theory further purports that through human interaction, relationships, and communication, a vocabulary is formed that allows us to understand and interpret our experiences.[28] In this radical departure from a bio-medical paradigm, one's perceived reality is socially constructed, including the apparent presence of psychopathological conditions. Although this perspective, emerging from the social sciences, is far from challenging the hegemonic psychiatric establishment, it should serve to remind diagnostic manual writers that psychiatric conditions have a long history of shifting characterizations and meanings.

Presently, researchers and clinicians, including those developing the fifth edition of the *Diagnosic and Statistical Manual*, recognize the need for multidimensional assessment of individuals' experience and display of the symptoms and features of mental disorders.[29] Clinicians are encouraged to note not only the nature of their patients' distress and impairment but also its severity and any contributing psychosocial factors.[29] Rather than limiting their attributions to the broad concept of culture in evaluating what have been previously referred to as culture-bound syndromes, clinicians and researchers might focus on these psychosocial, and/or "context variables," to account for cultural differences when they occur[30] (p. 4). Cultural competence requires not only a deep understanding of the patient's culture but also a keen awareness of the clinician's own worldviews and biases, including those that are intricately woven into the culture of psychiatry.[31]

REFERENCES

1. American Psychiatric Association (2000). *Diagnostic and statistical manual of mental disorders* (4th ed., text rev.). Washington, DC: Author.
2. Marsella, A. J., & Yamada, M. (2010). Culture and psychopathology: Foundations, issues, directions. *Journal of Pacific Rim Psychology, 4*(2), 103–15.
3. Lewis-Fernandez, R., & Kleinman, A. (1995). Cultural psychiatry: Theoretical, clinical, and research issues. *Psychiatric Clinics of North America, 18*, 433–448. As cited in Widiger, T. A., & Sankis, L. M. (2000). Adult psychopathology: Issues and controversies. *Annual Review of Psychology, 51*, 377–404.
4. Widiger, T. A., & Sankis, L. M. (2000). Adult psychopathology: Issues and controversies. *Annual Review of Psychology, 51*, 377–404.
5. Adamopoulos, J., & Lonner, W. J. (2001). Culture and psychology at a crossroad: Historical perspective and theoretical analysis. In D. Matsumoto (Ed.), *The Handbook of Culture and Psychology* (pp. 11–34). New York, NY: Oxford University Press.
6. Canino, G., & Alegria, M. (2008). Psychiatric diagnosis—is it universal or relative to culture? *The Journal of Child Psychology and Psychiatry, 49*(3), 237–250.
7. Draguns, J. G., & Tanaka-Matsumi, J. (2003). Assessment of psychopathology across and within cultures: Issues and findings. *Behaviour Research and Therapy, 41*, 755–776.
8. World Health Organization (2010). *Mental health and development: Targeting people with mental health conditions as a vulnerable group.* Retrieved October 19, 2012 from http://whqlibdoc.who.int/publications/2010/9789241563949_eng.pdf
9. Fabrega, H. (1996). Culture diagnostic validity in psychiatric illness: Its application to schizophrenia. In Mezzich, J. E., Kleinman, A., Fabrega, H., Parron,

D. L. (Eds.), *Culture and psychiatric diagnosis: A DSM-IV perspective* (pp. 3–14). Washington, DC: American Psychiatric Press.

10. Flaskerud, J. H. (2009). What do we need to know about the culture-bound syndromes? *Issues in Mental Health Nursing, 30,* 406–407.

11. Giosan, G., Glovsky, V., and Haslam, N. (2001). The lay concept of "mental disorder": A cross-cultural study. *Transcultural Psychiatry, 38*(3), 317–332.

12. Norvilitis, J. M., and Fang, P. (2005). Perceptions of ADHD in China and the United States: A preliminary study. *Journal of Attention Disorders, 9*(2), 413–424.

13. Jahoda, G. (2001). Beyond Stereotypes. *Culture & Psychology 7*(2), 181–197. As cited in Adamopoulos, J., & Lonner, W. J. (2001). Culture and psychology at a crossroad: Historical perspective and theoretical analysis. In D. Matsumoto (Ed.), *The Handbook of Culture and Psychology* (pp. 11–34). New York, NY: Oxford University Press.

14. Alarcon, R. D. (2009). Culture, cultural factors and psychiatric diagnosis: Review and projections. *World Psychiatry, 8,* 131–139.

15. Lee, Y-J., & Bursztyn, A. M. (2011). Understanding childhood disabilities through culturally diverse families' perspectives (pp. 15–36). In A. M. Bursztyn (Ed.), *Childhood Psychological Disorders: Current Controversies.* Westport, CT: Praeger Books.

16. Marsella, J. A. (1988). Cross-cultural research on severe mental disorders: Issues and findings. *Acta Psychiatrica Scandinavica, 344,* 7–22.

17. Sundbom, E., Jacobsson, L., Kullgren, G., & Penayo, U. (1998). Personality and defenses: A cross-cultural study of psychiatric patients and healthy individuals in Nicaragua and Sweden. *Psychological Reports, 83,* 1331–1347.

18. Tseng, W. (2006). From peculiar psychiatric disorders through culture-bound syndromes to culture-related specific syndromes. *Transcultural Psychiatry, 43*(4), 554–576.

19. Jablensky, A., & Sartorius, N. (1988). Is schizophrenia universal? *Acta Psychiatrica Scandinavica, 78,* 65–70.

20. Al-Issa, I. (1995). The illusion of reality or the reality of illusion: Hallucinations and culture. *British Journal of Psychiatry, 166,* 368–373.

21. Kirmayer, L. J., Young, A., & Hayton, B. C. (1995). The cultural context of anxiety disorders. *Psychiatric Clinics of North America, 18*(3), 503-21. As cited in Widiger, T. A., & Sankis, L. M. (2000). Adult psychopathology: Issues and controversies. *Annual Review of Psychology, 51,* 377–404.

22. Triandis, H. C., & Suh, E. M. (2002). Cultural influences on personality. *Annual Review of Psychology, 53,* 133–60.

23. Miranda, A. O., & Fraser, L. (2002). Culture-bound syndromes: Initial perspectives from individual psychotherapy. *Journal of Individual Psychology, 58,* 422–33.

24. Guarnaccia, P. J., & Rogler, L. H. (1999). Research on culture-bound syndromes: New directions. *American Journal of Psychiatry, 156,* 1322–1327.

25. Bursztyn, A. M. (2011). *Childhood psychological disorders: Current controversies.* Westport, CT: Praeger Books.

26. Maier, T., & Straub, M. (2011). "My head is like a bag full of rubbish": Concepts of illness and treatment expectations in traumatized migrants. *Qualitative Health Research, 21*(2), 233–248.

27. Tanaka-Matsumi, J. (2001). Abnormal psychology and culture. In D. Matsumoto (Ed.), *The handbook of culture and psychology* (pp. 265–286). New York, NY: Oxford University Press.

28. Walker, M. T. (2006). The social construction of mental illness and its implications for the recovery model. *International Journal of Psychosocial Rehabilitation, 10*(1), 71–87.

29. Reynolds, C. F., Lewis, D. A., Detre, T., Schatzberg, A. F., & Kupfer, D. J. (2009). The future of psychiatry as clinical neuroscience. *Academic Medicine, 84*(4), 446–450.

30. Matsumoto, D. (Ed.). (2001). *The handbook of culture and psychology.* New York, NY: Oxford University Press.

31. Bursztyn, A. M. (2006). Qualitative methods in multicultural psychology. In Yo Jackson (Ed.), *Encyclopedia of Multicultural Psychology.* Thousand Oaks, CA: Sage.

Chapter 15

Parapsychology, Sects, Cults, and Religious Fundamentalism

Naji Abi-Hashem

In this chapter we will explore topics and activities that are not frequently discussed in the mental health literature, like paranormal phenomena, mystic appearances, unique social derivation, pseudo- and quasi-religious movements, sectarian cultism, group indoctrination, legalism, fundamentalism, and fanaticism. We will attempt to define each of these and explain what they actually are and what they are not. We will review the limited literature about some of them and will also discuss each concept or trend from a cultural and spiritual perspective. Finally, we will examine the potential impacts of these on the mental-emotional health and the psycho-social functioning of people who are involved and consider what educators, clinicians, and caregivers can do to implement possible prevention and intervention strategies.

PARAPSYCHOLOGY

Parapsychology is an intriguing topic, yet it has no agreed-upon definition or unified connotation. It is a multi-level approach to the study of abnormal occurrences and extrasensory phenomena in life. Parapsychology, as a profession, claims to be the exploration of the paranormal and the metaphysical and also what is referred to as psychic energies, untapped mental abilities, and spiritualistic powers. In addition, it is the observation of certain people who might possess inexplicable abilities, unusual faculties, or pseudo skills that enable them to perform astonishing acts or displays and therefore impact their surroundings and social settings.[1]

Parapsychology is an interdisciplinary attempt to discover the para-natural domains, examine the beyond-the-normal spheres, and study the atypical events in life. There is not a unique method to its procedures or analytical work. Rather, due to its various interests, parapsychology covers multiple arenas and channels, accommodates differing views, and stretches through wide perspectives.[2,3,4]

It is a field that basically resides outside the range of one single academic discipline or scholarship. It melds together a variety of fields like anthropology, religion, psychology, sociology, numerology, physiology, ritualism, and scientific inquiry.[5,6] Therefore, and to some degree, parapsychology has developed its own vocabulary, which sets it apart from other fields.[7,8] Its wide interpretation of psychic and irregular phenomena has been characterized in many ways, as one or more of the following: anomalous experiences, psi powers, déjà vu, apparitions, intuitiveness, auras, altered states of consciousness, psychokinesis, telepathy, elusivity, automatism, bilocations, clairvoyance, premonitions, precognition, postcognition, crystal gazing, unorthodox healing, channeling, mediumship, past-life recalls, and reincarnation.

Since ancient times, humans have been fascinated by the mysterious, the powerful, the unusual, and the extraordinary. These happenings or forces have caused people of all backgrounds, cultures, and races, through all centuries and civilizations—and regardless of place and time—to fear, adore, worship, or serve these phenomena. At times people used some of the new features, abilities, or powerful maneuvers they observed and learned for their own benefit or to actually subdue others under their own control. People repeatedly have tried to influence the natural realm by manipulating the unnatural and supernatural cues and then teach those skills (or tricks) to the next generations. These activities ranged from practicing the simple "mind over body" exercises to engaging in the mysterious practice of *spiritualism* or *occultism*.

Some social thinkers consider parapsychology as a branch of the mainstream psychology because it attempts to study a group of events and abilities that are conceivably mental, perceptual, and behavioral in nature yet have no tangible or physical correlates to them (collectively known as psi).[7,8] However, for other academicians, the study of such mental abilities, whether actual or purported, has not been fully adoptable by the framework of mainstream scholarship or the conventional methods of science. Occasionally, parapsychologists struggle to give a comprehensive explanation of their work and unconventional fields of study.[9,10,11]

It appears that for some paranormal researchers, subjective reporting, intuition, and spontaneous cases, even when unsystematically collected, are a major source of their study. For other PSI researchers, measurable data and objective laboratory experimentations, as in controlled studies, are more practiced and a reliable form of study. Obviously, parapsychology has supporters and critics, and both appear to consent that there are two sides to the discipline—a more popular and soft side and a more serious and scientific side.[9,12,13] Due to the lack of clear boundaries and the presence of several branches and derivatives, most literature on the topic is inconsistent and reflects a mixture of approaches and methodologies. In addition, there has been some disagreement on how to clearly define someone as a *parapsychologist*. Therefore, for mainstream academia in general and for social and behavioral sciences in particular, parapsychology remains controversial because of its historical origin and later its inability to replicate many conducted or documented studies. In addition, it is controversial because of its strong emphasis on life coincidences, synchronicity of events, personal moods and temperaments, human intuitions, and a speculative metaphysical ontology.[5,7,8,14,15]

In parapsychology, PSI refers to a transfer of data or energy in unconventional mechanisms. PSI phenomena include *extrasensory perception* (ESP), which is supposedly the process of acquiring knowledge without any mediation of the sensory apparatus. *Psychokinesis* (PK) is the ability to cause physical objects to move without actually touching them. *Clairvoyance*, on the other hand, is the awareness of objects or entities that have no physical or tangible presence and are not available to any sensory field of knowledge. *Telepathy* is an assumed ability to communicate across distance via thought transference and without any direct use of the human senses. *Postcognition* refers to the ability to vividly recapture past events while *precognition* refers to the ability to experience future events before they occur in actual time. Some of these *extrasensory* abilities are also referred to as the *sixth sense*.[4,6,16]

Some of the topics and features that parapsychology is interested in examining may not be purely parapsychological in nature after all. They appear to be more philosophical, existential, theological, and spiritual in nature and have been discussed and expanded for centuries, that is, life after death; the dynamic relationship of body, mind, and soul; theology of culture; mythology; unexplained miracles; spiritual transcendence; eschatology and curiosity about predicting the future; the power of belief and prayer; existential and supernatural hope; etc.[12,17] However, parapsychology claims many of such topics as its own fields of inquiry. Modern parapsychology is also concerned with the extraordinary manifestations and pseudo-natural happenings called apparitions, psychic healing, uncommon visions, haunting, divination, fortune telling, out-of-body experiences, time-displaced activities, alien abduction, medium spirits, and near-death experiences.[1] Historically, parapsychology and its related branches can be traced to the establishment of the Society for Psychical Research (SPR) in London, England, in 1882. The early efforts of this group were to dissociate *psychical* phenomena from superstition or spiritualism and to investigate an assortment of mediums and their claims to evoke apparitions. SPR attempted to study also ectoplasm poltergeists, automatic writing, and levitation. Shortly after, an American Society for Psychical Research was founded in 1885. Then, much later, another organization followed, the Parapsychological Association (PA), which was established in 1957 and grew to become an international group. The PA website claims that it represents only professionals who are engaged in a rigorous analysis of the psi phenomena and anomalous manifestations from a purely scholarly and scientific perspective.

Investigators who are active in psychic-paranormal movements seem to be convinced that their work is valid, up to date, and compelling. They believe that plenty of unusual and irregular experiences or metaphysical and spiritualistic events are still happening around the world today. Although some of these occurrences may be *folk* in nature, to parapsychologists they are real and should be analyzed and documented.[4,11,16] At the same time, most parapsychologists admit that these phenomena cannot be proven in the usual scholarly and systematic way due to the small research sample used, rarity of the incident, and the quick disappearance of the evidence. Therefore, abnormalists argue that although such trends are beyond natural laws, they do happen, do have social impact and psychological consequences, and furthermore, are safe to observe, interact with, and closely study.[3,16] Psychologists of the New Age orientation usually try to defend these views and positions. However, for mainstream psychologists, educators, philosophers, theologians, psychiatrists, and other clinical and mental health caregivers, these assertions create serious concern about the risks involved. Even when perceived as generic extrasensory incidents, these strange activities, experiences, and inexplicable events could in reality be socially disturbing, mentally unsettling, emotionally upsetting, and psychologically disorienting.[18] Naturalistic professionals, who basically reject any idea of the supernatural or divine, explain such incidences and reports as mere tricks of the biological brain, lack of orientation in time or space, lapses of memory, overlap of recollections, overwhelming unconscious material, hallucinations, delusions, and the like.[1,9,11,13]

Even though parapsychology has seriously tried to present itself as a subspecialty of universal psychology and to project an image of professionalism as in other fields, it has repeatedly faced skepticism from recognized disciplines and established university and seminary research centers, both on the basis of theoretical-scientific grounds and applied-therapeutic grounds.[8,11] For example, some of the objections facing parapsychology have been as follows: (a) parapsychology challenges the laws of nature and physical realm; (b) it encourages the fusion of boundary or the loss of ego-identity; (c) its subject matters are not only controversial but considered taboo in some societies; (d) it tends to spread anxiety and fear among average people that someone or some groups with an extra psychic ability can influence their minds, their families, and their lives;

(e) it can lead to medieval superstitions; and (f) it can present a subtle danger to communities and societies at large.[10,11] On the other hand, the most recent and scientific branch of parapsychology totally refuses these claims and repeatedly distances itself from any superstitious beliefs or activities, though they admit that these have existed in the beginning and early stages of the profession.

Traditional cultures and communities have their own set of values, habits, beliefs, norms, and practices. Through the ages, they have developed views regarding life and death, health and sickness, myth and reality, good and evil, etc. Virtually, what is normal and natural in one culture may be completely abnormal and pathological in another. Cultural anthropology and cultural relativity are major factors in determining these sensitive matters. People groups have also developed remedies for most individual and social ills. Some interventions are popular and folk in nature; others are more technical and progressive. Thus, interventions may range from the modern and medical to the spiritual and magical. For example, in some parts of the Middle East, people still do believe in the powerful attack of the black or evil eye, referred to as *saybit el aayin*. For protection, they carry or attach to their possessions a large blue glass bead with an eye drawn on it. Some seek a psychic (*arraaf*) for the sake of fortune telling (*tabseer*) or astrology (*tangeem*), for palms/cards/boards reading, for crystal ball gazing, and for calling or manipulating the spirits. In addition, people at times seek clergy, a guru, or spiritualistic practitioner for a veiling (*hijaab*), which is a form of secret writing (*kitaab*), that both articulates and agrees to carry a statement to fulfill a hurtful wish against someone else or another situation. The verdict pronounces condemnation or evil on the subject, is wrapped in a piece of cloth, and is to be hidden in a secret place in proximity to the target. These healers are also sought by individuals to reverse any suspected script written against them by either writing a counter-script or by offering prayer or administering a set of rituals in order to bring healing for illnesses or break the power of any curse or evil tendency. Some people make a pilgrimage (*hajj*) to shrines of all sorts, folk types or mainstream religious centers, where they utter an oath (*nider*) and make a commitment to the place if their prayer is answered and desire fulfilled. Such practices are very common in the Middle East today, both as a way of intervention and prevention. Certainly, these activities and phenomena are worth observing and studying, but deciding what method or approach to use and how and when to use it can be real, challenging questions. Some practices can be merely cultural-traditional, religious-spiritual, or cultic-magical in nature . . . or simply an overlap of all these factors and spheres.[19]

When the interest in paranormal occurrences and odd, inexplicable mysteries are emphasized and legitimized, curious people and younger generations become attracted and may want to look for or attempt some of them. Those who are vulnerable can get themselves into trouble when dealing with the *paranormal* and the *psi* activities without prior training, guidance, or supervision. They may lose touch with reality or fall victim to powerful suggestions and external spiritualistic influences.[12,15,17] Naturally, people are always attracted to the unknown, those who seek thrill and adventure, who thrive on risks and dangers, or who are just innately curious with a hunger for wonderment. Endeavors like black magic, connecting with the dead, ghost hunting, mediumship, out-of-body experiences, etc., can be very tempting to experiment with and see what happens. Therefore, it is difficult to draw a safe line between what is innocent or scholarly and what is risk-glorifying and damaging on an anomalous-sensational level. Thus, the need is for caution when practices fall outside the areas of normative human reasoning and experiences and of the established emotional apparatus and socio-cultural realms.[1]

With the availability of Internet resources and online searching capabilities, parapsychology has a better chance to introduce itself and share its literature, studies, and findings. Integrative and interdisciplinary approaches to knowledge have increased the exposure of paranormal psychology and helped decrease the misconceptions and the unfavorable impressions about that profession. However, many reviewers and critics still believe that parapsychology is somewhat polarized and divisive. Apparently, the debate for complete recognition of parapsychology and its related fields will remain active and unresolved for years to come.[7,15]

SECTS AND CULTS

In this section, we will define the concepts of sect and cult, review their various types and kinds, compare their similarities and differences, explain their roles and functions, and find out why people do join them and who is more vulnerable to become a member or an affiliate. Finally, we will describe the challenges facing ex-members when they attempt to leave such groups and their struggle to readjust again to the broader society—a task that they may not accomplish alone but for which they may require the assistance of therapeutic helpers and caregivers.

A sect can be defined as a derivation from the mainstream religious establishments and other conventional and social movements. It is formed by a group of individuals who are, by nature, non-conformists and who have separated themselves from the larger society. They hold different beliefs, observances, and practices that are usually labeled as heretical. Being a part of a sect can be a part-time or a lifetime commitment.

Cults, on the other hand, are made of small groups characterized by a strange way of life, a skewed doctrine, and a set of rituals. They are totally devoted to a particular system of operation or to a prominent figure or leader. They manifest a blind dedication to a certain object, entity, or ideology and are known to have an intense loyalty to the founder(s) of the assembly. A cult can be a deviant social unit or quasi-religious organization with exclusive ideology and skewed practices, using deceitful and manipulative psychosocial strategies to recruit new members and to control the rest of its followers.[20,21]

The terms *sects* and *cults* are often used interchangeably in the literature. The mass media and the general public usually tend to label any odd movement or strange group as a sect or a cult. Even on an academic level, it is difficult to formulate a commonly accepted definition for either one because there are overlapping characteristics and dynamics among these groups. Although there are many similarities between sects and cults, social scientists consider sects as a mild form of social deviances and cults as a more severe and dangerous type of alienated groups. However, it is hard to penetrate and study any of these groups from within because most are sealed and secluded. The majority of examinations have been done from the outside, based on the accounts and experiences of ex-members, who after a time of investment have felt their group quite disillusioned and confused.[22]

In the world today, there appears to be an increase in the number of unconventional groups, deviant assemblies, and new religious movements (NRM).[23] This could be due, on one hand, to the rise of human isolation, social boredom, and personal loneliness, and to peer pressure, available free information on the Internet and, on the other hand, to a desire to try something new and seek thrilling adventures, especially among the younger generation. Although it is difficult to fully distinguish between the many types and variations of such groups, there are several traits that remain in common among them all: a) they all seem to function as cluster movements, b) they are unconventional, unorthodox, and atypical in their nature, and c) they tend to have self-appointed leaders. Normally, the founders and leaders of these groups tend to claim to have a special divine mission and power and are charismatic, articulate, smart, and able to formulate a visionary dogma that is innovative and exclusive, and they expect unquestionable allegiance from followers at all times—and occasionally they tend to exploit the young and the vulnerable among members.[20]

The terms sects and cults seem to carry negative connotations in modern society. Mild and irregular movements can be passive, isolated, and peaceful, but strong and eccentric ones can be aggressive and forceful in approach. Severe deviational groups may range from the cultist to the occultist in nature and display pathological and dangerous features. Virtually, many sects and cults are derivations from social norms and exhibit psychological disturbances in spite of their original appeal to be normal community groups. According to some researchers, there appears to be a progression in the formation of sects and cults.[24,25] The stages of development could start with a mild form of a mainstream branch or an off-shoot activity, which then becomes a serious derivation, then progresses to an established sect, then moves into a cult level or classification, and then perhaps becomes an occultic group, with antisocial attitudes, pathological rituals, and/or violent behaviors. Other observers have noticed the presence of these elements in all kinds of sects and cults, regardless of their type or degree of severity. Actually, there is no single criterion of evaluation or diagnosis available as a standard tool to be used in dealing with sects and cults.[24,25,26]

Certain groups are basically psychological in nature. They emphasize personal growth, inner transformation, and self-actualization. Others are socially or politically oriented, emphasizing inter-group formation and mass solidarity. Yet others represent a quite novel and fascinating movement combining Far Eastern philosophies and mysticism blended with practices of spiritualism and scientism. *Sects* are viewed as derivations and breakaway movements from the acceptable and normative establishments due to ethnic, doctrinal, organizational, or cultural reasons. Some are classified as *deviations*, because they lean toward becoming cults in their own way. Naturally, each group-type possesses a unique level of complexity and intensity that sets it apart from others. Depending on their kind, ideology, zeal, and resources, groups range from generic and harmless to radical and toxic. Some groups are totally ignored by local authorities and the larger society, while others are watched and monitored closely.[20,21,27]

People who join such movements share in common characteristics and predisposing factors. Individuals or families who are emotionally vulnerable, relationally disconnected, socially struggling, or experiencing major life changes and crises are usually strong candidates. In addition, those who are very dependent, frequently disappointed, or with a marked sense of inadequacy are also prospects. Teenagers and young adults who, by nature, are idealistic, intelligent, seeking affiliation and meaning, and looking for a new emotional thrill or spiritual ecstasy are also prone. Some of the joining members are innately impulsive, angry at society, searching for a cause to adopt, and requiring a rigid structure to function well. They prefer to be in a totalitarian environment.

Some long-term members of radical sects or cults, and the children who were born and raised within such an environment, may have seen or experienced multiple abuses and traumas. They could have been exposed to bloody initiations and shocking rituals, a common practice of many secretive groups. Certain sects, cults, assemblies, and street gangs prefer to practice their rituals in the dark, behind closed doors, or deep in the woods, away from the public eye and observation. Therefore, participants would begin to split their lives and operate in two ego states, one openly in public and the other secretly in private. Another kind of severe emotional disturbance is experienced when a member or a family decides to leave the questioned group. Probably they would break away after an intense period of ambivalence and feelings of guilt and confusion, and perhaps after being put down by other members or officially ex-communicated by the leadership of that group. Later on, these members will find themselves unable to function well and not really belonging anywhere. They will certainly face an identity crisis and an existential dilemma, and their road to psycho-emotional recovery and socio-cultural reintegration will usually be long.[21,28]

Today, there is plenty of literature on these topics attempting to examine the nature, function, mindset, subculture, and behavior of sects and cults. Some material provides *awareness* of the risks and dangers involved and exposes the agendas of fanatic movements, deviant assemblies, and cultic leaders. Other literature focuses on *intervention* to help former members restore natural functioning and participation within the larger society again. Such efforts have resulted in what is known as *the counter-cult movement* (CCM).[29] Breaking away from a longtime commitment to an exclusive group is extremely complicated and difficult. Handling mental disillusionment over the former affiliations and grief over the losses of a well-established identity, a structured lifestyle, and a deep psychological attachment can be heavily intense. Many former members experience a tormenting cognitive dissonance. The recovery process can be slow and challenging, for ex-members have to relearn how to trust and show confidence in others, rebuild a balanced belief system and worldview, establish new socio-emotional attachments, and integrate themselves again within the community and larger society.[26,28]

Still more research is needed in this domain to learn additional insights and dynamics about sects and cults: What motivates them and what holds them together? How do they attract others to join them? Also, more clinical studies are needed to examine the predispositions of prospective members, the various experiences of active members, and the challenges facing previous members. Currently, there are many therapists, mentors, counselors, and pastors who specialize in helping former sect and cult members, yet there is a continual need to find the best therapeutic approaches and to share the effective interventions in order to help the victims of harmful sects and cults in their process of recovery and restoration. They will need all available coaching and support in their journey of mental adjustment, family reconciliation, social integration, and spiritual healing.[20]

RELIGIOUS FUNDAMENTALISM

Religious fundamentalism is basically concerned with the preservation of the moral-ethical values, the spiritual dogmas, and the set of ideals, as inherited from past generations or as discovered by modern-day teachers. It is an attempt to preserve old traditions and beliefs of a community even at the cost of isolating themselves and alienating others. It is found in every denominational branch of every mainstream religion, across time, place, and culture (Judaism, Christianity, Islam, Buddhism, Hinduism, etc.).[30,31]

In every society, there are many individuals, clans, and parties who have an innate desire to hold on to their heritage. They tend to lock themselves blindly to their doctrine or their past without sorting the complex matters, finding a middle ground, and modifying the stands. Their own values, norms, truths, practices, doctrines, and legacies represent their cherished tradition. Thus, they cling to these, rigidly unwilling to negotiate the relevancy of their beliefs and traditions to modern-day times. Fundamentalists have a need to be faithful to their own history, stay on the right side of the issues, have clear-cut answers to the difficult questions of life, and remain within the sphere of the familiar and accustomed norms. These needs and drives are as old as human nature itself.[32]

Fundamentalism can manifest itself in many different ways. It can be mild, moderate, or severe, depending on the location, people involved, and issues at hand. When the discussion of sensitive and controversial topics becomes a debate and when the people involved begin to develop passionate opinions with intense feelings, the result is divisive and polarizing, often leading to arguments, negative attitudes, and increased tensions. Another reason extremism can flourish within a certain group or community is that individuals begin to feel threatened, invaded, or attacked, especially in their core value or belief system. Virtually, it all depends on the group's understanding of their causes, sense of duty, sacred texts, perceived mission, sense of calling, and projected destiny. Also, it depends on their level of emotional maturity, stage of moral development, and their kind of cognitive reasoning and global worldview. However, if the ideological differences are not quickly resolved and the relationship restored, then the strain can easily escalate to become social unrest, ethno-political conflict, violent behaviors, or actions of hostility—known as *religious militancy*.[30,31]

Fundamentalism is not only found among religious groups or faith-based circles but also in many other areas of regular life and civic society, like governments and political parties, trades and large corporations, science and academia, athletics and sports, community programs and social movements, and defense strategies and military doctrines. Extreme secular humanism and radical atheism have their own versions of fundamentalism as well. Religious fundamentalism is not identical to a *cultism* in the literal sense but can become one when the movement builds excessive rhetoric and rigidity, calls for unconventional and fanatic methodologies, and uses somewhat brain-washing and indoctrinating approaches. Both lay and professional people normally possess tender spots and pushbuttons that, when manipulated or triggered, will elicit an unrealistic reaction or overreaction. Basically, *fundamentals* and *passions* are natural and necessary for any healthy value system, but when they become very skewed, narrowly rigid, or markedly acute, then they could lead to a dysfunctional mentality or a pathological lifestyle.[30,31]

Mainly, religious fundamentalism is an excessive form of conservation aimed at preserving the strict tenets of faith with no room for negotiation or compromise. The modern interpretation of the term has taken different connotations and flavors since the incidents of September 11. Often in the public discourse, fundamentalism is used interchangeably with extremism, radicalism, and terrorism; however, it is not exactly identical to these terms. Fundamentalism is a strict effort to dwell on the complete truths and to avoid any potential faults or errors in matters of beliefs and convictions or in matters of social conducts, habits, and lifestyles (or both). Legalistic movements do not encourage openness, tolerance, diversity, or pluralism, as these will challenge their inner- and inter-group cohesiveness and endanger their memberships to outside exposure. Therefore, conformity and loyalty to the leaders and to core principles are very essential.[33]

In the process of protecting heritages, values, customs, and traditions, families and communities tend to focus on the past and detach themselves from the present context, the social settings around them, and the reality at large. Most fundamentalists are not skewed in all areas of life and intellect. Rather they are passionate and inflexible in certain spheres only (and that is true for political affiliations, social activists, secular lifestyle defenders, etc.). When challenged, they tend to over-react with apprehension, intensity, and resentment. Interestingly, the majority of them remain quite pleasant, reasonable, and functional in other areas of life and public domains. However, when hot topics are brought up and discussed, their core beliefs and sensitivities become stirred up and activated, so they react strongly in obsessive, defensive, and judgmental ways. Religious fundamentalists call for a strict observance of their scriptures and of the interpretations/teachings of the founding fathers of their religious faith. They claim a full grasp of the truths as related to the matters of doctrine and life. However, fundamentalists can also be *nationalists* who are zealous about a certain political ideology, local ethnicity, economic system, and lineage of ancestry. They may consider a certain governmental party as their adopted cause and therefore promote its programs as their nationalistic goal and exclusive way of governing their country.

Throughout the generations, some individuals and communities were able to integrate the ancient with the contemporary and to reconcile tradition with modernity. Others, however, were not quite successful and remained struggling with intrapsychic conflicts, cultural tensions, and mental-emotional dissonances. They seemed unable or unwilling to accommodate any new developments or advances, labeling all progress and modification as threat or corruption. Fundamentalist, legalist, extremist groups consider their thoughts, ways, and interpretations as quite superior to any other group, so they reinforce their position and further inflate each other's ego status and sense of entitlement. Although such groups are not alike, they do share some common characteristics. They offer considerable safety and security, enough structure and discipline, and a sense of community and solidarity. These attractive qualities lead vulnerable individuals and those seeking substantial meaning and significance in their lives to join the movement and subscribe to its ideology. However, when the fanatic tendency is carried away, it can lead to close-mindedness, psycho-social splitting, and antagonistic behaviors. Often, fundamentalists display an air of arrogance and chauvinism. They feel they have a monopoly on the *truth* and they possess the ultimate answers to the hard questions of life. They pride themselves as exclusive and purists, who have arrived at the distilled understanding of knowledge and found the best application to all matters of practical living.[34]

Who is attracted to fundamentalist movements? Mainly individuals and families who are needy, lack exposure, and prefer a black-and-white approach to reality. They usually have restricted emotions, a weak imagination, and a critical attitude. Such movements attract people who are searching for belonging and a cause or are looking for affirmation in their various assumptions and convictions. People find there a defined structure, a crisp value cadre, and a protective environment. The lists of expectations, performances, and ideals are very clear (beliefs, privileges, responsibilities). In addition, fundamentalist groups appeal to individuals who by nature are linear, impulsive, and controlling. Eventually, some of these dedicated persons may very well advance to become leaders in their own given assembly.[30,31]

Although fundamentalism, in its various forms, has been present in all phases of history, it is still a growing phenomenon in our world today. In the mindset of its supporters, it represents a direct stand and an existential answer to the invasion of secularism and materialism, both on a local and global level. It is an extreme form of *traditionalism*, blended with *legalism* and *fanaticism*, with a strong tendency for self- and group-preservation. Fundamentalism emphasizes moralism, dogmatism, and purism in the face of modern trends like consumerism, hedonism, and dissipationism. Thus, the world is experiencing two major waves and two sharp polarities opposing and competing with each other. It seems that, with the constant social changes, rapid technological advances, increased mixture of cultures, and fast unfolding of globalization, these conflicting movements have not exhausted themselves yet. Therefore, as many observers have concluded, these opposing polarities are not going away any time soon.[35,36,37]

When group members discover that their affiliation and involvement in such movements are rather unhealthy, they struggle with the decision of how and when to leave. Breaking former associations is not easy, especially if they have a long history with the group. Even if they succeed in breaking the ties, they will face the struggles of re-orienting and re-establishing themselves anew. They will need help and assistance (coaching, guiding, mentoring) so they can begin to recover, regroup, and restore a normal and healthy psychosocial functioning.

Clinical caregiving and counseling will help those coming out of any type of a fundamentalist background to gradually repair their mindset and emotional rigidity, widen their horizon and worldview, and expand their psychosocial repertoire without making them feel they are compromising their core identity or value system. Therapy for grief and trauma-related experiences is also necessary.

Caregivers, educators, and providers are in a good position to notice any early signs of fanaticism or extremism in young people, students, and clients, in a small family unit or among any unconventional circle of friends. It is crucial to intervene and offer help early in the process before the trends become entrenched in their system. Also, catching potential candidates is the best way of prevention before they become too involved, unreachable, or actually unyielding. Modeling sound outlook and flexibility, promoting balanced affiliation and community, helping to navigate life's grey areas and ambiguity, and advocating healthy spirituality and religiosity all are essential to raise the next generation and constitute a sound strategy for prevention-intervention in an age of potential legalism and increased fundamentalism.

CONCLUSION

Thus, we have discussed sensitive topics and unconventional subjects that are usually not very common or well treated in the professional literature. We have studied phenomena, explored movements, described mentalities, analyzed attitudes, and reviewed activities that are considered marginal to the mainstream society. We have also examined their impact on the individual, familial, and communal levels alike. Although these trends and topics are ancient in their roots, they are contemporary in their forms and manifestations. The challenge that is facing academicians and caregivers presently is to know what is considered acceptable and what is considered unacceptable, what is normal and what is abnormal, and what is eventually cultural-typical-natural versus clinical-atypical-pathological. Such fine distinctions are not easy to construct or conclude.

Virtually, being able to differentiate between healthy and unhealthy behaviors, sound and skewed mentalities, enlightening and misleading spiritualities, natural and unnatural experiences, and realistic-normal and unrealistic-irrational emotional reactions (or personal intuitions) is a major skill that perhaps requires years to develop and master. It will be the result of a lifetime journey of continual keen observance, eager learning, substantial patience, rich experience, spiritual insight, wisdom and discernment, and attitudinal and cultural humility.

REFERENCES

1. Abi-Hashem, N. (in press). Parapsychology. In K. D. Keith (Ed.), *Encyclopedia of cross-cultural psychology*. Malden, MA: Wiley-Blackwell.
2. Broughton, R. S. (1992). *Parapsychology: The controversial science*. New York, NY: Ballantine Books.
3. Cunningham, P. F. (2011). *Bridging psychological science and transpersonal spirit: A primer of transpersonal psychology*. Retrieved from http://www.rivier.edu/faculty/pcunningham/Research/A%20Primer%20of%20Transpersonal%20Psychology.doc
4. Henry, J. (Ed.). (2005). *Parapsychology: Research on exceptional experiences*. New York. NY: Routledge.
5. Beyerstein, B. L. (1995). *Distinguishing science from pseudoscience*. Victoria, BC: Center for Curriculum and Professional Development. Accessed from http://www.sld.cu/galerias/pdf/sitios/revsalud/beyerstein_science_vs_pseudoscience.pdf
6. Irwin, H. J., & Watt, C. A. (Eds.) (2007). *An introduction to parapsychology* (5th ed.). Jefferson, NC: McFarland & Company.
7. Boeving, N. (2010). Paranormal experience. In D. Leeming (Ed.), *Encyclopedia of psychology and religion*. New York, NY: Springer. Retrieved from http://www.springerreference.com/docs/html/chapterdbid/70528.html
8. Schmeidler, G. R. (2008). Parapsychology. *International Encyclopedia of the Social Sciences*. Retrieved from http://www.encyclopedia.com/topic/parapsychology.aspx
9. Hui, C. (2010). Extra-sensory perception (ESP). In D. Leeming (Ed.), *Encyclopedia of Psychology and Religion*. New York: Springer. (www.springerreference.com) Springer-Verlag Berlin Heidelberg. DOI: 10.1007/SpringerReference_70354 2012-09-04 14:12:40 UTC
10. Mandrake (2004). *Parapsychology*. Accessed from http://www.mandrake-press.co.uk/Definitions/parapsychology.html
11. *Parapsychological Association* (2011). Why is parapsychology so controversial? Retrieved from http://www.parapsych.org/articles/36/56/why_is_parapsychology_so.aspx
12. Griffin, D. R. (1997). *Parapsychology, philosophy, and spirituality: A postmodern exploration*. New York, NY: State University of New York Press.
13. Scharfetter, C. (1998). Occultism, parapsychology and the esoteric from the perspective of psychopathology. *Fortschritte der Neurologie-Psychiatrie, 66* (10), 474–482.
14. Utts, J. (1991). Replication and meta-analysis in parapsychology. *Statistical Science, 6* (4), 363–403.

15. Zingrone, N. L. (2001). Controversy and the problems of parapsychology. *Journal of Parapsychology, 66* (1), 3–30.
16. Rhine, J. B., & Pratt, J. G. (1962). *Parapsychology: Frontier science of the mind.* Springfield, IL: Thomas/Bannerstone.
17. Leech, D. (2011). Relating spiritual healing and science: Some critical reflections. In F. Watts (Ed.), *Spiritual healing: Scientific and religious perspectives* (pp. 153–166). Cambridge , UK: Cambridge University Press.
18. Rhine, J. B. (1933). *Extrasensory perception.* Boston, MA: Society for Psychical Research.
19. Abi-Hashem, N. (2008). Arab Americans: Understanding their challenges, needs, and struggles. In A. Marsella, P. Watson, F. Norris, J. Johnson, and J. Gryczynski (Eds.), *Ethnocultural perspectives on disasters and trauma: Foundations, issues, and applications* (pp. 115–173). New York, NY: Springer.
20. Abi-Hashem, N. (2012). Cults and sects. In C. Figley (Ed.), *Encyclopedia of trauma: An interdisciplinary guide.* Thousand Oaks, CA: Sage.
21. Langone, M. D. (1999). Cults, psychological manipulation and society: International perspectives—An overview. Accessed from http://content.iskcon.org/icj/7_2/72langone.html
22. Zablocki, B., & Robbins, T. (2001). *Misunderstanding cults: Searching for objectivity in a controversial field.* Toronto, Ontario: University of Toronto Press.
23. Lewis, J. R. (Ed.) (2004). *The Oxford handbook of new religious movements.* Oxford, UK: Oxford University Press.
24. Bainbridge, W. S., & Stark, R. (1979). Cult formation: Three compatible models. *Sociology of Religion: A Quarterly Review, 40* (4), 283–295.
25. Goldman, M. S. (2006). Cults, new religions, and the spiritual landscape: A review of four collections. *Journal for the Scientific Study of Religion, 45* (1), 87–96.
26. Sirkin, M. I. (1990). Cult involvement: A systems approach to assessment and treatment. *Psychotherapy: Theory, Research, Practice, Training, 27* (1), 116–123.
27. Barret, D. V. (1998). *Sects, 'cults' and alternative religions: A world survey and sourcebook.* London, UK: Blandford.
28. Chen, N. N. (2003). Healing sects and anti-cult campaigns. *The China Quarterly, 174,* 505–520. [Cambridge University Press] doi: 10.1017/S0009443903000305
29. Giannini, T. (2000). New religions and the anti-cult movement: Online resource guide in social sciences. *Online databases in the humanities and social sciences.* Accessed from http://rand.pratt.edu/~giannini/newreligions.html
30. Abi-Hashem, N. (2012). Religious fundamentalism. In C. Figley (Ed.), *Encyclopedia of trauma: An interdisciplinary guide.* Thousand Oaks, CA: Sage.
31. Abi-Hashem, N. (in press). Religious fundamentalism and terrorism. In D. A. Leeming (Ed.), *Encyclopedia of psychology and religion.* New York, NY: Springer. (www.springerreference.com)
32. Caplan, L. (1987) (Ed.). *Studies in religious fundamentalism.* London: Macmillan Press.
33. Hood, R. W., Hill, P. C., & Williamson, W. P. (2005). *The psychology of religious fundamentalism.* New York, NY: Guilford.

34. Santosh, C. S. (Ed.) (2004). *Religious fundamentalism in the contemporary world: Critical social and political issues.* Lanham, MD: Lexington Books.
35. Almond, G. A., Appleby, R. S., & Sivan, E. (2003). *Strong religion: The rise of fundamentalisms around the world.* Chicago, IL: University of Chicago Press.
36. Armstrong, K. (2005, January). Fundamentalism is here to stay. *Global Agenda,* 234–236.
37. Barzilai-Nahon, K., & Barzilai, G. (2005). Cultured technology: The Internet and religious fundamentalism. *Information Society, 21*(1), 25–40.

About the Editor and Contributors

EDITOR

Thomas G. Plante, PhD, ABPP, is the Augustin Cardinal Bea, S.J., University Professor and professor of psychology at Santa Clara University and adjunct clinical professor of psychiatry and behavioral sciences at Stanford University School of Medicine. He has served as psychology department chair, acting dean of the school of education, counseling psychology, and pastoral ministries, and is director of the Spirituality and Health Institute at Santa Clara University. He recently served as vice-chair of the National Review Board for the Protection of Children and Youth for the U.S. Conference of Catholic Bishops and president of the psychology and religion division (division 36) of the American Psychological Association. He has authored, co-authored, edited, or co-edited 16 books, including *Religion, Spirituality, and Positive Psychology: Understanding the Psychological Fruits of Faith* (2012, Praeger), *Sexual Abuse in the Catholic Church: A Decade of Crisis, 2002–2012* (2012, Praeger), *Sin against the Innocents: Sexual Abuse by Priests and the Role of the Catholic Church* (2004, Praeger), *Bless Me Father For I Have Sinned: Perspectives on Sexual Abuse Committed by Roman Catholic Priests* (1999, Praeger), *Faith and Health: Psychological Perspectives* (2001, Guilford), *Do the Right Thing: Living Ethically in an Unethical World* (2004, New Harbinger), *Contemporary Clinical Psychology* (1999, 2005, 2010, Wiley), *Mental Disorders of the New Millennium* (Vols. I, II, and III, 2006, Praeger), *Spirit, Science and Health: How the Spiritual Mind Fuels Physical Wellness* (2007, Praeger), *Spiritual Practices in Psychotherapy: Thirteen Tools for Enhancing Psychological Health* (2009,

American Psychological Association), and *Contemplative Practices in Action: Spirituality, Meditation, and Health* (2010, Praeger), as well as published over 175 scholarly professional journal articles and book chapters. He has been featured in numerous media outlets including *Time Magazine*, CNN, *NBC Nightly News*, the *PBS News Hour*, *New York Times*, *USA Today*, British Broadcasting Company, National Public Radio, among many others. He has evaluated or treated more than 700 priests and applicants to the Catholic and Episcopal priesthood and diaconate and has served as a consultant for a number of Church dioceses and religious orders. His undergraduate degree in psychology is from Brown University while his MA and PhD degrees are in clinical psychology from the University of Kansas. His clinical internship and postdoctoral fellowship are from Yale University. He maintains a private practice in Menlo Park, CA.

CONTRIBUTORS

Naji Abi-Hashem, PhD, is a clinical and cultural psychologist and an independent scholar. He is Lebanese-American and is involved in international service, teaching, writing, editing, training, conference presentation, volunteer work, consultation, global networking, and caring for the caregivers. Formerly a staff psychologist with the Minirth-Meier New Life Clinics in Seattle, WA (1992–2003), he has served as a visiting scholar at the Graduate School of Intercultural Studies, Fuller Theological Seminary in Pasadena, CA (2006–2007), and at the Graduate Theological Union in Berkeley, CA (2006–2008). He is an active member or a diplomate in a number of organizations and associations. He has taught and lectured at many institutions in the United States and abroad. He writes and speaks on matters related to culture, psychology, religion, globalization, immigration, fundamentalism, politics, counseling, pastoral care, and spirituality. He divides his time between Beirut, Lebanon, and the United States.

Sarah Gathright Afonso, MS Ed, is a graduate of the School Psychology program at CUNY, Brooklyn College. She graduated from the University of Miami with a bachelor of music in music therapy and served both general and special education students as a music therapist in the Jersey City Public Schools. Ms. Afonso currently works as a school psychologist with emotionally disturbed middle and high school students at the Essex Valley School in West Caldwell, NJ.

Kimberly Black, MS Ed, NCSP, is a graduate of the School Psychology master's program at Brooklyn College. She is a 2012 New York State Association of School Psychologists' Ted Bernstein Award winner for outstanding professional promise in the field of school psychology. Her research interests include examining the impact of social technology on student social-emotional development as well as the assessment and application of executive functioning skills. She is currently a practicing school psychologist in the Boston area.

Phillip Brownell, MDiv, PsyD, is a licensed psychologist in North Carolina and Oregon and a clinical psychologist registered in Bermuda. He is an ordained clergyman and writes a weekly column on integrative issues for *The Royal Gazette,* Bermuda's largest daily newspaper. He is currently a staff psychologist at Benedict Associates, Ltd., where he offers a broad range of assessment and counseling services to child, adolescent, and adult populations, including individual, couple, family, and group therapy. He is editor of the *Handbook for Theory, Research, and Practice in Gestalt Therapy* (2008), author of *Gestalt Therapy: A Guide to Contemporary Practice* (2010), co-editor of *Continuity and Change: Gestalt Therapy Now* (in press), co-editor of *Gestalt!,* the official journal of the Association for the Advancement of Gestalt Therapy (AAGT), a consulting editor at the *European Journal for Qualitative Research in Psychotherapy,* and co-chair of the AAGT's Research Task Force. He is a member of the New York Institute for Gestalt Therapy, the American Psychological Association, and the AAGT.

Alberto M. Bursztyn, **PhD,** is professor of School Psychology at Brooklyn College and of the doctoral program in Urban Education of the Graduate Center—CUNY. His research focuses on psychological assessment of English language learners, family/school relations, multicultural education, and urban special education. Recent consultations and training activities include the New York City Department of Education, Nassau BOCES, Mid-Hudson area BOCES, and the Henry Viscardi School. His latest significant publications include *Childhood Psychological Disorders: Current Controversies* (Praeger, 2011). He is the editor of the *Handbook of Special Education* (Rowman & Littlefield, 2007). He also co-edited *Teaching Teachers: Building a Quality School of Urban Education* (Peter Lang, 2004) and *Rethinking Multicultural Education* (Praeger, 2002). Dr. Bursztyn is a licensed psychologist who received his doctorate in counseling psychology from Columbia University. He also holds graduate degrees in science education (Brooklyn College), school psychology (Brooklyn College), and educational leadership (NYU).

Enoch Callaway, MD, is emeritus professor of psychiatry, University of California, San Francisco. He has written over 100 edited technical papers, three books, and a monograph. He has also published an article on fly fishing, a novel (*The Mating Flower: A Botanical Murder Mystery*), and memoirs of a psychiatric residency from 1948–1950 (*Asylum: A Mid-Century Madhouse and Its Lessons about Our Mentally Ill Today*, Praeger, 2011). He is also past president of the Society for Biological Psychiatry and the Society for Psychophysiological Research, and he has been a recipient of the Royer Award for the outstanding neurologist or psychiatrist in the San Francisco Bay Area.

Brooke J. Cannon, PhD, is professor of psychology at Marywood University in Scranton, PA. She teaches a psychology in film course and has authored numerous articles related to movie portrayals of psychopathology. In addition, Dr. Cannon created the psychmovies.com website in 1999, offering summaries of hundreds of movies related to psychology, as well as resources for instructors.

Mark S. Carlson, **PhD, LP,** is an assistant professor of clinical psychology at Argosy University—Twin Cities, where he is the lead faculty of their history and systems of psychology course. He has over thirty years of experience as a psychotherapist and has presented widely on topics ranging from Weaving the Other into the History of Psychology to Human Rights Issues at a World Council of Churches conference in Harare, Zimbabwe.

Diane E. Dreher, PhD, is professor of English at Santa Clara University, where she is enrolled in the master's program in counseling psychology. She has a PhD in Renaissance English literature from UCLA as well as credentials in spiritual counseling and holistic health. She has published numerous books and articles on Renaissance literature and literary history as well as positive psychology studies of hope and vocation. Her nonfiction books, from the best-selling *Tao of Inner Peace* to her latest, *Your Personal Renaissance*, apply insights from Eastern and Western philosophy to the challenges of contemporary life. Diane blogs for *Psychology Today* and offers personal coaching based on research in positive psychology.

Aaron J. Jeffrey, PhD, LMFT, is an assistant professor at Minnesota State University, Mankato in the department of counseling and student personnel. He is also a licensed marriage and family therapist and has a part-time practice in southern Minnesota.

D. Brett King, PhD, is a senior instructor at the University of Colorado at Boulder. In addition to journal articles on the history of psychology, he has written two books in the area: *Max Wertheimer and Gestalt Theory* (co-authored with Michael Wertheimer) and *A History of Psychology: Ideas and Context* (co-authored with Wayne Viney and William Douglas Woody). He has won numerous teaching awards and, after only four years in the department of psychology and neuroscience, he was named the "University of Colorado's Best Professor" in a student survey conducted by the UCB student newspaper. In addition to his academic work, King is also the author of two novels, *The Radix* (2010) and *The False Door* (2012), both blending his long-standing interest in psychology, history, and medicine. He is working on the fifth edition of his history of psychology textbook, scheduled for publication in 2013, along with his third novel.

Andrea Knestel, PhD, is an assistant clinical professor in the Counseling and Career Center at Brigham Young University. She holds a PhD in clinical psychology from Syracuse University, with an emphasis in clinical health psychology. Andrea is interested in studying the relationships between spirituality, religiousness, and health. Her clinical interests include working with trauma, chronic health conditions, somatization, and religion/spirituality concerns.

Genomary Krigbaum, PsyD, was professionally trained in psychology in the Dominican Republic, prior to migrating to the United States; she is multilingual (primarily Spanish and English). In the United States, she completed a BA in psychology at Carroll College (Helena, Montana), an MA in clinical psychology, and a PsyD in clinical psychology at Argosy University/Phoenix. Dr. Krigbaum completed her pre-doctoral internship in the psychology department at Barrow Neurological Institute–Phoenix Children's Hospital, and her post-doctoral fellowship, as a staff psychologist, at the Arizona State University Counseling Services. Her undergraduate honors thesis on a psychosocial rehabilitation treatment for schizophrenia and her doctoral dissertation on an analysis of the sensitivity-specificity of the Standard-Spanish Version of the Culture-Fair Assessment of Neuro-Cognitive Abilities (S-S CANA) have been published. She holds the copyright for the S-S CANA. Presently, Dr. Krigbaum provides consultations and advocacy services in these areas of interest (though she is not limited to them): cross-cultural neuroscience research (i.e., design & protocols), multicultural issues, and systemic-organizational dynamics. Dr. Krigbaum trains physicians and other professionals, as well as the general population, in the United States and Latin America (i.e., the Dominican Republic). She is also an adjunct professor at Grand Canyon University, in both the College of Doctoral Studies and the College of Arts and Sciences. In addition, she adjunct-teaches at Estrella Mountain Community College in Arizona. Dr. Krigbaum is dedicated to scholarly and research activity. She is invested in contributing to literature in clinical psychology, evidence-based interventions, and frameworks. Dr. Krigbaum participates in research protocols, both as a primary and co-investigator, in the areas of seizures and brainwaves respectively.

Alexandra Elisabeth Maddi is an undergraduate student at the University of Colorado at Boulder. She is pursuing a bachelor's degree in psychology and serves as an officer in UCB's chapter of Psi Chi, the International Honor Society in Psychology. As an undergraduate teaching assistant, she leads a general psychology recitation for nearly fifty students at the University of Colorado. Following graduation, she plans to attend a doctoral program in clinical psychology.

Janet R. Matthews, PhD, ABPP, is professor of psychology at Loyola University New Orleans as well as partner with her husband in a private psychology practice. She currently serves as associate editor of *Professional Psychology: Research and Practice* and has served for many years on the editorial board of *Teaching of Psychology*. She has published four books, including *Introduction to Clinical Psychology* (2008, Oxford), as well as numerous book chapters and journal articles. Her history of professional service includes being president of Southwestern Psychological Association, president of APA's Divisions 2 (teaching) and 31 (state, provincial, and territorial psychological association affairs), chair of many APA boards and committees, serving three terms on the APA Council of Representatives and one term on the APA Board of Directors. She received the 2011 Distinguished Psychologist Award from the Louisiana Psychological Association.

Lee H. Matthews, PhD, ABPP, is in independent practice in both rural and urban Louisiana. He serves as a consultant to the inpatient programs for both general and geriatric psychiatric units. He is currently program director for a grief resources program that provides bereavement programs within the community for adults, adolescents, and children. His academic experience includes part-time undergraduate psychology teaching at three universities, developing and running training programs for medical students and interns in both behavioral medicine and psychiatry, and running continuing-education workshops for allied mental health professionals. He has published numerous book chapters and journal articles. His most recent chapter was "Applying for Clinical and Other Applied Jobs" (2011, Sage). His professional service has included serving as president of the New Orleans Neuropsychological Society and secretary-treasurer of APA's Division 1 (general). He is currently serving as chair of the Louisiana State Board of Examiners of Psychologists.

Linda A. Mayers, PhD, is past director of training of the Institute of the Postgraduate Psychoanalytic Society, where she was a training and supervising analyst. She has also been an adjunct associate professor at LaGuardia Community College and the City University of New York. She is a former adjunct clinical professor at City University, Teachers College—Columbia University, and Yeshiva University. She is a founder and vice-chair of Psychoanalysis, Art and Creativity, a member organization of the International Society for Art and Psychology. She has published in the area of art and psychoanalysis and was co-editor of the *Psychoanalytic Inquiry* issue on adoption. She is a member of the International Federations of Psychoanalytic Societies and is in private practice in New York City.

Anne Bliss Niess earned a bachelor's degree in psychology from the University of Colorado at Boulder. As an advocate for a local mental health center, she developed a passion for working within family systems and with adolescents. She has held several positions working on behalf of local and international communities. She currently works as a mental health counselor at Children's Hospital Colorado in addition to volunteering with children on the oncology floor.

Eva D. Papiasvili, PhD, ABPP, is a clinical faculty member and a supervisor in the doctoral program of clinical and counseling psychology, Columbia University, Teachers' College; she was also the past executive director of the Institute of the Postgraduate Psychoanalytic Society, where she has been a training and supervising analyst since 1996. She is the founder and chair of Psychoanalysis, Art and Creativity, a member organization of the International Society for Art and Psychology. Dr. Papiasvili originally received her PhD in clinical psychology from Charles University in Prague, Czech Republic. Her landmark dissertation was the first major-scale study of the effectiveness of the psychotherapeutic programs in Eastern Europe, excerpts of which were published internationally. Over the last 30 years, she has published professionally in the *International Journal of Group Psychotherapy*, *International Journal of Therapeutic Communities*, *International Forum of Psychoanalysis*, *Psychoanalytic Inquiry*, and others. Her full-time private practice in New York City and Westchester is in clinical psychology, psychoanalysis, psychotherapy, and supervision.

Layne S. Perkins is an undergraduate student at the University of Colorado at Boulder. She is studying psychology with a minor in integrated physiology and plans to earn a doctoral degree in clinical psychology. She serves as vice president in the UCB chapter of Psi Chi, the International Honor Society of Psychology, and is also actively involved in a leadership position with her sorority, Alpha Phi, as a representative in the Greek community.

Amy Pitchforth, PhD, received her doctorate in clinical psychology from Loma Linda University. She is currently a postdoctoral fellow at the VA Pacific Islands Health Care System. Amy's professional interest is in health psychology.

Santiago Valenzuela Sosa, MD, is a medical doctor with a practice in neuro-surgery. He obtained his medical degree and graduated magna cum laude from the Universidad Autonoma de Santo Domingo (Dominican Republic). He was trained in the neurosciences and as a neurosurgeon in France at the Faculty of Medicine in Marseille. Currently, he is a professor of neuroanatomy and neuro-surgery in the school of medicine at the Universidad Autonoma de Santo Domingo, as well as the Instituto Tecnologico de Santo Domingo; he also attends patients and trains future physicians in the residencies of surgery and internal medicine at the Hospital Universitario Padre Billini. He maintains a private practice at the Corazones Unidos and the Centro Medico Dominico-Cubano, where he sees patients of all social strata. His professional practices include cases of oncology, back-surgery, neuro-endoscopy, radiosurgery, epilepsy and neurology, psycho-surgery, and gamma-knife. Professional interests entail neuroscience research (including epileptic and neurologic disorders), cerebral tumors, and hydrocephalus, as well as psychological-psychiatric pathologies treated through neurosurgeries. He has been published in twenty books and magazines and has been invited to present in more than 50 congresses in the Dominican Republic and abroad (including the United States and France). For leisure activities, he goes to the gym, plays tennis, and enjoys family activities. He is the father of a young lady who recently graduated from medical school and a young man who is in his first year of law school.

James W. Sturges, PhD, is a psychology professor at California State Poly-technic University, Pomona. He was formerly a faculty member at the University of Mississippi Medical Center. His research has been in the areas of pediatric pain, smoking prevention, and HIV risk. He has a current interest in mindfulness and acceptance. He is also in private practice.

Index